REAL ESTATE LAW
&
ASSET PROTECTION

For Texas Real Estate Investors

By David J. Willis, J.D., LL.M.

First Edition Design Publishing
Sarasota, Florida

Real Estate Law & Asset Protection
For Texas Real Estate Investors

ISBN 978-1622873-95-1 PRINT
ISBN 978-1622-873-96-8 EBOOK

LCCN 2013949130

August 2013

Published and Distributed by
First Edition Design Publishing, Inc.
P.O. Box 20217, Sarasota, FL 34276-3217
www.firsteditiondesignpublishing.com

TABLE OF CONTENTS

PREFACE

This book is a pragmatic and creative approach to legal and asset protection issues faced by investors in Texas real estate, particularly investors in residential and smaller commercial properties. It is not intended to be a textbook or comprehensive academic treatise. Rather, it contains practical perspectives and techniques developed over the years in the course of advising and representing investors. Since there are usually as many opinions as there are lawyers in a room, it should be no surprise if other lawyers disagree with at least some of my conclusions. In response, I would point out that there is nothing theoretical in this book. Every strategy I describe has been tried and has succeeded in the real world. Having said that, readers should consult an attorney prior to implementing any of my suggestions in order to insure compatibility with individual circumstances. Business plans vary and so do investments and asset protection strategies. This book does not offer legal guidance to any particular person with regard to any particular case. Note also that the law changes and evolves, often rapidly. While cases and statutes are cited in this book, the reader should do independent research to ascertain the current status of the law before relying on any of these citations.

If you are a real estate investor who owns (or aspires to own) 10, 20, or 50 or more properties, then you should consider reading this book. If you use creative methods such as wraparounds and "subject to" transactions then you may find this volume very useful indeed. If, however, your goal is to assemble an international consortium to purchase Rockefeller Center or Trump Tower, then this is probably not the book for you.

All real estate investors should form the habit of doing thorough due diligence prior to investing in real estate. This includes consulting attorneys, accountants, insurance advisors, and other qualified professionals on overall methods and goals as well as specific transactions. Every investor should have a team of seasoned professionals available to answer questions, offer input, and provide customized services. A professional investor will also acquire a basic level of competence in searching and obtaining information and copies from real property and appraisal district records.

On the subject of transactional documentation, I urge readers to avoid most standard forms, especially those obtained from the Internet, except for contracts and addenda promulgated by the Texas Real Estate Commission and the Texas Association of Realtors. Consider all others suspect.

There are many resources for investors, not the least of which is the Texas Property Code. I suggest that every investor have a paperback copy of the Code on his or her desk and refer to it regularly (go to www.JonesMcClure.com). There are also a number of quality educational opportunities in the marketplace, including real estate schools and mentorship programs, enough so that there is no excuse for an investor not to master the trade.

Lastly, it has been my experience that good ethics make for good business. Avoid any transaction that even hints of fraud or deception. If it appears too good to be true it probably is.

I welcome comments and criticism. I can most easily be reached by email at LoneStarLandLaw@aol.com.

David J. Willis

CONTRACTS & CLOSINGS

Chapter 1

RESIDENTIAL SALES CONTRACTS

The TREC One to Four Family Residential Contract

The most commonly used residential sales contract in Texas is the One to Four Family Residential Contract (Resale) promulgated by the Texas Real Estate Commission as form number 20-11. The blank form is available at www.trec.state.tx.us. I will refer to it as the "TREC 1-4 contract." All licensed brokers and agents are required to use this contract and other TREC promulgated forms when representing clients in the purchase and sale of real property. Non-licensees and attorneys may use any format they wish.

Real estate investors will find that they are almost always better off using the TREC 1-4 contract with appropriate addenda rather than anything simpler that is supposedly designed or streamlined for investor use. This is true even though TREC forms are generally intended to be neutral one-size-fits-all documents. Accordingly, an experienced investor will become familiar with the various options and boxes to be checked in TREC forms and learn how to tailor a contract to his or her advantage.

The truth is, even when amicably conducted, the sale and purchase of real estate is by definition an adversarial transaction. From a lawyer's perspective, producing a contract and closing documents that advance the client's best interests is the whole point of the exercise.

Strike-Outs versus an Addendum

How should revision of the TREC 1-4 contract be accomplished? One way is to make changes on the form itself—strike, insert, and initial with pen. This is legally valid although it can get messy if there are lots of alterations. It is often cleaner to attach a special provisions addendum that supersedes any printed form provisions that may conflict. Only items to be altered are mentioned in the addendum. This method of modifying the contract has an obvious advantage in negotiations: It is immediately apparent to everyone which terms are being changed and which are not.

Another advantage to the addendum method is that brokers and agents are more comfortable with it, since the actual body of their familiar TREC contract has not been changed. Custom, non-standard contracts tend to push licensees out of their comfort zone, at least in the residential arena. Custom contracts are much more common in commercial transactions.

If your choice is to add a special provisions addendum, the wording "See Special Provisions Addendum attached hereto and incorporated herein" should be inserted in paragraph 11 (Special Provisions) of the TREC 1-4 contract. Also, in paragraph 22 (Agreement of Parties), the box "other" should be checked and "Special Provisions Addendum" inserted in the line that follows.

A further note as to paragraph 11 (Special Provisions): it is a blank space available for inserting extra comments, but its permitted use by brokers and agents is limited to "factual statements and business details applicable to the sale"—i.e., not modification of text or addition of provisions that are primarily legal in nature. It is therefore not the appropriate place to insert provisions that have legal implications, nor is it an acceptable substitute for a special provisions addendum when dealing with a creative transaction.

Typical Concerns of the Seller

The seller usually has the simpler side of the transaction. First and foremost, the seller wants to make sure that a buyer is serious and capable of following through. For this reason, the seller may want to require that the buyer submit a pre-approval letter with the contract. Also, a contract should arrive with sufficient earnest money and should show that the buyer will be making a substantial down payment. Other concerns of the seller include:

(1) *"As Is."* The seller usually wants to convey the property to the greatest extent possible "as is" without responsibility for repairs or any representations or warranties (other than warranties of title), particularly those that survive closing. The goal should be a transaction that is "as is in its present condition" with "no reps and warranties" and "no survival" of contract terms.

(2) *Buyer Due Diligence.* The seller should make it clear that due diligence duties are the sole obligation of the buyer (including obtaining inspections, determination of square footage, an appraisal, a title commitment or policy, legal advice, and the like). Reliance on any statements by seller or seller's agents should be expressly disclaimed.

(3) *Existing Survey.* If an existing survey is supplied by seller to buyer, the survey should be supplied "as is" without warranties. If the buyer

wants someone to hold liable for survey currency or accuracy, then the buyer should obtain a new one at the buyer's own expense. And there should be no automatic extension of the closing date for survey-related issues.

(4) *Specific Performance.* It is in the seller's interest to avoid the possibility of being sued for specific performance of the contract, which might result in a lis pendens being filed that could prevent sale of the property to anyone else—so specific performance as a buyer remedy should be struck. And since specific performance is generally an ineffective remedy for the seller, there is no reason (from the seller's point of view) not to strike specific performance all around.

(5) *Content of Legal Documents.* The seller should exercise at least some control over the content of the warranty deed that conveys title to the buyer (and for which the seller pays) instead of merely accepting an assembly-line version supplied by title company attorneys. For example, the seller may require inclusion of comprehensive "as is" language along with the buyers signature. The seller may also want to expand that section of the deed entitled "Exceptions to Conveyance and Warranty" to include "all matters of which Grantee has actual or constructive notice and all matters excepted from coverage in any owner's title insurance policy issued to Grantee in connection with this conveyance."

(6) *Assumptions.* In assumptions, the seller should assure that there will be a mutually acceptable deed of trust to secure assumption as well as an assumption agreement that specifies when and to whom the buyer will make payments, how casualty insurance will be handled, and so forth. The assumption agreement should also include disclosure of the potential future impact of any due-on-sale clause and provide a course of action in the unlikely event due-on-sale is invoked by the lender.

(7) *Seller Financing.* If there is seller-financing, it is in the seller's interest to control the terms and conditions of the note and deed of trust beyond what is provided in the TREC Seller Financing Addendum—and then, ideally, obtain early approval for all seller financing documents. By early, we mean well before closing. Last minute disputes about the form and content of legal documents have ended more than one transaction.

(8) *Wraparounds.* In the event the transaction is a wrap, there should be a wrap addendum that addresses pertinent details. Since there is no TREC or Texas Association of Realtors promulgated addendum for this, a

custom addendum is needed. As is the case with assumptions and seller financing, early approval of legal documents is preferred. Actually, the very best way to do this is to attach the preapproved legal documents to the sales contract itself, although this seldom occurs because the parties are usually in a rush and reluctant to pay an attorney to create documents at this early stage. Attaching preapproved docs happens more frequently in commercial transactions.

(9) *"Sub 2" Transactions.* In the case of a "subject to" transaction, precise language to this effect should be included in a custom addendum to the contract since there is no TREC or TAR addendum for a sub 2.

This is a partial list of seller concerns. There may be other items to consider based on the unique nature of a particular transaction. Each item can be effectively addressed by a customized special provisions addendum that is brief and to the point. It need not ramble on, page after page, with unnecessary legalese.

As an aside, be cautioned that the TREC 1-4 contract should *never* be used as a substitute for a contract for deed or other executory device. Given changes to section 5.061 et seq. of the Property Code, this practice, always dubious, is now out of the question.

Seller Disclosure

If a condition could reasonably affect the decision by an ordinary buyer to buy or not buy, then it should be disclosed, even if the conveyance is to be made "as is." That may mean going beyond the Seller's Disclosure of Property Condition if that form does not provide sufficient scope or detail. Failure to do so could violate the Deceptive Trade Practices-Consumer Protection Act ("DTPA"). *See* Tex. Bus. & Com. Code §§ 17.41 et seq. However tempting it may be for a seller to avoid disclosure of a material fact or condition, it is not worth risking a lawsuit that ends with a judgment for treble damages plus attorney's fees.

The Buyer's Side of the Transaction

A buyer's concerns are more complex. Generally, the buyer should want to know everything there is to know about the property, whether that information is derived from due diligence, a title commitment, a survey, disclosure by the seller, information provided by a broker, or even gossip from neighbors. "Buyer beware" still has considerable meaning in the purchase and sale of real estate.

There is no excuse for a buyer (particularly an investor) failing to do his or her homework on a property or failing to read documents before signing them. We live in an information society. Not putting forth a minimum effort to obtain information about a property one is buying (not having it professionally inspected, for instance) looks more and more . . . well, stupid—and judges and jurors are likely to see it that way. Yet there continue to be suits by buyers who claim they were absolved from their duty to inspect or read documents because they were rushed or pressured by the seller.

Specific items of concern to the buyer:

(1) *Financing Contingency*. A buyer should want the third-party financing contingency to be a true contingency governed by specific parameters, not just a vague notion subject to dispute by a seller who may argue that the buyer failed to "apply promptly" or make "every reasonable effort" to get a loan. Does the TREC language require application to one lender or four? In its attempt to be neutral, the text is silent. Moreover, nowhere in the contract or in the TREC Financing Condition Addendum is it spelled out what constitutes adequate evidence of failure to get financing. Can the buyer be sure that the seller will take the buyer's word and agree to return the earnest money? Does failure of the property to adequately appraise constitute denial of the buyer's loan application? It should. Failure to appraise should be considered a failure to satisfy the lenders' underwriting requirements and therefore permit the buyer to cancel the contract and obtain a refund. These issues may not be so compelling if the earnest money is only $500 . . . but what if it is $5,000 or $15,000, amounts that are not uncommon in sales of higher-end homes? It is also to the buyer's benefit to specify that providing a "turn down letter" shall be conclusive, indisputable evidence that financing was denied.

(2) *Assumptions, Seller Financing, and Wraps*. If the transaction involves an assumption, seller-financing, or wrap, there is always the issue of the specific content of legal documents that the buyer will be asked to sign at closing. We have discussed this from the seller's side, but in many cases it is just as important to the buyer. The TREC Loan Assumption Addendum and the TREC Seller Financing Addendum are reasonably detailed, but what if the seller's attorney includes unexpected or oppressive clauses in the note or deed of trust? Does the closing fail? Is there a breach? It is wise to anticipate and prepare for these issues well before closing. Again, a special provisions addendum may be useful.

As noted, there is no promulgated addendum for a wrap, yet many pesky details need to be addressed. Is the buyer fully informed about the particulars of the wrapped debt? Has the buyer seen a copy of the existing note? How can the buyer be sure the seller will pass monthly payments along to the first-lien lender? Will the buyer have the right to contact the lender or receive written evidence that payments are current? What happens if the lender exercises due-on-sale and accelerates the wrapped note? What about casualty insurance? Wrap issues should be addressed in a custom wrap addendum to the TREC 1-4 contract, followed by a detailed wraparound agreement signed at closing. Additionally, wrap deals may include extra seller-financing in the form of a second or third lien. What will the seller-financed note and deed of trust look like? The buyer's attorney should see all this coming and insist on reading draft legal documents early on. Ideally, no buyer should be ambushed at closing with documents that the buyer has neither seen nor agreed to.

(3) *Disclosure of Material Conditions and Defects*. Disclosure is often the buyer's biggest concern. A "Seller's Notice of Property Condition" is required by Property Code section 5.008, which states that "[a] seller of residential real property comprising not more than one dwelling unit located in this state shall give to the purchaser of the property a written notice as prescribed by this section or a written notice substantially similar to the notice prescribed by this section which contains, at a minimum, all of the items in the notice prescribed by this section." Section 5.008(d) goes on to say that the "notice shall be completed to the best of seller's belief and knowledge as of the date the notice completed and signed by the seller." There are exceptions, notably as to previously unoccupied new homes.

The Seller's Disclosure form has several problems from a buyer's point of view. First, the form states, right at the top, that "IT IS NOT A WARRANTY OF ANY KIND BY SELLER OR SELLER'S AGENTS." Why not? The form's utility as a disclosure tool is diminished by this statement. The buyer's attorney should consider using a special provisions addendum to convert the Seller's Disclosure into a set of express representations and warranties.

Second, disclosure of defects and conditions is limited to the seller's knowledge and awareness—not the highest standard. *What the buyer is concerned with is not what the seller knows or says he knows, but with what is actually true about the property.* It is just too easy for an unethical seller to later say, "Oh, I didn't know about that." Sometimes problems can be detected by inspections and other due diligence, sometimes not. Often, the truth is discovered only after subsequent conversations with neighbors—who may take perverse delight in reporting that not only did the seller know about water penetration behind that faux stucco, he *personally* patched and painted it to conceal the damage. The buyer should want to know about any such repairs and ask to see contractor paperwork to determine the extent of the work done as well as whether or not there is a transferable warranty. Broadly speaking, what a buyer wants is something stronger than what is offered by the Seller's Disclosure, namely an actual representation and warranty by the seller that certain negative conditions do not exist.

Finally, at no point does the seller state, swear, or affirm that the Seller's Disclosure is true and correct. Most everyone assumes that this is so since the seller signs the disclosure. *But look closely—the form does not say that.* This is another disappointment for the buyer. From the buyer's point of view, there is no substitute for maximum, unconditional disclosure backed up by meaningful recourse against the seller that survives closing.

What about previous inspection reports? Neither the contract nor the Seller's Disclosure obligates the seller to provide them. The buyer should therefore always request copies of these.

(4) *Joint Tenancy with Right of Survivorship.* The buyer also has an interest in the wording of the warranty deed. For example, unless otherwise instructed, title company attorneys will list the grantee as "John Jones and wife, Mary Jones," creating tenancy-in-common. This form of co-ownership does not provide for the surviving spouse to automatically inherit the entire property when the other dies. Title to the property vests in the surviving spouse only if the property is community property and the deceased had no children or, if there are children, all of them are the result of the marriage between John and Mary. Tex. Prob. Code § 45. Accordingly, if it is the desire of the buyer to use the deed to do some basic estate planning, the grantee should be listed as "John Jones and wife, Mary Jones as joint tenants with rights of survivorship and not as tenants in common." This adds value for the buyer at no cost to the seller.

(5) *Sub 2 Transactions.* Investor buyers will often want to take title "subject to" existing indebtedness. Express language (both in the buyer's addendum and in the deed) to the effect that the buyer will not be assuming the obligation to pay the existing debt—and therefore the seller will not be released from the loan until it is paid—is essential in forestalling subsequent claims by remorseful sellers who suddenly realize that they remain on the hook for their old loan with no control over whether or not the current owner makes monthly payments.

(6) *Survey.* It is usually in the buyer's best interest to delete the "survey exception" to title insurance coverage (and ask the seller to pay the fee for this service) by requiring that the "standard printed exception as to discrepancies, conflicts, shortages in area or boundary lines, encroachments or protrusions, or overlapping improvements shall be amended, at seller's expense, to read, "shortages in area." Unfortunately, the TREC 1-4 contract does not offer a box to be checked for this purpose so this item needs to be addressed in a special provisions addendum.

The buyer also wants flexibility as to whether or not to order a new survey if the seller fails to deliver the existing one. The contract says the buyer "shall" order a new survey; but this may not be necessary and the buyer should not be compelled by contract to do so. The buyer may want to specify that failure by the seller to supply the existing survey will, at buyer's election, be cause for termination and return of the earnest money. It may be advantageous to have an "out" for the buyer rather than a mere seller default. The difference? The first supplies a clean exit from the contract by the buyer (along with return of earnest money), but the second only gives the buyer grounds for a lawsuit—an expensive and time-consuming remedy.

(7) *Seller's Representations.* Because of concern with full disclosure, the buyer may not be satisfied with the language of paragraph 19 (Representations). This paragraph states that "If any representation of Seller in this contract is untrue on the Closing Date, Seller will be in default." Again, this merely provides grounds for a lawsuit; it does not facilitate expedient termination of the contract and return of the buyer's earnest money plus expenses.

What about asking the seller to declare that he or she has made full disclosure of any item that could materially affect buyer's decision to buy or not buy? Or what about openly declaring that the Seller's Disclosure of Property Condition is true and correct? Any deal where a seller refuses to agree to such terms should be avoided as if the property were radioactive (it just might be).

(8) *Restrictions.* Applicable covenants and restrictions should not be overlooked as part of the buyer's due diligence. Title companies like to provide these at closing, if at all, but by then it may be too late for the buyer to back out. If a specific use of the property is vital to the buyer (for instance, a day-care center in a neighborhood that is transitioning out of exclusively residential use) then a request for a copy of the restrictions should be made *during the option period.* The specific use should also be

expressly described in the blank at paragraph 6.D of the TREC 1-4 contract.

(9) *Final Walk-Through.* The buyer should have the unconditional right to do a final walk-through when the property is vacant and all furnishings removed. It is best to do this in the hours immediately prior to closing. If there is a material change, the buyer should have the right to terminate and receive the earnest money as well as compensation for expenses.

Investor/Licensee Disclosure

Whether in the capacity of buyer or seller, investors and real estate licensees should always disclose their status in the contract. The appropriate place to do this is the Special Provisions paragraph (or in a special provisions addendum) by using language similar to the following: "Buyer is a real estate investor [and/or licensee] engaging in this transaction for a profit. Seller should obtain professional advice." This disclosure mitigates any subsequent claim by lay persons that their relative innocence was exploited by a predatory professional. As discussed later, judges and juries do not favor investors if the transaction contains any hint of unfairness.

The Role of the Real Estate Attorney

Negotiating a real estate transaction presents multiple opportunities to favor one side or another, and not just on price. This is where it may be advantageous to consult a real estate lawyer. A real estate investor should always have (at least) three professionals on call: a CPA, an insurance agent, and a real estate attorney.

Why, might one ask, involve an attorney in preparing or advising on a TREC form that is available online and which is often completed by agents and brokers who are trained and licensed to do the job? Because lawyers can (1) modify the actual language of the form and (2) customize an addendum to favor a client. Brokers and agents cannot do this. Licensees are limited to checking appropriate boxes, filling in blanks, and attaching required addenda. They are not permitted to materially alter or supplement the contract text, which is considered the practice of law.

Another logical question: Why alter these contracts at all, since they were prepared by a broker-lawyer committee composed of experienced, practicing professionals? The answer is that no standard form can anticipate every condition or circumstance; and while many transactions are similar, no two are ever identical. Goals of sellers and buyers vary. Every transaction is unique. While some may say, "It's just a standard form, it's OK to sign it," no investor, and certainly no attorney, should ever be satisfied with *any* standard form. Neutrality is not good enough. The goal is negotiate and draft a contract that is in the investor's best interest.

Unfortunately, there is a common fear that bringing in an attorney will kill the deal. This is almost never the case with an experienced real estate lawyer, since lawyers know the difference between changes that are reasonable and those that are not—and they could not stay in business with a reputation for killing deals. Likewise, meticulous and ethical investors and realtors should see the wisdom of suggesting that an inexperienced person obtain legal advice, particularly when a transaction has non-standard aspects. This not only benefits the individual involved but shifts liability away.

A Buyer's Nightmare

A buyer goes to closing without doing a last minute walk-through. When the buyer arrives at her new home, she finds that the seller removed all the shrubbery and rose bushes—that very morning—and took them with him.

Moreover, the buyer discovers that the seller had, when showing the house, strategically positioned his artwork and oriental rugs to conceal sheetrock and slab cracks. The foundation will cost $15,000 to repair. The seller has moved to Missouri. The inspector has no E&O insurance.

Although the seller indicated on the Seller's Disclosure that *the house itself* had never been flooded, he neglected to mention that during heavy rains the entire lot is 18 inches underwater, all the way up to the weepholes. And weep the buyer does.

The buyer decides to repaper the bathroom and discovers black mold under the old wallpaper. Astonishingly, the Seller's Disclosure did not ask specifically about mold—only about "water penetration" or "any condition that materially affects the physical health or safety of an individual." When confronted by phone, the seller replies, "That mold never bothered *my* health."

Even after all these challenges, the buyer settles in. Suddenly, the front door opens and in walks the seller's estranged common-law wife (whose existence was not disclosed by the seller) and shouts "Honey, I'm home!"

Chapter 2

SELLER DISCLOSURE

Competing Interests of Seller and Buyer

As the previous chapter made clear, sellers and buyers have different needs and motivations when it comes to the transfer of real estate. One area that is often an issue is property condition. Sellers typically want to make the transfer "as is" without warranties and with no obligation for repairs. Buyers, on the other hand, have an interest in acquiring property that is in the best condition for the price. They also want full disclosure of adverse conditions, defects, and needed repairs.

Residential Sales

TREC promulgates a Seller's Disclosure of Property Condition form for use in residential real estate transactions (www.trec.state.tx.us/forms). This form (TREC OP-H) is filled out by the seller and attached to the TREC 1-4 contract. The form tracks section 5.008 of the Property Code which states:

> **5.008(a) A seller of residential real property comprising not more than one dwelling unit located in this state shall give to the purchaser of the property a written notice as prescribed by this section or a written notice substantially similar to the notice prescribed the his section which contains, at a minimum, all of the items in the notice prescribed this section.**

The purpose of the Seller's Disclosure is to make it clear what appliances, equipment, and features exist on the property; whether or not these items are working; if the seller knows of any defects or malfunctions in critical systems; if certain red-flag events like termite treatment, previous fires, or flooding have occurred; the need for repairs; and the existence of unpermitted additions, unpaid HOA fees, violations of deed restrictions, lawsuits, or conditions that "materially affect the health or safety of an individual."

Exceptions

Property Code section 5.008(e) excludes the following transactions from the requirement that a Seller's Disclosure be provided:

1. pursuant to a court order or foreclosure sale;
2. by a trustee in bankruptcy;
3. pursuant to a deed in lieu of foreclosure;
4. by a lienholder who has either purchased at a foreclosure sale or a sale pursuant to a court order or accepted a deed in lieu of foreclosure;
5. by a fiduciary in the course of an administration of a decedent's estate, guardianship, conservatorship, or trust;
6. from one co-owner to one or more other co-owners;
7. made to a spouse or to a person or persons in the lineal line of consanguinity of one or more of the transferors;
8. between spouses incident to divorce, legal separation or a property settlement agreement;
9. to or from a governmental entity;
10. a new residence of not more than one dwelling unit that has not been occupied for residential purposes;
11. of real property where the value of any dwelling does not exceed 5% of the value of the property.

Penalty

If the seller does not give the Seller's Disclosure as required, Property Code section 5.008(f) permits the buyer to "terminate the contract for any reason within seven days after receiving the notice." However, if the failure to give the notice is coupled with fraud or failure to disclose defects, then other penalties may arise pursuant to the Deceptive Trade Practices Act and/or the Statutory Fraud Act.

Commercial Sales

For commercial transactions, the Texas Association of Realtors has a Commercial Property Condition Statement that is an *optional* attachment to its standard commercial contracts. Its scope is broader than TREC's Seller's Disclosure since it addresses additional issues such as wetlands, underground storage tanks, toxic waste, and the like. Although the form is optional in commercial transactions, a careful buyer should always require that the seller provide it. Note that this and other TAR forms are available only to realtors.

Purpose of Disclosure Forms

The intent and purpose of both the residential and commercial disclosure forms is the same: to induce the seller to disclose material conditions, circumstances, and defects. For some reason, however, the drafters of these forms saw fit to insert a statement at the top to the effect that the contents of the form do not constitute a warranty by the seller. The TREC Seller's Disclosure states:

> THIS NOTICE IS A DISCLOSURE OF SELLER'S KNOWLEDGE OF THE CONDITION OF THE PROPERTY AS OF THE DATE SIGNED BY SELLER AND IS NOT A SUBSTITUTE FOR ANY INSPECTIONS OR WARRANTIES THE PURCHASER MAY WISH TO OBTAIN. IT IS NOT A WARRANTY OF ANY KIND BY SELLER OR SELLER'S AGENTS.

The TAR Commercial Property Condition Statement reads:

> THIS IS A DISCLOSURE OF THE SELLER'S KNOWLEDGE OF THE CONDITION OF THE PROPERTY AS OF THE DATE SIGNED. IT IS NOT A SUBSTITUTE FOR ANY INSPECTIONS OR WARRANTIES A BUYER OR TENANT MAY WISH TO OBTAIN. IT IS NOT A WARRANTY OF ANY KIND BY SELLER, SELLER'S AGENTS, OR ANY OTHER AGENT.

Both of these disclaimers confuse the intent and purpose of each disclosure form. Why? Is the seller making disclosures but then warning the buyer not to rely on them? Apparently so. At best, this is ambivalent legal drafting. It should be unsettling if not unsatisfactory from the buyer's point of view. A careful buyer may consider negotiating inclusion of a clause which makes it clear that the seller is standing behind the truth of the disclosures. Buyers, commercial or residential, should not leave a seller any wiggle-room on the disclosure issue.

Ongoing Duty to Disclose

The Seller's Disclosure does not in and of itself impose an ongoing duty to disclose matters that may come to the seller's attention after the form has been signed and delivered to the buyer. *Bynum v. Prudential Residential Servs.*, 129 S.W.3d 781,795 (Tex. App.—Houston [1st Dist.]

2004, pet. denied). Although this may be strictly true as it relates to the form, it would be unwise for a seller to withhold material adverse information that is subsequently discovered. There are too many statutory and common law avenues for an aggrieved buyer to pursue.

Broker Liability

Accurately completing the Seller's Disclosure is the responsibility of the seller, preferably in the seller's own handwriting. The seller's broker does not ordinarily become liable for the seller's wrongdoing in this regard. A broker "would have a duty to come forward only if he had any reason to believe that the seller's disclosures were false or inaccurate, and the only way he could be held liable for [the seller's] statement in the notice is if it were shown to be untrue." *Sherman v. Elkowitz*, 130 S.W.3d 316, 321 (Tex. App.—Houston [14th Dist.] 2004, no pet.).

The Deceptive Trade Practices-Consumer Protection Act (DTPA)

Failure to disclose material adverse conditions and defects is a violation of the DTPA. In Business & Commerce Code section 17.46(a), the statute declares:

> **False, misleading, or deceptive acts or practices in the conduct of any trade or commerce are hereby declared unlawful and are subject to action by the consumer protection division under sections 17.47, 17.58, 17.60, and 17.61 of this code.**

The DTPA also declares the following to be unlawful:

> **17.46(b)(5): representing that goods or services have sponsorship, approval, characteristics, ingredients, uses, benefits, or quantities which they do not have. . .**
>
> **17.46(b)(7): representing that goods or services are of a particular standard, quality, or grade, or that goods are of a particular style or model, if they are of another.**
>
> **17.46(b)(10): advertising goods or services with intent not to sell them as advertised.**
>
> **17.46(b)(24): failing to disclose information concerning goods or services which was known at the time of**

the transaction if such failure to disclose such information was intended to induce the consumer into a transaction into which the consumer would not have entered had the information been disclosed.

Have no doubt about it: The DTPA applies to real estate transactions. The cases consistently declare that real estate is a "good" within the meaning of the statute. *See Chastain v. Koonce*, 700 S.W.2d 579, 582 (Tex. 1985).

Additionally, a consumer may file suit if the consumer has relied to that consumer's detriment upon:

17.50(a)(2) breach of an express or implied warranty;

17.50(a)(3) any unconscionable action or course of action by any person.

Statutory language does not get any broader or more potentially damaging than that. Investor sellers beware: If you fail to disclose a material item, a jury can find that your action was "unconscionable" (an open-ended term by any definition) and award treble damages, attorney's fees, and court costs against you.

Statutory Fraud

The Statutory Fraud Act (Tex. Bus. & Com. Code § 27.01) is another potential pitfall for sellers who fail to make full disclosure:

(a) Fraud in a transaction involving real estate or stock in a corporation or joint stock company consists of a

(1) false representation of a past or existing material fact, when the false representation is

(A) made to a person for the purpose of inducing that person to enter into a contract; and
(B) relied on by that person in entering into that contract; or

(2) false promise to do an act, when the false promise is

> **(A) material;**
> **(B) made with the intention of not fulfilling it;**
> **(C) made to a person for the purpose of inducing that person to enter into a contract; and**
> **(D) relied on by that person in entering into that contract.**

(b) A person who makes a false representation or false promise commits the fraud described in Subsection (a) of this section and is liable to the person defrauded for actual damages.

(c) A person who makes a false representation or false promise with actual awareness of the falsity thereof commits the fraud described in Subsection (a) of this section and is liable to the person defrauded for exemplary damages. Actual awareness may be inferred where objective manifestations indicate that a person acted with actual awareness.

(d) A person who (1) has actual awareness of the falsity of a representation or promise made by another person and (2) fails to disclose the falsity of the representation or promise to the person defrauded, and (3) benefits from the false representation or promise commits the fraud described in Subsection (a) of this section and is liable to the person defrauded for exemplary damages. Actual awareness may be inferred where objective manifestations indicate that a person acted with actual awareness.

(e) Any person who violates the provisions of this section shall be liable to the person defrauded for reasonable and necessary attorney's fees, expert witness fees, costs for copies of depositions, and costs of court.

Observe the language in *Coldwell Banker Whiteside Associates v. Ryan Equity Partners*, 181 S.W.3d 879, 888 (Tex. App.—Dallas 2006, no pet.): "A misrepresentation may consist of the concealment or nondisclosure of a material fact when there is a duty to disclose. The duty to disclose arises when one party know that the other party is ignorant of the true facts and does not have an equal opportunity to discover the truth. A fact is material if it would likely affect the conduct of a reasonable person concerning the transaction in question." That is very straightforward language, as far as court opinions go.

Exemplary or punitive damages are available to plaintiffs who prevail. A plaintiff is entitled to recover exemplary damages in cases of statutory fraud if the false representation is made with actual awareness of the falsity of the representation. *Hines v. Hash*, 843 S.W.2d 464 (Tex. 1992).

Common-Law Fraud

The Statutory Fraud Act does not preclude a deceived buyer from filing suit on grounds of common-law fraud as well. In other words, the two causes of action can be pursued side-by-side. What is the difference? Read *Trinity Indus. v. Ashland, Inc.*, 53 S.W.3d 852, 867 (Tex. App.—Austin 2001, pet. denied): "The elements of statutory fraud under section 27.01 . . . are essentially identical to the elements of common law fraud except that section 27.01 does not require proof of knowledge or recklessness as a prerequisite to the recovery of actual damages."

Any competent plaintiffs' attorney will include as many causes of action as possible in his lawsuit against a nondisclosing seller. This is known as the "shotgun approach" and is designed to insure that, when the dust settles, at least some lines of attack will have found their mark.

Additional Liability for Real Estate Licensees

Agents and brokers who are also sellers need to be especially concerned about failing to make full disclosure. The Real Estate License Act ("RELA," found in Occupations Code section 1101.652), allows TREC to revoke or suspend the license of a broker or salesperson if the licensee is convicted of any offense involving fraud or engages in misrepresentation, dishonesty, or untrustworthy behavior. RELA Section 1101.652(b)(3) provides that a licensee may be sanctioned for making "a material misrepresentation to a potential buyer concerning a significant defect, including a latent structural defect." Section 1101.652(b)(4) specifically adds failure to disclose a significant defect to the list. Accordingly, investors who have a real estate license have a heightened level of potential liability.

"As Is" Transactions

It is important to observe that the TREC 1-4 contract contains an optional "as is" clause, and the transaction becomes "as is" if the box at paragraph 7D(1) is checked. Problem is, not all "as is" clauses are equally thorough and effective (see below).

Here is the central question: Is it lawful to transfer property without disclosing material defects if the contract states that the transaction is "as is?" In other words, does use of the words "as is" or similar phraseology relieve the seller of the obligation to disclose? The answer, as is true in many areas of the law, is *it depends*—but probably not.

The foundational case in this area is *Prudential Insurance Co. v. Jefferson Associates Ltd.*, 896 S.W.2d 156 (Tex. 1995), which upheld "as is" clauses in certain narrow circumstances. Two things are critical if such a clause is to be upheld: the specific wording and whether or not the buyer obtained an inspection. Also, in evaluating an "as is" transaction, courts look not just at these two factors but at the totality of the circumstances. Note that if the buyer consults an attorney before agreeing to an "as is" clause then a court is more likely to find the clause enforceable. Courts dislike situations where the parties are unequally informed of their rights. For this reason, it is more likely that an "as is" provision will be upheld in a commercial rather than a residential transaction since commercial buyers are presumed to be more sophisticated.

In 2007, the Dallas Court of Appeals said the following with regard to "as is" transactions involving residences: "The nature of the transaction and the totality of the circumstances surrounding the agreement must be considered. Where the 'as is' clause is an important part of the basis of the bargain, not an incidental or 'boilerplate' provision, and is entered into by parties of relatively equal bargaining position, a buyer's affirmative agreement that he is not relying on the representations of the seller should be given effect." *Kupchynsky v. Nardiello*, 230 S.W.3d 685, 690 (Tex. App.—Dallas 2007, pet. denied).

The commercial landlord-tenant case of *Italian Cowboy Partners, Ltd. v. Prudential Insurance Co. of America*, 341 S.W.3d 323 (Tex. 2011), involved lease of a restaurant with a history of chronic sewage odor. The landlord's manager, who knew of the problem, fraudulently induced the tenant into a lease by orally declaring that the premises were in "perfect condition." Even though *Italian Cowboy* is a commercial lease case, it is likely that a similar theory of liability would be applied against a seller of residential property who made such false statements.

Willful Concealment and Fraudulent Inducement

The general take-away from this discussion is that an "as is" clause will not protect a seller in a case of willful concealment, and it will certainly be no protection if the seller engages in fraudulent inducement. *Ritchy v. Pinnell*, 357 S.W.3d 410 (Tex. App.—Texarkana 2012, no pet.).

Example? A seller knows that there is foundation settlement because of cracks in the sheetrock and floor tile. So the seller positions a picture over the wall crack and a rug over the cracked tile (willful concealment) and then goes on to tell the prospective buyer that there are no serious defects in the condition of the house (fraudulent inducement).

Determined "As Is" Sellers

What if a real estate investor is determined to sell "as is" and minimize any duty to disclose? In the residential context, of course, this is difficult because the Seller's Disclosure is a required document. In commercial transactions, however, the situation is more fluid. Note, however, that an "as is" clause designed to comply with the standards of the *Italian Cowboy* case was upheld in *Dragon Fish, LLC v. Santikos Legacy, Ltd.*, 383 S.W.3d 175 (Tex. App.—San Antonio 2012, no pet.), so a well-drafted "as is" clause is most definitely effective in Texas.

In order to be safe, it is suggested that (1) there be an effective "as is" clause in *both* the earnest money contract and the warranty deed, and this clause should be clear, unequivocal, and conspicuous; (2) the language should go further than merely stating that the transaction is "as is"—it should clearly reject any duty of disclosure on the part of the seller; (3) neither the seller nor his broker should make any assurances or promises (oral or written) relating to property value, use, or condition; and (4) the buyer should sign the warranty deed. A sample seller-oriented "as is" clause would be:

> **SELLER SELLS AND BUYER UNCONDITIONALLY ACCEPTS THE PROPERTY "AS IS," IN ITS PRESENT CONDITION, WITH ALL DEFECTS, KNOWN OR UNKNOWN, PATENT OR LATENT, AND WITHOUT REPRESENTATIONS OR WARRANTIES, EXPRESS OR IMPLIED. SELLER HAS NO OBLIGATION TO DISCLOSE MATERIAL FACTS INCLUDING DEFECTS OR ADVERSE CONDITIONS. BUYER AGREES. BUYER RELIES SOLELY ON BUYER'S INSPECTIONS AND OTHER DUE DILIGENCE IN EVALUATING PROPERTY CONDITION. ANY PRIOR ORAL OR WRITTEN STATEMENTS CONCERNING CONDITION OF THE PROPERTY,**

WHETHER MADE BY SELLER, SELLER'S AGENTS, OR THIRD PARTIES, ARE EXPRESSLY DISCLAIMED. NO REPAIRS, REMEDIATION, OR TREATMENT WHATSOEVER ARE REQUIRED TO BE PERFORMED BY SELLER. THIS "AS IS" CLAUSE IS A MATERIAL TERM BUT FOR WHICH THE SELLER WOULD NOT HAVE AGREED TO SELL THE PROPERTY TO BUYER. THE CONSIDERATION PAID FOR THE PROPERTY REFLECTS THE "AS IS" NATURE OF THIS CONVEYANCE. PROVISIONS OF THIS "AS IS" CLAUSE SHALL SURVIVE CLOSING AND SHALL NOT MERGE. IF BUYER IS UNCERTAIN ABOUT THE MEANING AND EFFECT OF THIS "AS IS" CLAUSE, THEN BUYER SHOULD CONSULT AN ATTORNEY. BUYERS INITIALS: _________

The practical question, of course, is whether or not a buyer will be willing to accept such strict language. As is true with many contract terms, it may come down to price.

"As Is" in the Real World

Generally speaking, "as is" transactions as a means of avoiding seller disclosure are problematic at best and should be avoided. No one, especially juries, likes a liar—whether the lie is by commission or omission. The best advice an attorney can give a seller is *disclose, disclose, disclose*. If an "as is" clause is going to be included in a contract, the seller should get a real estate attorney to draft it.

Investor clients often ask, "Can they sue me if . . . ?" For lots of reasons, this is the wrong question, since anyone can sue anyone for anything and incur little or no liability for doing so, at least in this country. The better approach is to deter suits in the first place by being open and aboveboard.

Buyers confronted by a seller who insists on an "as is" clause while attempting to avoid disclosure should be suspicious. In such a situation, the best course of action for the buyer may be to walk away. *Not every deal can or should be made.* On the other hand, an "as is" clause combined with full disclosure by the seller may not be a problem so long as the buyer realizes that the he or she should thoroughly inspect the property. Whenever a seller wants to include an "as is" clause in a sales contract, the buyer should respond by including a provision to the effect that such a clause does not relieve the seller of the obligation to disclose material conditions and defects. If the seller balks, then it may be time for an investor to look elsewhere for a deal.

Chapter 3

TITLE INSURANCE

Title Companies—a Blessing and a Curse

Title insurance is available to protect owners and lenders from loss resulting from defects in the title to real estate. Title policies and regulations are a complicated and evolving area and we are not offering a comprehensive treatise on the subject here. This chapter is designed only as an introductory overview for investors. Further information may be obtained at the websites for the Texas Land Title Association (www.tlta.com) and the Texas Department of Insurance (www.tdi.state.tx.us).

Closing at a title company that issues a title insurance policy to both buyer and lender is the usual way to do business in Texas, but it is not the only way. Closings can occur without title insurance—for example, in a lawyer's conference room or even at the kitchen table of one of the parties. There are good reasons, however, why obtaining title insurance is customary:

(1) The title company maintains a database of real estate resources that can be searched in order to produce a "title commitment," which is a review of the status of title and an important part of the preclosing process.

(2) The title company acts as a clearinghouse for closing documents that need to be signed and recorded, as well as for funds to be collected and disbursed at closing. The "closer" is the contact person who assembles the file (which is assigned a file number or "GF" number), prepares the HUD-1 settlement statement, and supervises the execution and notarization of documents on the day of closing.

(3) The title policy provides an avenue of recourse and recovery in the event either lender or buyer sustains a monetary loss as a result of a title defect. What kind of monetary loss? Well, suppose the title company missed a valid lien and the lienholder comes to collect; or suppose there

is a previously unknown heir who appears and claims an interest in the property. The title company will work to resolve such issues or, if appropriate, pay compensation. In many respects, a title company is like any other insurance company.

The Title Commitment

The title commitment is produced after the title company has received a copy of a signed sales contract and a check for earnest money. The commitment reviews the status of title, lists title issues and defects that need to be addressed or cured before closing, and states any other preconditions to issuance of a title policy.

The commitment also shows existing liens on Schedule C, and the title company routinely requires release of these. Other miscellaneous requirements may apply, such as a marital status affidavit, a not-same-name affidavit if there is a judgment in a name similar to that of the seller, and the like. If there are more serious issues like mechanic's liens, judgments against the seller, tax liens, lawsuits affecting title, heirship issues due to a previous owner dying without a will, or gaps in the chain of title, the commitment will indicate these and what must be done if title is to be cleared.

Role of the Earnest Money Contract

The title company's duties commence when it receives the executed sales contract and a check for earnest money. For residential transactions, Paragraph 6 of the TREC 1-4 contract entitled "Title Policy and Survey" applies. Although it is customary for the seller to pay for the title policy, this is not required, and paragraph 6 provides the opportunity to check the buyer as the paying party. The title company has 20 days to produce the commitment with an automatic 15 day extension if needed.

Paragraph 6.D provides a blank for insertion of a time period during which the buyer may object to issues raised by the commitment. The period inserted in this blank is usually seven to ten days. If the buyer does not make timely objections, any such issues are waived. Despite the buyer's waiver, however, the title company may insist that Schedule C items be cured before a title policy issues. It is, after all, the title company's liability that is on the line. If the buyer timely raises objections, then the seller must cure them or the TREC contract terminates.

Policies of Title Insurance

Two policies are usually issued: one for the buyer (the T-1 Owner Policy of Title Insurance) for the sales price of the land and improvements, which remains in effect so long as the new owner retains an interest in the property; and one for the lender (the T-2 Loan Policy of Title Insurance, formerly called the "Mortgagee Policy") for the value of the property or the amount of its loan, whichever is less. The loan policy terminates when the note matures and the four-year statute of limitations for foreclosure on the lien expires. An investor will not get a loan on Texas real estate from an institutional lender without a T-2 loan policy, so plan on using a title company if the intent is to borrow purchase money from a bank. A private hard-money lender may do the deal without title insurance, however, since the private market is far less regulated.

A title insurance policy insures "good and indefeasible" title, which is a slightly lesser standard than "good and marketable" title. The distinction goes back to the Great Depression when many properties were sold at sheriff's sales. Issues of marketability were raised, and this led to Texas adopting the "good and indefeasible" title rule—stating, in effect, that one's title is better than anyone else claiming it.

In the case of a construction loan, title companies do not cover mechanics' liens filed during construction, although one can and should request a down-date endorsement to the policy for an extra fee.

Remember, an owner policy is not required by law. It is always possible to do a title search or obtain a title report or abstract of title, thereby providing a comfort level regarding the status of title, the absence of liens, and the like—and then proceed on that basis. Many investors do just that and then close their deals. In fact, savvy pros learn how to do their own informal title searches at the courthouse and consult with their attorneys about what they find, reducing delays and costs.

Title Insurance Rates

The cost of title insurance is set by the Texas Department of Insurance which regulates this industry pursuant to Title XI of the Texas Insurance Code (the "Texas Title Insurance Act"). The form of a title insurance policy and the various available amendments are prescribed. The basic premium for a $100,000 policy is less than a $1,000, which is a one-time fee for coverage that lasts as long as the buyer has an insurable interest in the property. A formula applies for amounts higher than that. Hearings on rate increases occur biennially in even-numbered calendar years. Further information is contained in the Texas Title Insurance Basic Manual which can be found at tdi.texas.gov/company/titleman.html.

It is customary in Texas for the seller to pay the cost of the owner's policy. However, this is negotiable. It is all a question of price.

Differences between Title Companies

Since rates are regulated, there is nothing to gain from comparing title companies for the cheapest policy. Title companies do, however, vary in at least two significant respects: first, in the level and quality of service they (or a particular closer) may provide; and second, in their willingness to "insure around" certain potential defects or insure nonstandard transactions (wraparounds, trusts, and the like). Title companies are by nature conservative institutions. If a title company refuses to do a transaction, or sets out requirements that are difficult or impossible to satisfy—and this happens—then it may be necessary to shop title companies until one is found that is willing to do the more creative deals.

Some law offices enter into an arrangement with title underwriters to act as "fee attorneys," meaning that these attorneys can close transactions in their offices and issue title policies as an agent for the underwriter. While this may seem convenient, prominent real estate attorney Chuck Jacobus and others argue that it is a conflict of interest—that the lawyer's job is to advocate for the buyer or seller, not act as neutral escrow officer in order to collect insurance premiums and fees. We agree. The interests of buyers and sellers differ, sometimes immensely. Real estate documents can often be highly customized to favor one party or another. A lawyer trying to represent everyone may mean that no one gets adequate representation.

Exclusions and Exceptions to Owner's Coverage

As with any insurance policy there are exclusions and exceptions. The residential owner's policy expressly excludes such items as building and zoning ordinances; condemnation; title problems created by or undisclosed by the insured, or arising from fraud by the insured; title problems that result in no actual loss; access issues; refusal of anyone to lend money; and physical condition of the land.

Exceptions are specific limitations on coverage. These include standard printed exceptions on Schedule B—restrictive covenants and deed restrictions; the survey exception ("discrepancies, conflicts, or shortages in area") which can (and, for buyers should) be deleted for a fee; homestead, community, and survivorship rights; the exception for riparian rights, water-rights, and tidelands; the tax exception, including rollback taxes; the mechanic's lien exception; the exception for leases and subordinate liens; the rights of parties in possession; and, if there is no survey, easements and encroachments. The title company may also add special exceptions that it deems necessary after doing its research.

Title companies do not insure fraudulent conveyances or preferential transfers (transfers made to avoid payment of creditors). Excluded is "any claim, by reason of the operation of federal bankruptcy, state insolvency, or similar creditors' rights laws, that the transaction vesting the Title as shown in Schedule A is (a) a fraudulent conveyance or fraudulent transfer, or (b) a preferential transfer for any reason not stated in Covered Risk 9 of this policy." So if one is engaged in edgy asset protection, do not look to a title company for assistance.

The Title Company's Duty to Defend

If a title defect or lien appears after closing, the title company must investigate and

1. commence legal proceedings to clear title;
2. indemnify the insured pursuant to the policy;
3. reinsure the title to the property at current value;
4. indemnify another insurer if another company does there insuring; or
5. cure the defect or obtain a release of the lien.

If the title company does not take one or more of the above actions, it can be sued by the insured for breach of contract. Note that the company's duty to defend is contingent upon the insured providing timely written notice of the defect or lien. The duty to defend is not triggered by claims of money and the like that do not constitute a true cloud on the title.

Recovery under an owner's policy is limited to the owner's actual money loss or the amount of the policy, whichever is less. The insured must give the title company prompt notice and cooperate in furtherance of the claim. The old requirement that the policy itself be produced in order to recover has been eliminated. Payment must be made by the company within 30 days of determination of liability and the extent of the loss. If the title company settles a covered claim, it is subrogated to the rights of the insured as to that claim (i.e., it assumes the insured's right of recovery).

Minerals

Title insurance companies are not required to insure the mineral estate. *See* Tex. Ins. Code § 2703.0515. Prior to this statute, minerals and mineral rights were generally excepted under Schedule B of the policy. Title companies have traditionally taken the view that the job of determining title to minerals belongs not to title insurers but to landmen and oil and gas attorneys, although the title company will provide copies of mineral leases and conveyances if a buyer or the buyer's attorney wishes to review them prior to closing (never a bad idea). Since minerals in producing regions have usually long-since been conveyed away (especially in the typical urban residential setting) the sole concern of a homeowner is use of the surface of the land (surface estate) by a mineral-interest holder to gain access to the minerals. Optional endorsements are available that will protect against damage to the surface estate (T-19.2 or T-19.3). The Texas T2-R already protects lenders against such surface damage. This is an evolving area currently under review by the Department of Insurance.

Community Property and Heirship Property

Texas is a community property state and, as such, all property acquired by either spouse during marriage is presumed to be community. It is common for a title company to either require joinder of a seller's spouse on a deed or, in the alternative, a marital status affidavit and/or a nonhomestead affidavit.

If someone in the chain of title died without a will, you may also expect that the title company will require a conveyance of some kind (usually a special warranty deed) from each and every heir and, if an heir is deceased, from the heirs of that heir. Alternatively, the title company may be satisfied with an affidavit of heirship if there are no other heirs and the circumstances of family history can be sufficiently well established. It can get complicated and expensive to cure defects in heirship property. See the chapter on affidavits of heirship.

Chapter 4

EARNEST MONEY DISPUTES IN RESIDENTIAL TRANSACTIONS

The Process for Release of Earnest Money

Disputes over earnest money usually arise when either buyer or seller perceive the other to be at fault for failing to close. The parties can be emotional, unreasonable, and determined to stand on principle, all common shortcomings in persons who are unacquainted with the costs and burdens of litigation. In fact, "fault" in the subjective sense is not usually the issue, at least as to earnest money, since its disposition is expressly governed by the TREC 1-4 contract and its addenda. Problems and the potential for litigation arise when an aggrieved party refuses to do what the contract says.

This chapter does not address what occurs when earnest money is not deposited at all, except to observe that this constitutes a breach of the contract (a default by the buyer). It does not, as some believe, cause the contract to fail altogether.

Buyer Withdrawal Because of Failure to Obtain Financing

A common area of dispute is failure by the buyer to obtain financing. Note that although paragraph 4.A(1) makes the TREC 1-4 contract contingent upon financing, the TREC Third-Party Financing Condition Addendum contains a blank for a *specific time* during which the buyer must notify the seller of his inability to obtain financing. If this notice is not timely given, the contingency is waived. Buyers often miss this detail and insist on their continuing right to get their earnest money back if their loan application is denied, even after the specified time has run.

Sellers, on the other hand, may believe that the buyer did not make "every reasonable effort to obtain credit approval" (as required by the TREC addendum) and therefore should not be entitled to return of earnest money even if notice is given within the prescribed period. Unfortunately for this point of view, the addendum does not go into detail about what "every reasonable effort" means.

Contract Provisions Relating to Release of Earnest Money

Whatever the cause of the dispute, paragraphs 18.C through E address the procedure for release of earnest money:

> C. DEMAND: Upon termination of this contract, either party or the escrow agent may send a release of earnest money to each party and the parties shall execute counterparts of the release and deliver same to the escrow agent. If either party fails to execute the release, either party may make a written demand to the escrow agent for the earnest money. If only one party makes written demand for the earnest money, escrow agent shall promptly provide a copy of the demand to the other party. If escrow agent does not receive written objection to the demand from the other party within 15 days, escrow agent may disburse the earnest money to the party making demand reduced by the amount of unpaid expenses incurred on behalf of the party receiving the earnest money and escrow agent may pay the same to the creditors. If escrow agent complies with the provisions of this paragraph, each party hereby releases escrow agent from all adverse claims related to the disbursal of the earnest money.
>
> D. DAMAGES: Any party who wrongfully fails or refuses to sign a release acceptable to the escrow agent within 7 days of receipt of the request will be liable to the other party for liquidated damages in an amount equal to the sum of: (i) three times the amount of the earnest money; (ii) the earnest money; (iii) reasonable attorney's fees; and (iv) all costs of suit.
>
> E. NOTICES: Escrow agent's notices will be effective when sent in compliance with Paragraph 21. Notice of objection to the demand will be deemed effective upon receipt by escrow agent.

The contract is clear. Upon failure of the contract for any reason, the party desiring the earnest money must make written demand upon the title company. A copy of the demand should be sent to the other party. The written demand triggers a 15-day window during which the other party may make written objection to the title company. Phone calls, almost always legally insufficient in real estate for notice purposes, will not meet the requirements of the contract. Email or fax would be sufficient, but certified mail to both the title company and the other party is best, particularly if litigation is a possibility. There is nothing like being able to show a signed green card in court in order to prove notice.

The language of the contract is vague about *which* demand—demand from the party desiring the earnest money versus demand from the title company—triggers the 15- and 7-day periods, but it is prudent to be conservative and assume that these periods begin when the first party makes written demand.

What happens next?

The title company will follow up with a notice of its own that written demand has been made and enclosing a release form for signature. It must be signed by all parties and their brokers. Although fifteen days are permitted in order to make written objection, paragraph 18.D imposes liquidated damages of three times the amount of the earnest money if a party "wrongfully" refuses to sign a release within seven days. Attorney's fees and costs could be added to this amount as provided in paragraph 17.

What happens next depends on whether or not the remedy of mediation was checked in paragraph 16. If it was, mediation must precede the filing of litigation to recover earnest money. Filing suit prior to mediation will likely result in the court abating the case (putting it on hold) until the mediation requirement is fulfilled.

Lawsuit Remedy in Justice Court

Lawsuits may be filed in justice court so long as the total amount claimed (including attorney's fees) does not exceed $10,000. If total damages exceed that amount, then suit may be filed in the county court at law. Named defendants should include the party refusing to sign the release *and* the title company holding the earnest money. Title companies will usually respond by interpleading the earnest money (depositing it into the court's account) which removes them from the merits of the litigation. The title company may then seek dismissal from the case or decide to remain in an attempt to recover attorney's fees from the party at fault.

Before filing a legal action concerning earnest money, it is useful to consider the practical reality that attorney's fees and costs, once added up, can easily exceed the amount of earnest money in dispute. As a consequence, many earnest money disputes are resolved by the parties' splitting the funds and going their separate ways, respective claims of principle notwithstanding.

Chapter 5

AFFIDAVITS OF HEIRSHIP

An Inexpensive Alternative to Probate

If a person dies without a will, and the deed does not expressly include joint tenancy with survivorship language, then issues may arise as to which persons have title and in what percentages. Such property is often referred to as "heirship property." It is essentially unsellable as it is, and a title company will not issue title insurance until heirship issues are addressed and resolved. This is usually accomplished by either a probate proceeding in county court (resulting in appointment of a personal representative of the estate and ultimately a judgment determining heirship) or by an affidavit of heirship followed by a "curative deed" or "consolidation deed" (our terms) signed by the surviving heirs.

Note that this is not a book on probate law, although we occasionally refer to sections of the Probate Code. If an investor is faced with probate issues, then an attorney who is a board-certified specialist in that area should be consulted.

Title Company Requirement

This is the typical title company requirement where heirship property is involved: *We are to be furnished with an affidavit executed by an immediate member of the family and corroborated by at least two disinterested parties containing the marital history of the deceased and his spouse and a complete list of heirs, together with an original death certificate attached.*

The title company is asking here for an affidavit of heirship. The purpose of the affidavit in an intestacy case (no will) is to describe family history and name the likely heirs pursuant to the appropriate provision of the Probate Code. The affidavit must be signed under oath by a person familiar with these facts (usually but not always a family member) and attested to by disinterested witnesses (using three witnesses is prudent) who have no personal or financial stake in the outcome. It is then filed in the real property records of the county where the property is located.

Intestate Succession

When a person dies intestate, the rules of intestate succession take over. Essentially, the State of Texas has made a will for intestate decedents.

If the intestate decedent is unmarried, then Probate Code section 38 applies, providing that property goes in equal shares to the children if there are any. If not, then the property goes in equal shares to the parents. If the decedent was married, then community property is involved and section 45 applies, which can be complicated to understand and apply:

> **§ 45. Community Estate**
>
> **(a) On the intestate death of one of the spouses to a marriage, the community property estate of the deceased spouse passes to the surviving spouse if:**
>
> > **(1) no child or other descendant of the deceased spouse survives the deceased spouse; or**
> >
> > **(2) all surviving children and descendants of the deceased spouse are also children or descendants of the surviving spouse.**
>
> **(b) On the intestate death of one of the spouses to a marriage, if a child or other descendant of the deceased spouse survives the deceased spouse and the child or descendant is not a child or descendant of the surviving spouse, one-half of the community estate is retained by the surviving spouse and the other one-half passes to the children or descendants of the deceased spouse. The descendants shall inherit only such portion of said property to which they would be entitled under section 43 of this code. In every case, the community estate passes charged with the debts against it.**

A well-drafted affidavit of heirship will refer to specific sections of the Probate Code and reach a conclusion as to the identity of the heirs.

Two-Step Process: Affidavit then Deed

Curing title (resolving heirship issues) outside of probate court is usually a two-step process. First, the affidavit of heirship must be prepared and signed by someone with first-hand, personal knowledge of family history (marriages, births, and deaths). Probate Code section 52A offers a suggested form for this affidavit, although the form is only a minimal guideline. Crafting a thorough and effective affidavit is both art and science and should be left to an attorney who will assure its contents will be both admissible and persuasive in any future litigation. Accordingly, Internet forms should *never* be used for this or any other serious legal purpose.

Probate Code section 52 provides that an affidavit of heirship will be presumed to be true "if the affidavit or instrument has been of record for five years or more in the deed records of any county in this state in which such real or personal property is located[.]"

The purpose of the affidavit of heirship is to reach conclusions as to the identity of the rightful heirs and the amount of their respective interests.

Preparation of the Deed

The second step in the process, after drafting and execution of the affidavit, is a deed that focuses title into a single heir who may then keep the property or sell it. Alternatively, all heirs may sign conveying the property to a third-party buyer.

The deed is usually a special warranty deed or deed without warranties, but not a quitclaim deed, which is to be avoided because title companies will likely not insure it. All heirs named in the affidavit (or their legal guardians) must sign. Both documents are filed in the real property records in the county in which the property is located—the affidavit first, and then the deed.

What the Attorney Needs from the Client

The attorney needs basic information from the client in order to proceed, including:

> (1) an explanation of family history and circumstances (e.g., who married whom and who had children, who died with a will or without, who got divorced and re-married, and so on);
>
> (2) a copy of the existing recorded deed to the property and, if available, a copy of a title commitment;

(3) the names and addresses of all relevant parties; and

(4) an explanation of the client's intent. Is the goal to consolidate title into one or more heirs? Or sell the property to a third party?

In many cases heirs are spread across the country and may have lost touch. Some heirs may not sign unless they are paid to do so—and financial issues between family members can get ugly. Clients are often disappointed when they discover how difficult and expensive the process can be. Heirs may attempt to resolve heirship and title issues on their own, without an attorney (often using junk forms from the Internet), and are left with an incorrect result. Affidavits and deeds may then have to be reprepared and refiled, prolonging the process and increasing expense.

Family Values

A prospective client calls an attorney and says "My mother died six months ago, and I need to get a deed to her ranch. How much do you charge for preparing a deed?"

The attorney needs to know a great deal more information before he or she can respond, starting with asking, "Did she die with a will?" The client admits that he hasn't seen his mother in ten years, but he believes there was no will. He goes on to ask, "But I can still get my deed can't I?" Further questions from the attorney reveal more information about the family. The mother was a widow. The father died two years earlier, also without a will. In addition, it turns out that the client has several siblings, one of whom was from the father's prior marriage. Another has dropped out of sight and has not been heard from in years. There are rumors he is homeless on the streets of Los Angeles. Another sibling recently passed away, leaving two small children who are currently in foster care because their remaining parent is in prison. Also, the youngest sibling was living with Mom and taking care of her at the time of Mom's death, and she continues to occupy the property, now claiming it as *her* homestead and threatening to use a shotgun on anyone who enters without her consent. She contends that Mom promised that the house would be hers in exchange for care during her final illness.

The attorney is forced to tell the client he is *not* going to get a deed, at least not until heirship issues are straightened out, beginning with the father and which persons were entitled to inherit from him, and then moving on to the mother and her heirs. The client is suspicious. He says, "Look, your secretary told me that the fee for a deed is $225. It sounds like you're just trying to charge me more money. I'm the oldest, and I was always told the property would be mine one day. I want my deed now!" Unfortunately, that is just not possible given the facts of the case. The attorney is not a miracle worker, nor is a law office a court of law where differences can be adjudicated.

Because of the complexities of the case and the necessity of attempting to contact, negotiate with, and perhaps buy out other surviving heirs who also might want the property, legal fees and expenses could reach into the many thousands of dollars—with no guarantee of success. Other attorneys could become involved. The case might have to be decided in court and take years to resolve.

Chapter 6

LIS PENDENS

Are These a Proper Device to Stop a Closing?

A lis pendens (or more properly, a "notice of lis pendens") is an affidavit filed in the county clerk's real property records announcing that a lawsuit involving local real estate is pending in a certain court. A lis pendens indicates that a civil action is pending pertaining to title to real property, the establishment of an interest in real property, or enforcement of an encumbrance against real property. These are specific statutory categories. Another way to say this is that the law will not support the filing of a lis pendens unless *the property itself* is truly the subject of the suit. A notice that indirectly affects the property is not valid. For instance, a suit seeking only monetary damages would not justify the filing of a lis pendens, nor would a suit to specifically enforce or set aside an earnest money contract, because none of these pertain to the property itself—only to a breach of contract to convey the property, a subtle but meaningful legal distinction.

If a lis pendens is wrongfully filed, a court may order it canceled. Damages for wrongful filing, while not expressly provided by statute, cannot be precluded.

Rule Relating to Bona Fide Purchasers

Although a lis pendens is not a lien, it is often viewed in a similar light and can therefore have the effect of stopping a sale. Why? Because constructive notice of litigation has now been given to potential buyers. If this were not the case, the rule regarding a bona fide purchaser ("BFP") would apply—i.e., a buyer who purchases real property for valuable consideration without notice of a disputed claim or prior interest does so free of that claim or interest. Accordingly, if a notice of lis pendens is properly filed, then a buyer (by definition) cannot be a BFP; at best the buyer becomes a purchaser pendente lite, meaning that he or she would take title subject to the outcome of the litigation. Additionally, a title company will not usually issue an owner's policy of title insurance to a buyer until the lawsuit is cleared up and/or the lis pendens is canceled.

The result is that a seller involved in litigation concerning a property cannot easily get rid of the problem by selling that property to someone else. Without this rule, the parties could be prevented from justly resolving their litigation and the authority of the courts defeated.

Note that if a prospective purchaser has actual notice of a pending suit, then the lis pendens doctrine applies whether or not a statutory notice has been filed in the real property records. A buyer cannot know about a lawsuit (from whatever source) and still claim to be a BFP.

Governing Law

The law governing lis pendens arises from equitable common law but has been significantly enhanced by statute. Property Code sections 12.007, 12.0071, and 12.008 state that the notice itself must contain specific facts. Section 12.007(b) and (d) state:

> **(b) The party filing a *lis pendens* or the party's agent or attorney shall sign the *lis pendens*, which must state**
>
> **(1) the style and number, if any, of the proceeding;**
> **(2) thc court in which the proceeding is pen-ding;**
> **(3) the names of the parties;**
> **(4) the kind of proceeding; and**
> **(5) a description of the property affected.**
>
> **(d) Not later than the third day after the date a person files a notice for record under this section the person must serve a copy of the notice on each party to the action who has an interest in the real property affected by the notice.**

A notice that does not satisfy the requirements of the statute may, upon motion, be ordered canceled or expunged by the court. Property Code section 12.0071 contains the requirements for a motion to expunge. Section 12.008 further addresses the subject of cancellation:

> **(a) On the motion of a party . . . the court hearing the action may cancel the *lis pendens* . . . if the court determines that the party seeking affirmative relief**

can be adequately protected by the deposit of money into court or by the giving of an undertaking.

Duration of a Lis Pendens

"A *lis pendens* operates only during the pendency of the [underlying] suit, and only as to those matters that are involved in the suit. It terminates with the judgment, in the absence of an appeal." *Rosborough v. Cook*, 108 Tex. 364, 367, 194 S.W. 131, 132 (1917). A timely appeal or motion for new trial extends the operative effect of the lis pendens. In other words, a lis pendens has no life of its own apart from the lawsuit that underlies it. A property owner may nonetheless legitimately demand that a lis pendens be terminated by the filing of a formal cancelation, even after dismissal or resolution of the suit.

Penalties for Wrongful or Fraudulent Filings

The Property Code does not grant an express penalty for filing a wrongful or fraudulent lis pendens. As a result, "courts have given a broad reading to § 12.008, so as to grant an effective remedy." *See Prappas v. Meyerland Cmty. Improvement Ass'n*, 795 S.W.2d 794, 798 (Tex. App.—Houston [14th Dist.] 1990, writ denied).

Although lis pendens are generally considered to be privileged (even if filed with malice), this protection does not extend to the underlying suit. Rule 13 of the Texas Rules of Civil Procedure provides sanctions if lawsuits are "groundless and brought in bad faith or groundless and brought for the purpose of harassment. . . . 'Groundless' for purposes of this rule means no basis in law or fact and not warranted by good faith argument for the extension, modification, or reversal of existing law." Annoy a judge with a frivolous lis pendens and watch how quickly Rule 13 sanctions will be imposed.

It is also worth looking at Civil Practice and Remedies Code section 12.002 which addresses "liability related to . . . a fraudulent lien or claim filed against real or personal property." Since a lis pendens could be interpreted as a claim of sorts, or at least the memorandum of one, the filer could potentially incur liability under this statute if aspects of the lis pendens or the underlying suit are found to be fraudulent. A person who knowingly and intentionally files a fraudulent lien may be held liable in civil district court for the greater of $10,000 or actual damages, exemplary damages, and recovery of attorney's fees and costs. It is also a criminal offense. *See* Tex. Penal Code § 37.01. If applicable, a cause of action under Chapter 12 should be included in any suit against the filer of the lis pendens.

There is also the matter of civil liability for consequential damages. What if a wrongfully or fraudulently filed lis pendens causes a transaction to fail, perhaps resulting in substantial monetary loss to the seller? It is likely that the seller's attorney will be looking for someone to hold responsible.

Additionally, the filing of a fraudulent lien or claim may under certain circumstances form the basis of a cause of action under the Deceptive Trade Practices Act, Tex. Bus. & Com. Code §§ 17.44 et seq.

Lis pendens are a useful tool but are subject to abuse as well as potential liability. They must be employed in strict compliance with the statute and not merely to gain advantage in a dispute over a real estate closing.

OWNERSHIP & TRANSFER OF TEXAS REAL ESTATE

Chapter 7

CO-OWNERSHIP OF PROPERTY

Including Comments on Joint Tenancy with Rights of Survivorship

For purposes of most investor transactions, co-ownership is generally "tenancy-in-common" although other legal categories exist. This means that the interest of a co-owner, absent express provision to the contrary, passes directly to that person's heirs—who may or may not be the other co-owner(s). And disregard the common meaning of "tenant" and "tenancy." Traditional legal language can be misleading. In this context, these terms refer to owners not renters.

Attorneys often face co-ownership issues when advising on inheritance and probate avoidance. Inheritance in such cases may be determined by express language in a deed or a last will and testament, or in the absence of either, by intestacy provisions of the Probate Code. In some circumstances a co-owner may have no survivorship rights at all. This may come as a surprise to those who rashly assume that Texas law will rule as they wish, or even logically, in such matters.

Another area is the common request from clients that someone be "added" to a deed which, unfortunately, is not as simple as it sounds. This topic is discussed below.

Co-Owners Who Are Spouses

Does a surviving spouse inherit the entire interest in the home when the other dies? Not necessarily. It is first necessary to determine if the deceased spouse died "testate" (with a will) or "intestate" (without a will). If a spouse dies intestate, property automatically vests 100% in the surviving spouse *only* if the property is community property *and* the deceased had no children—or, if there are children, all of them are the result of the marriage between these two spouses (i.e., there are no children from a prior marriage, an increasingly uncommon circumstance). See Probate Code section 45 for further explanation.

Co-Owners Who Are Not Spouses

Texas law presumes that if two nonspouses are named as co-owners, and nothing more is said, then they are tenants-in-common. This means they each person owns an undivided one-half interest in the property *but there is no automatic right of survivorship.* When one co-owner dies, the interest of the deceased co-owner goes directly to that person's heir or heirs, either by will or by intestate succession. The recipient may or may not be the other co-owner. The line of succession is more likely to be vertical than horizontal.

Joint Tenancy with Rights of Survivorship (JTWROS)

Probate Code section 46(a) states that "[t]he joint owners may agree in writing . . . that the interest of any joint owner who dies shall survive to the surviving joint owner or owners, but no such agreement shall be inferred from the mere fact that the property is held in joint ownership." The simplest way to accomplish JTWROS is to recite language in the deed which expressly establishes survivorship rights. *This language must be included at the time that both persons receive their interest in the property.* If the required language is present, a joint tenancy is created which will result in the surviving co-owner automatically inheriting the entire interest of the deceased co-owner, without necessity for probate or other legal action. This is true even if the co-owners are not spouses.

An example of a grantee clause that creates joint tenancy is "John Smith and wife, Mary Smith, as joint tenants with rights of survivorship and not as tenants in common." The intent and agreement of the co-owners is stated plainly. This achieves a survivorship arrangement that has been dubbed the "poor man's will."

Probate Code section 47(d) imposes a caveat: In order for a joint tenant to inherit, the survivor must survive the deceased by at least 120 hours. If this does not occur, then "these assets shall be distributed one-half as if one joint owner had survived and the other one-half as if the other joint owner had survived."

Note that if property is currently held by two persons as tenants-in-common, they can convert this to joint tenancy by means of a survivorship agreement as provided in Probate Code section 46. However, this method does not physically change the warranty deed, and many persons are looking for just that—a single title document that states both names and makes survivorship clear.

The Role of a Last Will and Testament

Even if a deed contains no survivorship language, each co-owner may make his or her wishes plain by executing a valid will that provides for inheritance of the deceased's interest. The Probate Code is a fallback that comes into effect by default, in the absence of a will. Failing to make a will is equivalent to asking the State of Texas to determine how your property will be disposed of. *See* Tex. Prob. Code §§ 38 et seq.

Deeds Prepared by the Title Company

When buyers arrive at a title company to close, they are often handed an assembly-line deed that contains no extra clauses favorable to them—unless, of course, their own attorney has negotiated the inclusion of such clauses. This is unfortunate, since a warranty deed is qualitatively different from the routine forms and disclosures that title companies prepare. It is the sole document that evidences title to the property and may also set forth significant conditions upon which the seller is selling and the buyer is buying. It is far more important than, say, a MUD disclosure.

It is worth the effort to customize the warranty deed so it suits one's purposes. Generally, one should not expect the title company to assist with this. Title companies are *insurance companies*. They and their attorneys look out for themselves, not you. It is astonishing how many people, even investors, naively believe that the title company is concerned with their best interests and will draft documents accordingly. Not necessarily so.

If buyers want to hold title as joint tenants with rights of survivorship, they must specifically ask in advance of the closing that appropriate wording be included in the deed. Ideally, this intent should be reflected on the earnest money contract they sign to purchase the property.

Heirship Property

What happens if a person dies both without a will *and* without a joint tenancy clause in their deed? Such property is often referred to as "heirship property" and, without curative measures, may be unsellable except perhaps privately by means of a deed without warranties or quitclaim.

A title company will not issue title insurance until heirship issues are first addressed and resolved. An affidavit of heirship is often used for this purpose, followed by a consolidating deed signed by the heirs. The affidavit recites relevant facts concerning family history, identifies the heirs, and is usually signed by a family member with personal knowledge. The deed is then signed by the heirs with the goal of moving title into a single heir or perhaps a third-party buyer. Both documents should then be filed in the proper order in the real property records.

Adding Someone to the Deed

Clients often ask that another person be added to their deed so that this other person will have co-ownership and inheritance rights. There are two methods:

> (1) The existing owner can execute a deed to the other person for a percentage of fee-simple ownership (e.g., 50%). The result is that each person becomes a co-owner, although this status is reflected in two documents, not one. Again, Texas law presumes that the two persons here are tenants-in-common.
>
> (2) The second method is for the owner to transfer the property out to a third party (the attorney or some other trusted individual) who then transfers the property back into the two desired names with JTWROS language. This is the only way both names wind up on the same piece of paper.

If the intent is to achieve JTWROS in a single instrument, then this must be created when title is taken by both persons simultaneously. The second method described above is the only way to achieve this. Title must be conveyed out to a third party and then conveyed back as JTWROS, requiring that two deeds be executed and filed back-to-back.

Regardless of whether the result is tenancy in common or JTWROS, the added person does *not* become liable on the loan on the property. Liability on a loan occurs only when a note is signed. No signature on a note, no liability to the bank.

If a client wants to add someone to a deed, then he or she should let the attorney know which of the two methods is preferred; provide a copy of the existing warranty deed to the property; and supply all pertinent names, addresses, and the marital status of the parties.

Percentage Ownership

If one investor owns 60%, another owns 20%, and a third owns 20%, then it is appropriate to specify these percentages in the deed by which the property is acquired. Alternatively, the three owners could form an entity (an LLC or a trust) to hold title, and the records of the LLC would reflect the varying membership interests or, if a trust is used, the varying beneficial interests. An LLC is preferred if the parties are concerned with potential liability, a trust if the principal concern is anonymity. Percentage ownership is not available in the case of JTWROS.

The Living Trust Alternative

A living trust achieves the objectives of joint tenancy and more. It is designed to hold property (primarily real estate) during the life of the trustor (the person conveying the property into trust) in order to avoid probate and potentially reduce estate/inheritance taxes at the time of the trustor's death. Read our chapter on living trusts.

Chapter 8

DEEDS IN TEXAS

An Overview for Investors

What is a deed?

A deed is a written document that conveys legal and equitable title to real property. It is difficult to imagine a more important document to the real estate investor, and yet its preparation is often left to a title company attorney who represents neither buyer nor seller and who, accordingly, has no incentive to produce anything other than an inexpensive, basic form.

A deed is to be distinguished from a promissory note (or real estate lien note) which is a promise to pay a sum of money, and from a deed of trust, which provides the lender with remedies (including foreclosure) if a borrower defaults on the note. A warranty deed, note, and deed of trust are the three principal documents in most Texas residential real estate transactions.

There is no standard form for a deed although Texas does have certain rules that apply if a deed is to be valid. For instance, the parties should be named, the intent to convey property must be clear from the wording, the property must be sufficiently described, and the deed must be signed and acknowledged by the grantor. *Gordon v. W. Hous. Trees, Ltd.*, 352 S.W.3d 32 (Tex. App.—Houston [1st Dist.] 2011, no pet.). Having said this, it is not true that all deeds are created equal. In particular, when a grantor intends to accomplish a specific objective and limit liability in doing so, the wording of a deed can be critically important. Similarly, if a buyer wishes to limit liability for an existing loan or for taxes due, a basic title company deed may not be adequate.

This chapter briefly describes different types of deeds commonly used in connection with real estate investment in Texas. It is not intended to be an exhaustive academic review of the topic.

Must deeds be recorded to be valid?

There is no requirement that a deed be recorded in the county clerk's real property records in order to be valid—only that it be executed and delivered to the grantee (this may be done privately), at which time the transfer is fully effective between the grantor (seller) and the grantee (buyer). Recording merely gives notice to the world of the transfer and, of course, establishes priority in the event an unscrupulous seller conveys the property twice.

Recording makes it easier for title companies to research and insure the chain of title. Title companies insist on recording for this reason. Recording also informs the taxing authorities where ad valorem tax bills should be sent.

Executing and delivering a deed without immediately recording it can be a useful, inexpensive estate planning device—sometimes called "the deed in the drawer." If, for example, a parent wants to insure that property is transferred to a child without probate or other difficulty, then he or she can sign and deliver a deed with the intention that it be held and not recorded until death. This is entirely legal.

One more item relating to timing—the doctrine of "after-acquired title." If I give you a deed today to property that I do not yet own, it of course has no effect; but if I acquire that same property next week, then the deed I gave you comes to life and the property is yours.

Must deeds show the actual purchase price?

No. In fact, in Texas, it is customary to recite that the consideration paid is "ten dollars and other valuable consideration." Why? Confidentiality. While recording gives the public notice that a transaction has occurred, and therefore preserves the integrity of the chain of title, it is Texas tradition that it is not the public's business what the purchase price was. Of course, the parties can always choose to show the actual price if they wish.

Who signs the deed?

The deed must be signed and acknowledged before a notary by the seller. The buyer's signature is not usually required, but it may be advisable to include it if the deed contains specific agreements on the part of the buyer. In order for these to be clear and enforceable in contract, they should be set out in the deed and the buyer should execute the deed before a notary.

Sale of Property Subject to Existing Indebtedness

Can title to property be transferred if money is owed to a lender? Yes. Title and debt are different and divisible concepts.

A "subject to" deed refers to acquiring title to property while expressly providing that the buyer assumes no liability for existing debts and liens.

It is a common device used by investors in order to buy property, fix it, and then flip it for a profit, all without promising to pay the existing debt or taking any liability for it.

The sub 2 concept may be better understood by reading the following sample sub 2 deed clause: "This conveyance is made subject to any and all indebtedness of Grantor and liens against the Property, including but not limited to that certain indebtedness and liens securing same evidenced by a note in the original principal amount of $______, dated ______, executed by Grantor and payable to the order of ___, which note is secured by a vendor's lien retained in deed of even date recorded at Clerk's File No. ___ in the Official Records of Real Property of ______ County, Texas, and is additionally secured by a deed of trust of even date to ___, Trustee, recorded at Clerk's File No. ___ in the Official Records of Real Property of ______ County, Texas. Grantee does not assume payment of this or any other indebtedness of Grantor."

Sale of Property "As Is"

A grantor may be willing to sell only on an "as is" basis. In such a case, "as is" refers to the condition of the property rather than the condition of the title. In other words, an "as is" deed may also be a warranty deed. The two are not mutually exclusive. Express and implied warranties of title may be and usually are present; however, there are no warranties made in an "as is" deed as to the state or condition of the land or any improvements upon it.

This is a sample brief "as is" clause: **"THE PROPERTY IS CONVEYED AND ACCEPTED "AS IS," IN ITS PRESENT PHYSICAL CONDITION, WITH ALL FAULTS AND DEFECTS, KNOWN OR UNKNOWN, AND WITHOUT WARRANTIES, EXPRESS OR IMPLIED, EXCEPT FOR WARRANTIES OF TITLE AS MAY BE EXPRESSLY SET FORTH AND LIMITED HEREIN."** The "as is" aspect of a conveyance is often more important in commercial transactions where the clause can be much more detailed and lengthy.

Does the presence of an "as is" clause negate any duty on the part of the seller to disclose defects? Probably not. Read our chapter on seller disclosure.

General Warranty Deed

The term "warranty deed" refers to a deed that contains both express and implied warranties (There is also a deed without warranties, discussed below.) A general warranty deed is the preferred form of deed for a buyer because it expressly warrants the *entire* chain of title all the way back to the sovereign, and it binds the grantor to defend against title defects, even if those defects were created prior to the grantor's period of ownership.

Here is a sample general warranty clause: "Grantor binds Grantor and Grantor's heirs, executors, administrators, successors and assigns to warrant and forever defend all and singular the Property to Grantee and Grantee's heirs, executors, administrators, successors, and assigns against every person whomsoever lawfully claiming or to claim the same or any part thereof, except as to the Reservations from Conveyance and the Exceptions to Conveyance and Warranty."

What are implied warranties? Mostly what one would expect. An example is the "covenant of seisin"—a warranty that the grantor presently owns the property that is conveyed, i.e., that he has not previously conveyed it to someone else. Another is the "covenant against encumbrances" which refers to undisclosed liens that diminish the monetary value of land. Property Code section 5.023 spells out these implied warranties. Note that the scope of any warranty may be limited by a "subject to" provision which might state, for example, that a conveyance is being made subject to a boundary dispute involving a certain section of the property. A provision of this type is intended to protect the grantor against a claim for breach of warranty.

General warranty deeds predominate in sales of residential property.

Special Warranty Deed

In a special warranty deed, title is warranted *only* from the grantor and no further back than that. The grantor's liability for title defects is therefore limited to his period of ownership up to and including conveyance to the grantee. Example: "Grantor binds Grantor and Grantor's heirs, executors, administrators, successors and assigns to warrant and forever defend all and singular the Property to Grantee and Grantee's heirs, executors, administrators, successors, and assigns against every person whomsoever lawfully claiming or to claim the same or any part thereof, when the claim is by, through, or under Grantor, but not otherwise, except as to the Reservations from Conveyance and the exceptions to Conveyance and Warranty."

Commercial properties are typically conveyed by special warranty deed. Deeds into an LLC may be either with general or special warranty, depending on the circumstances.

Deed without Warranties

A deed without warranties is just that—a conveyance of real property without warranties, express or implied, as to any matters whatsoever.

This is a sample no-warranties conveyance clause: "Grantor, for the consideration and subject to the Reservations from Conveyance and Exceptions to Conveyance and Warranty, grants, sells, and conveys to Grantee the Property, together with all and singular the rights and appurtenances thereto in any way belonging, to have and to hold it to Grantee and Grantee's heirs, executors, administrators, successors, and assigns forever, without express or implied warranty. All warranties that might arise by common law as well as the warranties in section 5.023 of the Texas Property Code (or its successor) are excluded."

Why would anyone make or accept such a conveyance? The usual case is when the parties are unsure as to the extent of the grantor's interest, and/or if the grantor is willing to enter into the conveyance only on the condition that there is no liability for doing so. A deed without warranties may transfer the entire interest in a certain property, or it may not. The parties assume the risk of this uncertainty. A deed without warranties is therefore a lower form of deed, but it nevertheless is effective in transferring title.

Quitclaims

Clients often call a lawyer's office and say they need a quitclaim deed. The lawyer's response should almost always be "No, you don't." Why? For one reason, a quitclaim may not be a true deed at all; it merely conveys whatever interest the grantor may have in a certain property, if any such interest exists. Secondly, from a practical standpoint, title companies disdain quitclaims and will frequently require that a warranty deed be obtained instead. One does no favor to the chain of title by inserting a quitclaim into it. If a grantor is unable or unwilling to provide any warranties, then a deed without warranties should be used instead of a quitclaim.

Assumption Deed

Assumption deeds usually contain covenants of general or special warranty. The difference is that assumption deeds expressly provide that the grantee will assume liability for existing indebtedness and promise to discharge one or more existing liens against the property.

The consideration clause in an assumption deed might read as follows:

> "Ten dollars ($10.00) and other valuable consideration, the receipt and value of which is hereby acknowledged, including Grantee's assumption of and promise to pay, according to its terms, all principal and interest remaining unpaid on that certain note (the "Assumed Note") in the

> original principal amount of $____, dated ______, executed by_______ and payable to the order of ___ (said payee together with its successors and assigns being referred to herein as "Lender"), subsequently assigned to and now held by ___. The Assumed Note is secured by an express vendor's lien and superior title retained in deed of even date recorded at Clerk's File No. ___ in the Official Records of Real Property of_______ County, Texas, and is additionally secured by a deed of trust of even date (the "Deed of Trust") in favor of ___, Trustee, recorded at Clerk's File No. ___ in the Official Records of Real Property of_______ County, Texas. As further consideration, Grantee promises to keep and perform all of the covenants and obligations of the Grantor contained in the Assumed Note and the Deed of Trust and to indemnify, defend, and hold Grantor harmless from any loss, attorney's fees, expenses, or claims attributable to a breach or default of any provision of this assumption by Grantee. Grantee shall commence payments on the Assumed Note on or before the next regular due date under the Assumed Note."

Again, separate the concept of *title* from the concept of *debt*. They are related but different, and they can be divided, at least when discussing respective obligations of grantor and grantee. One can take title to property without becoming liable to pay the underlying debt. Of course, debts secured by liens against the property remain in place even if title is transferred.

Under an assumption deed the grantee declares his assumption obligation to the grantor—but, it should be pointed out, not to the lender, since the grantee has not signed the lender's note. Similarly, the grantor has not been released from the existing note unless the lender has approved the assumption and expressly released the grantor in writing, which is so rare as to be nearly nonexistent. Expect a release only in response to full payment.

An assumption deed may be accompanied by a deed of trust to secure assumption which enables the grantor to make payments if the seller discovers that the buyer has failed to do so. The seller may then recover these advancements from the buyer. This enables the seller to proactively mitigate loss and preserve good credit. If reimbursement for advancements is not made, foreclosure may follow.

Can assumptions occur without the lender's consent? Yes, and they often do, in spite of the due-on-sale clause contained in paragraph 18 of the widely-used FNMA deed of trust.

Deed in a Wraparound Transaction

A wraparound transaction is a form of creative seller-financing that leaves the original loan and lien on the property in place when the property is sold. The buyer makes a down payment and signs a new note to the seller (the "wraparound note") for the balance of the sales price. This wrap note, secured by a new deed of trust (the "wraparound deed of trust"), becomes a junior (subordinate) lien on the property. The buyer makes monthly payments to the seller on the wrap note and the seller in turn makes payments to the original lender. The original lender's note is referred to as the "wrapped note," and it remains secured by the "wrapped deed of trust." The buyer receives a warranty deed (general or special) which transfers title to the property into the buyer's name.

The consideration clause in a wraparound deed reads something like this:

> "Ten dollars ($10.00) and other valuable consideration, including execution of a note (the "Wraparound Note") of even date in the principal amount of $___, executed by Grantee, and payable to the order of Grantor. The Wraparound Note is secured by a vendor's lien retained in this Wraparound Deed and by a Wraparound Deed of Trust of even date from Grantee to ___, Trustee."

Lots of details need to be addressed, so a wraparound agreement should accompany the wraparound deed and other wrap documents. Wraps are complex transactions that should be undertaken only with the guidance of an attorney knowledgeable in this area.

Foreclosure Deed or Trustee's Deed

A trustee's deed is delivered by a lender's trustee to the successful bidder at a foreclosure sale. The lender often bids the amount of the debt (plus accrued fees and costs) and acquires the property in this way. If the sale generates proceeds in excess of the debt, the trustee must distribute the excess funds to other lienholders in order of seniority and the remaining balance, if any, to the borrower.

Property Code section 51.009 states that a buyer at a foreclosure sale "acquires the foreclosed property 'as is' without any expressed or implied warranties, except as to warranties of title, and at the purchaser's own risk; and is not a consumer." It is also certain that the trustee's deed itself will contain its own disclaimer along the following lines:

> **THE PROPERTY IS CONVEYED AND ACCEPTED "AS IS," IN ITS PRESENT PHYSICAL CONDITION, WITH ALL FAULTS AND DEFECTS, KNOWN OR UNKNOWN. THE TRUSTEE MAKES NO REPRESENTATIONS OR WARRANTIES, EXPRESS OR IMPLIED, ORAL OR WRITTEN, AS TO TITLE, POSSESSION, QUIET ENJOYMENT, MERCHANTABILITY, MARKETABILITY, USABILITY, HABITABILITY, FITNESS OR SUITABILITY FOR ANY PARTICULAR PURPOSE, OR ENVIRONMENTAL CONDITION OF THE PROPERTY OR AS TO ANY OTHER MATTER RELATING TO THE PROPERTY. IMPLIED WARRANTIES AND ORAL STATEMENTS ARE EXPRESSLY DISCLAIMED AND EXCLUDED. THE TRUSTEE SPECIFICALLY DISCLAIMS THE VERBAL OR WRITTEN STATEMENTS OR INFORMATION INCLUDING REPRESENTATIONS AND WARRANTIES THAT MAY HAVE BEEN MADE OR PROVIDED BY AGENTS, BROKERS, INVESTORS, OR OTHER THIRD PARTIES.**

Even with these limitations, a foreclosure deed is probably the cleanest title obtainable, though it does not eliminate taxes owed.

Deed Incident to Divorce

A divorce deed is typically a special warranty deed that contains a clause similar to the following:

> "Consideration for this transaction is the division of property pursuant to a Final Decree of Divorce dated ___ entered in Cause No. ___, IN THE MATTER OF THE MARRIAGE OF ______AND ______, in the ___ District Court of ______ County, Texas."

The deed may also include an "owelty of partition" that creates a lien in favor of the grantor to secure payment of a certain sum from the other spouse. This is used to equalize the overall division of property.

The parties to a divorce should not rely on the final decree to transfer title to real property. A special warranty deed (often accompanied by a deed of trust to secure assumption) should be executed and recorded.

Deed in Lieu of Foreclosure (DIL)

A traditional deed in lieu of foreclosure is a specialized instrument designed to transfer property to a lender in satisfaction of a debt and in exchange for a full and complete release. The clauses contained in DILs can be quite technical. They begin with a general statement such as "This Deed is executed and delivered by Grantor and accepted by Grantee in lieu of Grantee demanding and collecting the Indebtedness and in lieu of the necessity for Grantee to give notice of default, notice of intent to accelerate, notice of acceleration, notice of posting for foreclosure, and conduct of a foreclosure sale of the Property." Much additional detail is then added.

Few institutional lenders today accept DILs as a means of avoiding foreclosure. The reason is that the foreclosure process itself is advantageous to the lender since it cleans up title by eliminating junior liens and clearly establishes a deficiency amount (the difference between the price at foreclosure and the balance on the note) for which the lender can then sue. *See* Part II, ch. 10: *Deeding Property to the Lender.*

Correction Deed

A correction deed is a supplementary filing that relates back in time to an original deed which contained some error or mutual mistake, often a scrivener's error in the legal description. It corrects the mistake but leaves other terms of the conveyance intact. No new consideration is required for a correction deed. Generally, a correction deed should be signed by both grantor and grantee.

Corrections deeds are appropriate for correcting errors only. If the parties intend to alter fundamental terms of the original conveyance, then a new instrument—not a correction deed—is required. Title companies will occasionally require a correction deed if their researchers discover an error in a previous deed.

Here is a sample correction deed clause:

> "This deed is made as a correction deed ("Correction Deed") to that certain General Warranty Deed ("Corrected Deed") dated ___, executed by Grantor herein to Grantee herein, and recorded under Clerk's File No. ___ in the Official Records of Real Property of ______ County, Texas, for the purpose of correcting the following: [e.g., error in

> the property description]. This Correction Deed correctly describes the Property that was intended to be conveyed and should have been conveyed by the Corrected Deed. Other than this stated correction, this Correction Deed is intended to restate in all respects the Corrected Deed, and the effective date of this Correction Deed relates back to the effective date of the Corrected Deed."

The 2009 Texas Supreme Court case of *Myrad Properties, Inc. v. LaSalle Bank N.A.*, 300 S.W.3d 746 (Tex. 2009), provided guidelines for what would be considered "correctable," including errors in a metes and bounds description or an erroneous description of a party's capacity. According to the Court, other more substantive items (adding or deleting a parcel, for instance) could not be cured with a correction deed. This case prompted the Texas legislature to enact Property Code sections 5.027 et seq., which add considerably more detail and differentiate between material and nonmaterial corrections.

Deeds Involving Co-Ownership

This topic has already been extensively covered. The primary point to remember here is that co-ownership in Texas is presumed to be as tenants-in-common, meaning that heirs of each owner will inherit that owner's respective interest upon death. The decedent's interest (likely) passes vertically. This is contrasted with JTWROS which provides that a co-owner will inherit the other co-owner's interest upon death—a horizontal transfer. JTWROS must be expressly created by specific wording when the property is acquired. Married buyers should consider taking title as JTWROS as basic estate planning.

Deeds with Life Estate Reserved

It is possible that an investor may encounter a situation where an older person is willing to sell but wishes to retain the right to reside in the property until his or her death. This may be an excellent investment if the property is likely to appreciate. A deed with life estate reserved should contain wording substantially similar to the following: "Grantor reserves, for Grantor and Grantor's assigns, a legal life estate in and to the Property for the remainder of Grantor's life, including rights to full possession, benefit, use, rents, revenues, and profits of and from the Property, until the death of Grantor (the "Life Estate") at which time full legal and equitable title to the Property shall automatically vest in Grantee, free of any interest of Grantor, Grantor's successor, heirs, and/or assigns. Grantor shall have the right to reside in the Property without rent or charge during the Life Estate."

Fraudulent Deeds

A fraudulent deed is a void deed, but action must generally be taken in order to establish that the deed is fraudulent. Section 51.901 of the Government Code requires a county clerk to act if there is "a reasonable basis to believe in good faith that document or instrument previously filed or recorded or offered or submitted for filing or for recording is fraudulent." One way to trigger such action is for an aggrieved party to file an affidavit which includes the property's legal description, send a copy of the affidavit to the perpetrating party, and demand that the fraudulent deed be canceled. If this strategy is unsuccessful, a suit alleging fraud (both common law fraud and statutory fraud under Business & Commerce Code section 27.01) and requesting rescission and/or a declaratory judgment should be filed.

Note also that Civil Practice & Remedies Code section 12.002 provides that a person who knowingly and intentionally files a fraudulent lien or claim against real property may be held liable in civil district court for the greater of $10,000 or actual damages, exemplary damages, and recovery of attorney's fees and costs.

Deeds and the Earnest Money Contract

The variety of deeds along with the choice of different clauses that can affect the conveyance and alter the liability of the parties make it advisable to a consult a real estate attorney, and do it early in the process. If an investor knows in advance that certain wording will be required in a deed then a provision to this effect should be included in the sales contract or special provisions addendum. Otherwise, the wording may become a matter of last-minute negotiations with potential to cause the closing to fail.

What the Attorney Needs from the Client

When an investor needs a deed prepared, the existing warranty deed to the property should be provided to the attorney along with the names and mailing addresses of seller and buyer. And, since Texas is a community property state, the client should supply the marital status of the parties and the names of spouses. If the property will be deeded into a series LLC, then the attorney will need to know which series (Series A or B, etc.).

Chapter 9

DEEDING PROPERTY TO AN LLC

An Essential Step in Asset Protection

A primary purpose of an LLC, whether a traditional LLC or a series company, is to provide protection from personal liability for its members. For this reason, any property that could potentially generate a lawsuit or other liability, especially investment and rental property, should be held in the name of an LLC—*never* in a personal name and *never* reflecting personal information such as the homestead address (POBs are recommended for LLC business).

Ideally, property ownership should reside in a dedicated holding company while management functions (including entering into contracts, collecting rent, and payment of expenses) are performed by a separate, shell management LLC. This accomplishes separation of assets from activities, a core principle of asset protection derived from the legal concept of privity.

Theory of Asset Protection

Asset protection (1) creates barriers to personal liability with one or more LLCs, at least one of which should be a series company (we prefer Texas and Nevada, two top AP states with similar statutes); (2) maximizes anonymity in the public records; (3) utilizes homestead protections afforded individuals by the Texas Constitution and Property Code; (4) deters lawsuits and judgment creditors; and (5) in the event of suit, exhausts their determination and resources. Planning ahead is critical, since the range and benefit of asset protection measures decrease significantly after suit is threatened or filed.

Deeding Property to an LLC

If possible, rental or investment property should be acquired directly in the name of an LLC. In a two-company structure, the optimum plan would be to acquire properties in the name of the management company and then, after closing and rehab, transfer them into individual series of the holding company. Lenders, however, often require that an investor take title to the property in his or her personal name for underwriting reasons. If that is the case, the property should nonetheless be moved *without delay* into the investor's series holding LLC after closing.

The series LLC is now the vehicle of choice for many real estate investors. Unlike a traditional LLC (which owns its assets in a single pool) a series company permits the LLC to hold multiple properties in separate, insulated compartments—Series A, Series B, and so forth. The assets and liabilities of each series are confined to that series only and are segregated from the assets and liabilities of other series. So if there is a lawsuit or a foreclosure that affects property in Series A, then other series (Series B, Series C, and so forth) *are not affected or liable for the outcome*. When deeding property into a series company, the deed should specifically reflect which series the property is going into—for example, "ABC LLC—Series A." Failure to do this will result in the property being acquired as an asset of the company at large, thereby losing series insulation and protection. Recitals from the Business Organizations Code that put the public on notice of the unique nature of a series company should, in our view, be included in the deed.

Due-on-Sale Issues

Will the lender call the note due if the property is transferred into an investor's LLC? There are two points to note on this subject. First, the standard due-on-sale clause contained in the Fannie Mae deed of trust *prohibits nothing*; it merely gives a lender the option to accelerate a note if a transfer of title occurs, so it is *not* correct to say that such a transfer "violates" or "breaches" the due-on-sale clause. Lenders may choose whether or not to act under this clause—that is all.

Second, lenders seldom act when property is transferred into the borrower's personal company (we have *never* seen that happen, actually) and in any case they are far more concerned with loans that are in monetary (rather than technical) default—although, as pointed out, transferring title is *not* a default, not even a technical one. Some lenders will send a threatening letter, but little will likely come of it so long as the note remains current.

What should be done with the homestead?

It is neither necessary nor advisable to transfer a homestead into an LLC that holds investment properties. As a general rule, homestead-exempt assets should be kept separate from investment assets. Why? First, the homestead is already protected by the Texas Constitution and Property Code against forced sale or execution upon a judgment. Second, mixing the homestead with investment assets that are prone to incur liability and lawsuits is just not a good idea. The homestead should be kept out of the line of fire.

Our recommendation is to transfer the homestead into a living trust (also called an inter vivos trust). Trusts do not provide a liability barrier, but this is not a problem here because the homestead is already protected. What the living trust accomplishes is probate avoidance (since the trust cannot die), providing for automatic transfer of the beneficial interest in the property without delay or expense. Even considering that Texas has expedited probate procedures, this is a real benefit. There is nothing to lose and everything to gain from using such an arrangement. A pour-over will should be executed along with the living trust to complete the picture.

General Warranty Deeds versus Special Warranty Deeds

Deeds into an LLC may be made by deed with either general or special warranties, depending on the situation. In most cases, there is no reason for an investor not to use a general warranty deed when conveying property into a personal company. Under no circumstances, however, should a quitclaim be used, since these can create problems with the chain of title. If one is determined to avoid warranties, use a deed without warranties rather than a quitclaim.

Clauses in the Deed

One factor that should be considered in deeding property into an LLC is whether or not the property is to be transferred with an assumption of the existing loan or "subject to." This choice has accounting implications—for instance, whether or not the company intends to carry the loan on its books as a company debt. Most transfers into an LLC are made "subject to," but this can vary with the circumstances. The best practice is to include an appropriate clause specifying assumption or "subject to" in the deed. Consult a CPA.

It is also advisable to include an "as is" clause in the deed. This should be routine for all business transactions in which in which an investor is the seller. If the property is rented it may also be appropriate to assign the security deposit to the LLC—if so a clause should be included addressing this issue. Consideration should be given to assigning any escrow account as well.

For married investors, it is the preferred practice for both spouses to sign the deed into the LLC, since Texas is a community property state. If that is not done, it is possible that a future title company will ask for a marital status or non-homestead affidavit.

Transfers Made for the Purpose of Defrauding Creditors

It is preferable to transfer assets into an LLC *before* trouble arises. Otherwise the usefulness of doing so may be limited by rules against fraudulent transfers that reach back up to two years. Such transfers are generally indicated by so-called "badges of fraud" including:

1. transfers to a family member;
2. whether or not suit was threatened before it was filed;
3. whether the transfer was of substantially all of the person's assets;
4. whether assets have been removed, undisclosed, or
5. concealed;
6. whether there was equivalent consideration for the transfer; and
7. whether or not, after the transfer, the transferor became insolvent as a result (made his cash disappear).

Such transfers are called "preferences" in bankruptcy court.

If one did not move property into an LLC *prior* to a lawsuit or judgment, can it be done after? The answer is a qualified *yes*, if it is done for consideration and in the ordinary course of business. Since most investment properties carry indebtedness, an example of adequate consideration might be payment of $5,000 (a random number, but one with substance) plus an agreement on the part of the LLC to assume and pay the existing indebtedness on the property. Such a transfer made by an investor into his or her LLC should be defensible as a transfer for consideration made for business reasons having nothing to do with the lawsuit.

Chapter 10

DEEDING PROPERTY TO THE LENDER

The Merits of Strategic Default

Foreclosure is the involuntary transfer of property from a borrower, usually to the lender. But what about relinquishing property voluntarily and unilaterally? Since a lender cannot be forced to foreclose (and some lenders drag their feet) an option may be for the owner to unilaterally deed the property to the lender and walk away. It may be more cost effective to let an underwater property go and instead direct resources to profitable investments, a cheaper housing alternative, or toward paying off homestead-exempt assets.

Effects of Foreclosure

So what are the potential benefits of a unilateral DIL? To answer, one must consider the alternative and examine the negative after-effects of foreclosure. These include adverse credit impact for seven or more years; the potential for a deficiency lawsuit by the lender; and the prospect that the IRS will deem the deficiency amount to be ordinary income taxable to the borrower. That could be a whopping number (deficiencies in the $100,000 range are not uncommon) and the borrower must take that amount as ordinary income all in one year. For an investor, the IRS consequences may be the worst aspect of the foreclosure process.

In 2008 Congress made homestead deficiencies exempt from the deemed-income problem, but that does not help investors who may be looking at numerous underwater investment properties.

Effects of *Non*foreclosure: Zombie Titles

Surprisingly, a significant percentage of banks are choosing *not* to foreclose after borrowers default. Why? These lenders have considered the negative factors involved in taking foreclosed properties into inventory (maintenance and insurance costs, carry time, etc.) and decided that it is more financially favorable to sell the defaulted note to a collector and write off the loss. These lenders walk away, effectively dumping the abandoned property onto the local municipality. The nightmare result for the homeowner (who was under the impression from lender notices that a foreclosure was imminent) is that he or she is relentlessly pursued by a third-party collector who now owns the note, by local taxing authorities seeking unpaid ad valorem taxes, and by cities and homeowners associations who either sue or impose liens for trash removal, health and safety code violations, and demolition. After all, since the lender decided not to go through with the foreclosure sale, the homeowner *still owns title* and is therefore responsible for the property. In this scenario, the best option may be a unilateral DIL to the lender enabling the borrower to assert nonownership of the property as a defense against circling vultures.

What is a deed in lieu of foreclosure?

Executing and delivering a deed from the owner of real property to the lender/lienholder has traditionally occurred in the context of a bilateral DIL, which is designed to transfer property to the lender in satisfaction of the debt and in exchange for a release of lien. The customary DIL occurs when both parties expressly consent to the mutual benefits of this arrangement. *Morission v. Christie*, 266 S.W.3d 89 Tex. App.—Ft. Worth 2008, no pet.). The problem is that few lenders nowadays will agree to accept a DIL and give a release in exchange. They would rather use the foreclosure process to wipe out junior liens and acquire a deficiency judgment, which then appears as an asset on the lender's books. So a traditional, bilateral DIL is often not an available option.

This chapter examines the benefit to deeding property to the lender *anyway*—even if the lender has not expressly agreed to discharge and release the debt in exchange. What happens if a borrower executes a unilateral DIL, records it, and then sends a copy to the lender saying "Here, the property is yours now, and by the way, I consider the debt paid in full?

Conveyance to the Noteholder

A DIL should convey the property to the current owner and holder of the note. This can be confusing, since ownership of the note is often split from the servicing function. In order to maximize the unilateral DIL strategy, the homeowner should deed the property to the actual holder of the note, not the servicer.

The 80-20 Problem

What if there are two liens against the property and two different lienholders? There is no perfect solution in such a case, but the most effective strategy is to give a DIL to the senior lienholder since it likely holds the largest debt. If one must choose, it makes sense to defend against the more significant threat, especially the possibility of IRS deemed income on a large deficiency.

Presumption of Acceptance

When a grantor transfers property, title to the property vests in the grantee upon execution and delivery of the deed. The grantee's acceptance is not usually indicated anywhere on the document. Acceptance is presumed. A showing that a deed was executed and delivered with an intent to convey the property is sufficient to establish that the deed vested title in the grantee. *Stephens County Museum, Inc. v. Swenson*, 17 S.W.2d 257, 261-62 (Tex. 1975). Proof that a deed was recorded creates a presumption of and establishes a prima facie case of delivery and intent by the grantor to convey the land. *Troxel v. Bishop*, 201 S.W.3d 290, 297 (Tex. App.—Dallas 2006, no pet.). Both cases are cited with approval in *Watson v. Tipton*, 274 S.W.3d 791 (Tex. App.—Fort Worth 2008, pet. denied).

However, there is another case that says acceptance of a deed by a lender in consideration for cancellation of a note will not be presumed. *Martin v. Uvalde Sav. & Loan Ass'n*, 772 S.W.2d 808 (Tex. App.—San Antonio 1989, no writ). This nonetheless leaves a lender who receives a unilateral DIL in an ambiguous and possibly hazardous position. If enough time goes by without action by the lender, is this still true? What if the lender, after receiving such a deed, refrains from filing a foreclosure or a deficiency suit—might not this inaction be construed as implied agreement with the stated terms of the deed (i.e., discharge of the debt)? After all, courts widely recognize the concept of an implied agreement based on conduct of the parties.

Because of these factors, the only safe and prudent course for a lender who truly does not want to accept title to property in exchange for discharge of the debt is to take the affirmative step of filing an instrument in the real property records rejecting the DIL. However, in filing dozens of deeds of this nature, this author has yet to see a lender take such action, even though lenders universally dislike the fact that the borrower has deeded property to them without their agreement. One lender responded by saying, "We find your correspondence to be incomprehensible and completely without merit. . . . We view the document provided as fraudulent and it provides no basis for debt relief." These protestations notwithstanding, title to the property has *still* been conveyed back to the lender as a matter of record. Their nasty letter does not reverse that. And as to the alleged "fraudulent" aspect of the DIL, that is nonsense. Fraud is *intentional concealment or misrepresentation.* Conveying property to the lender under these circumstances cannot by any reasonable standard be construed as fraud.

Property Code Section 51.006

What sort of instrument must the lender file if it wishes to reject a deed? Property Code section 51.006 may offer guidance. This statute "applies to a holder of a debt under a deed of trust who accepts from the debtor a deed conveying real property subject to the deed of trust in satisfaction of the debt." It expressly provides that a lender may record an affidavit voiding such a deed within four years if the grantor/debtor did not disclose liens of which the lender hand no personal knowledge. But this is narrowly focused. It applies only to this specific nondisclosure scenario.

The practical question is, if a lender already has a DIL in hand, will it expend time and money to formally reject it and proceed with foreclosure? Perhaps, perhaps not. Lenders vary in their response to this. Some (the minority) simply send the deed to their loss mitigation or REO department with instructions to list the property for sale and not bother with foreclosure. Others (the majority) continue with foreclosure in spite of having been given a DIL. Property Code section 51.006 expressly permits that "[i]f a holder accepts a deed in lieu of foreclosure, the holder may foreclose its deed of trust as provided in said deed of trust without electing to void the deed."

Potential Benefits Even if There is a Foreclosure

Accordingly, it is unlikely that deeding property to an unwilling lender will result in avoidance of foreclosure. But even if foreclosure occurs, might there be other significant benefits to executing a DIL? Given the potentially severe effects of both foreclosure and non-foreclosure, does the borrower have anything to lose by giving this method a try?

The first effect—the effect on credit—will not be avoided by executing a unilateral DIL if the lender chooses to go ahead and conduct a foreclosure sale anyway. That much is clear.

The second effect—avoiding or defending against a deficiency suit—presents more interesting possibilities. Say that the DIL contains language reciting that it was being executed and delivered in satisfaction of the debt. If the lender sues for the deficiency but has never filed anything of record rejecting the deed, might not the borrower be able to assert the deed as a defense (an "accord and satisfaction")? Essentially, the borrower could argue that *no deficiency exists.* It would be a creative argument.

Similarly, if the IRS declares that the deficiency amount is ordinary income and then demands that tax be paid, the borrower could produce the DIL and declare that since the lender accepted it (or, more precisely, never rejected it) there is *no* deficiency and therefore *no* taxable income. Would this argument prevail? No cases yet. However, it certainly has a fighting chance, which is a good deal more than most taxpayers have in this circumstance.

Lastly, in a nonforeclosure scenario (where the lender threatens to foreclose but then does not), the former homeowner can use the DIL to defend against suits from third-parties who are trying to collect taxes or enforce liens that have accumulated against a neglected property.

It goes without saying that a unilateral DIL must contain specific statements and recitals if it is to have any effect. A simple warranty deed to the lender will not do the job.

This Is *Not* Your Parents' Default

Texans are inclined by nature to honor their word and are reluctant to default on any obligation. However, consider that the world has changed; the top 1% of Americans now controls 80% of the wealth. The CEO of the bank holding the note you can no longer afford may be sitting on his yacht in the Bahamas, toasting his fellow Wall Streeters on their massive new wealth—*unprecedented in human history*—and laughing at poor souls who continue to make payments on their underwater notes.

Executing a unilateral DIL is not a perfect technique but it has interesting and potentially rewarding benefits. Even so, this strategy remains in the experimental category.

NOTEWORTHY
STATE & FEDERAL LAW

Chapter 11

EXECUTORY CONTRACTS IN TEXAS REAL ESTATE

A Snake Pit for Investors

Contracts for deed, lease-purchases, and lease-options have long been traditional tools of Texas residential real estate investors. Why? Because it was easy to induce tenant/buyers into such arrangements (with a minimal down payment) and easy to evict them using the forcible detainer process if they defaulted. No longer. Since 2005, these devices are considered "executory contracts" and are heavily regulated under Chapter 5 of the Property Code. The lender, if any, must give consent. Numerous initial and ongoing requirements must be observed, and the burden is on the seller to meet these. Violation entitles the purchaser to cancel and rescind the contract and receive a full refund of *all* payments made to the seller. That is not all, since a claim may also be made under the Deceptive Trade Practices-Consumer Protection Act which can result in treble damages plus attorney's fees. Add up the numbers and one can easily see that the potential downside is significant. Note that the statute contains *no significant defenses* for well-meaning sellers who thought they were giving the buyer a good deal, even if the whole arrangement was the buyer's idea in the first place.

Accordingly, the risks to an investor of engaging in executory contracts have nearly eliminated their use in the residential context.

What exactly is an executory contract?

Executory contracts include any transaction that defers material action by either party that pertains to ownership or possession of real property into the future. Think of it this way: an executed contract is one that is fully performed at closing. It is done, finished. An executory contract, on the other hand, leaves something dangling—usually the most important item of all, the delivery of a deed. The classic executory contract is the contract for deed (or land sales contact), which provides that the buyer gets title after making payments over a period of years. All such devices now fall under the extensive rules and penalty provisions of Property Code sections 5.061 et seq.

Contracts for deed, lease-purchases, and lease-options for longer than 180 days are unambiguously defined as executory contracts. Look closely at section 5.062(a)(2): "An option to purchase real property that includes or is combined or executed concurrently with a residential lease agreement, together with the lease, is considered an executory contract for conveyance of real property." The "180 days or less" exemption exists as an accommodation to real estate brokers, because otherwise the TREC 1-4 contract could violate this provision when combined with a TREC temporary lease.

Options that are not combined with a residential lease as well as options on commercial property are *not* affected by Property Code section 5.061.

Changes to the Investor Environment

Why did the Texas legislature make these changes? Because executory contracts had traditionally given a tremendous advantage to the seller, who technically retained "legal title" to the property. The buyer, on the other hand, had only "equitable title"—a fuzzy concept that requires filing an expensive lawsuit to enforce. A buyer under financial pressure was therefore more likely to abandon the property, along with the down payment, and move on. Unscrupulous sellers and investors used this situation to their advantage, disregarding buyers' equitable rights and representing to justices of the peace (the authority in eviction cases) that such buyers were ordinary tenants subject to ordinary leases. Evictions were obtained for minor or technical defaults and down payments were confiscated in the process, freeing the seller to move on to the next victim. The legislature rightly acted to stop such abuse.

Executory Contracts: Requirements for Validity

Make no mistake, one can still do a transaction by means of an executory contract, but many requirements now exist that did not apply before 2005. Property Code sections 5.069 and 5.070 contain a number of these requirements, which must be met *before* the executory contract is signed by the purchaser (i.e., before and not at closing):

5.069(a) (1) requires that the seller provide the purchaser with a survey which is no older than a year, or a current plat. Subsection (a) also requires the seller to notify the buyer that there "are no restrictive covenants, easements, or other title exceptions or encumbrances that prohibit construction of a house on the property. An additional notice is required advising the buyer to "obtain a title abstract or title commitment covering the property and have the abstract or commitment reviewed by an attorney before signing a contract of this type, and purchase an owner's policy of title insurance covering the property."

5.069(a)(2) requires that the seller provide the purchaser with copies of liens, restrictive covenants, and easements affecting the property.

5.069(a)(3) requires that a "Seller's Disclosure of Property Condition" be provided by the seller, just as in the case of an outright sale.

5.069(b) states that if "the property is not located in a recorded subdivision, the seller shall provide the purchaser with a separate disclosure form stating that utilities may not be available to the property until the subdivision is recorded as required by law."

5.069(c) pertains to advertising the availability of an executory contract. It requires that the advertisement disclose information regarding the availability of water, sewer, and electric service.

5.070(a)(1) requires the seller to provide the purchaser with a tax certificate from the collector for each taxing unit that collects taxes due on the property.

5.070(a)(2) requires the seller to provide the purchaser with a copy of any insurance policy, binder, or evidence that indicates the name of the insurer and insured; a description of the insured property; and the policy amount.

Cancellation and Refund

What happens if the foregoing requirements are not met? First, failure to do so is defined as a "false, misleading, or deceptive act or practice" pursuant to section 17.46 of the DTPA; second, the purchaser is entitled under Property Code section 5.069(d)(2) to "cancel and rescind the executory contract and receive a full refund of all payments made to the seller." *That includes any down payment plus all monthly payments that have been made.* It likely also includes any money expended by the buyer on permanent improvements to the property.

Also, Property Code section 5.074(a) entitles a purchaser to cancel an executory contract for any reason within 14 days of signing, even if all statutory requirements have been met.

Financial Disclosure Required

An additional preclosing requirement is imposed by Property Code section 5.071, which requires a seller to provide financial information similar to a RESPA disclosure:

> ***Before* [italics added] an executory contract is signed by the purchaser, the seller shall provide to the purchaser a written statement that specifies:**
>
> **(1) the purchase price of the property;**
> **(2) the interest rate charged under the contract;**
> **(3) the dollar amount, or an estimate of the dollar amount if the interest rate is variable, of the interest charged for the term of the contract;**
> **(4) the total amount of principal and interest to be paid under the contract;**
> **(5) the late charge, if any, that may be assessed under the contract; and**
> **(6) the fact that the seller may not charge a prepaying penalty or any similar fee if the purchaser elects to pay the entire amount due under the contract before the scheduled payment due date under the contract.**

There is some slight relief under this section (if you want to look at it that way) in that a violation by the seller is not defined as a DTPA violation.

The Seven-Day Letter

Another, related preclosing requirement is contained in Property Code section 5.016: "A person may not convey an interest in or enter into a contract to convey an interest in residential real property that will be encumbered by a recorded lien" without giving a seven-day notice to both lender and purchaser. The statute sets out the required content of this notice, which is quite technical, although no real penalties are imposed other than allowing the buyer a preclosing right of recission. After closing, there is no buyer remedy and no liability on the part of the seller. Result? The seven-day letter requirement is widely ignored. Anticipate that a future legislature may revisit this statute and insert penalties for non-compliance.

Punitive Fees and Clauses

Property Code section 5.073 prohibits these. Excessive late fees are banned, as are prepayment penalties and any clause that "prohibits the purchaser from pledging the purchaser's interest in the property as security to obtain a loan or place improvements." This codifies the traditional view from the justice court bench: Exorbitant late fees are almost never allowed in an eviction judgment.

Recording Requirement

In the past, lease options and other executory contracts did not need to be recorded. No longer. Section 5.076(a) states that "the seller shall record the executory contract, including the attached disclosure statement . . . on or before the 30th day after the date the contract is executed." Additionally, any instrument that terminates the contract must be recorded.

Annual Accounting Statement

Section 5.077 requires an annual accounting statement every January, which must include amounts paid, the remaining amount owed, the number of payments remaining, the amount paid in taxes, the amount paid for insurance, an accounting for any insurance payments by the insurer, and a copy of the current policy—a comprehensive status report to the buyer, in other words. There is no requirement that this be recorded.

What if the seller makes a good-faith error in the annual accounting statement? Does that trigger Draconian statutory penalties? Is that a DTPA violation? Probably not. "[A] timely but incomplete statement . . . 'does not, strictly speaking, trigger an award of "liquidated damages"' . . . unless the statement is 'so deficient as to be something other than a good faith attempt by the seller to inform the purchaser of the current status of their contractual relationship.'" *Morton v. Nguyen*, 369 S.W.3d 659 (Tex. App.—Houston [14th Dist.] 2012, pet. filed) (citation omitted).

Buyer's Right to Convert to a Deed

The buyer has an absolute right "at any time and without paying penalties or charges of any kind" to convert an executory contract to "recorded, legal title" under section 5.081. That means a deed, probably a general warranty deed, but no less than a deed without warranties. The seller has no choice in the matter so long as the buyer tenders the balance owed under the contract.

The SAFE Act Licensing Requirement

Executory contracts are a form of owner financing and, therefore, both the federal Secure and Fair Enforcement for Mortgage Licensing Act ("SAFE Act") and the Texas version ("T-SAFE") apply. However, the seller is required to be licensed only if the property is not the seller's homestead and/or the sale is not to a family member. The Commissioner of the Texas Department of Savings and Mortgage Lending ("TDSML") has ruled that T-SAFE will *not* be applied to persons who make five or fewer owner-financed loans in a year. Note that the T-SAFE licensing rule applies only to residential owner financing.

Dodd-Frank Law (Mortgage Reform and Anti-Predatory Lending Act)

Dodd-Frank and the SAFE Act were both born of the real estate collapse. Dodd-Frank requires that a seller/lender in an owner-financed transaction involving a residence make an informed determination that the buyer/borrower has the ability to repay the loan. The seller is therefore obligated to qualify the buyer/borrower in the same way any regular lender would. This law also has a de minimus exception that excludes persons doing no more than three owner-financed transactions per year, at least so long as the seller/lender is not in the building business. Although Dodd-Frank is roundly criticized by some politicians as an example of over regulation, there is no doubt that corrective action was necessary in order to avoid another epidemic of toxic loans.

Termination of Executory Contracts

It is not permissible to simply evict a buyer under an executory contract if there is a default. Why? Because the buyer has equitable rights and is more than a mere tenant. The Property Code therefore requires ample notice and opportunity for the buyer to cure the default. Sections 5.063 and 5.064 specify the content of the default notice, which must be followed *to the letter* if it is to be valid. The buyer must be allowed a 30-day unconditional right to cure the default before an eviction can be filed. If the judge grants possession to the seller at the eviction hearing, then and only then is the buyer's down payment forfeited.

There is also the "40 or 48 Rule" contained in Property Code section 5.066(a): If the buyer has paid in 40% or more of the purchase price, or the equivalent of 48 monthly payments, then a 60-day notice is required and, if the default is not cured, a traditional foreclosure (*not* an eviction) must be used to regain title. Clearly, the intent is to keep sellers from unfairly confiscating down payments and buyers' equity.

The Reality of the Courtroom

Why not just ignore the executory contract rules and march merrily forward? The reason is that courts and juries do not favor investors and landlords, who are often perceived as profiteers preying upon the weak and helpless. It does not matter how clever the investor's legal argument is. If a transaction does not pass the "smell test" a seller/landlord will likely lose. Even if the executory contract rules are found not to apply, the court can look to the laundry list of offenses under the DTPA, which prohibits "any unconscionable action or course of action by any person"—a very large hammer a jury can use against investors they do not like.

Note that pretending an executory contract is something else by renaming it will fool no one. A judge and jury may even be angry with an investor-seller who tries to pull a fast one with overly clever verbiage—and therefore more inclined to consider a finding of fraud, which brings the prospect of treble damages plus attorney fees.

Property Code section 5.073(a)(4) prohibits forfeiture of a buyer's down payment or option fee if a monthly payment is late. This is an important change, because it codifies what judges and juries have been telling lawyers for quite some time. They *hate* forfeitures. The trend in the law is to view any substantial forfeiture as unreasonable and unconscionable, whether within the context of an executory contract or not, if it results in a buyer losing either a large down payment or the home itself.

Landlords and sellers should generally avoid residential executory contracts because of the numerous requirements and potential liability for doing them improperly. Penalties fall entirely upon the seller, even if the purchaser was a willing participant in the transaction, and there are no significant defenses. Accordingly, such contracts are no longer advisable unless the property is paid for or used exclusively for commercial purposes.

Chapter 12

THE STATUTE OF FRAUDS

The Requirement of a Writing in Real Estate

This chapter addresses the requirement that agreements relating to real property be in writing, a requirement referred to as the "Statute of Frauds." Most investors are aware that they need a written contract when real estate is bought or sold. The issue of whether or not a signed writing must exist most often arises in connection with oral modifications, amendments, and extensions to a written contract. As an example, a lawyer may be asked if a handshake agreement to add thirty days to a designated closing date is binding. Generally, the answer is *no*, but there may be exceptions.

Applicable Law

Provisions of the Statute of Frauds applicable to real estate are found in the Business & Commerce Code sections 26.01 and 26.02(b):

> **26.01. Promise or Agreement Must Be In Writing.**
>
> **(1) A promise or agreement described in Subsection (b) of this section is not enforceable unless the promise or agreement, or a memorandum of it, is in writing;**
> **(2) And signed by the person to be charged with the promise or agreement or by someone lawfully authorized to sign for him.**
>
> **Subsection (a) of this section applies to:**
>
> **(1) a promise by an executor or administrator to answer out of his own estate for any debt or damage due from his testator or intestate;**
> **(2) a promise by one person to answer for the debt, default, or miscarriage of another person;**

(3) an agreement made on consideration of marriage or on consideration of nonmarital conjugal cohabitation,
(4) a contract for the sale of real estate;
(5) a lease of real estate for a term longer than one year;
(6) an agreement which is not to be performed within one year from the date of making the agreement;
(7) a promise or agreement to pay a commission for the sale or purchase of:
(A) an oil or gas mining lease;
(B) an oil or gas royalty;
(C) minerals; or
(D) a mineral interest; and
(8) an agreement, promise, contract, or warranty of cure relating to medical care or results thereof made by a physician or health care provider as defined in section 74.001, Civil Practice and Remedies Code.

26.02. Loan Agreement Must Be in Writing

A loan agreement in which the amount involved in the loan agreement exceeds $50,000 in value is not enforceable unless the agreement is in writing and signed by the party to be bound or by that party's authorized representative.

Section 26.02(b) is particularly important when those seeking loan modifications find themselves unwittingly foreclosed upon, despite an alleged oral agreement. These unfortunate homeowners likely have no recourse unless a written agreement signed by both borrower and lender was in existence at the time of the foreclosure.

Additional Statute of Frauds provisions are found in Business & Commerce Code section 2.201, but these apply to the sale of goods, not real estate.

Although not labeled as such, there is a second Statute of Frauds in Texas, Property Code section 5.021, which is sometimes referred to as the "Statute of Conveyances:"

§ 5.021 Instrument of Conveyance

A conveyance of an estate of inheritance, a freehold, or an estate for more than one year, in land and tenements, must be in writing and must be subscribed and delivered by the conveyor or by the conveyor's agent authorized in writing.

Exceptions

A discussion of the requirement of a signed writing would not be complete without addressing the equitable exceptions. "Equity" is that branch of the law which provides relief in cases where strict application of a statute or common-law rule would result in unfairness or injustice. In the case of the Statute of Frauds, the following exceptions apply: when enforcement of the Statute of Frauds would itself amount to an actual fraud (but not a mere wrong); when the doctrine of "promissory estoppel" applies, the three elements of which are a person makes a promise that he or she should have expected would lead another person to sustain some definite and substantial damage or injury, such damage or injury occurred, and the court must act to relieve or avoid the damage or injury; or when significant partial performance of an oral agreement has occurred and denying enforcement of the agreement at that point would amount to an actual fraud.

These exceptions are not found in Property Code section 26.01 but in case law that has evolved interpreting the Statute of Frauds. Their use is strictly limited since widespread allowance of these exceptions would effectively void the rule. *See Nagle v. Nagle*, 633 S.W.2d 796, 799-800 (Tex. 1982); *Birenbaum v. Option Care, Inc.*, 971 S.W.2d 497, 503 (Tex. App.—Dallas 1997, pet. denied); *Exxon Corp. v. Breezevale Ltd.*, 82 S.W.3d 429, 438 (Tex. App.—Dallas 2002, pet. denied).

Occurrence of Statute of Frauds Issues

Lawyers tend to encounter Statute of Frauds issues in two contexts: first, when a client inquires whether or not a certain oral agreement is legally enforceable; and second, in litigation, when a plaintiff seeks to enforce an oral agreement and the Statute of Frauds must be raised as an affirmative defense. If the Statute of Frauds is so raised, then the burden shifts back to the plaintiff to demonstrate how one of the exceptions would apply—a difficult task, inasmuch as these exceptions are narrowly construed.

An example of the strictness of the Statute of Frauds in Texas is found in a recent Fifth Circuit case where the court denied enforcement of a written contract merely because exhibits to the contract (describing oil and gas leases to be conveyed) had not been finalized. *See Preston Exploration Co. v. PEC P'ship*, 669 F.3d 518 (5th Cir. 2012). On the other hand, a Texas appeals court concluded that the failure of one party to sign a lease did not cause the lease to fail under the Statute of Frauds. *Thomas P. Sibley, P.C. v. Brentwood Inv. Dev. Co.*, 356 S.W.3d 659 (Tex. App.—El Paso 2011, pet. denied).

Property Description Issues

The Statute of Frauds is a factor in determining whether a contract adequately describes property to be conveyed. The description must be sufficient. *Pick v. Bartel*, 659 S.W.2d 636, 637 (Tex. 1983). How is "sufficient" defined? A property description is sufficient if the writing furnishes within itself, or by reference to some other existing writing, the means or data by which the particular land to be conveyed may be identified with reasonable certainty. *Wilson v. Fisher*, 188 S.W.2d 150, 152 (Tex.1945). This is Texas's reasonable certainty standard.

What about situations where a contract makes references to other documents? Again, the courts are strict. Only in limited circumstances may extrinsic evidence be used and then "only for the purpose of identifying the [property] with reasonable certainty from the data in the [writing]." *Pick*, 659 S.W.2d at 637 (quoting *Wilson*, 188 S.W.2d at 152). "The written memorandum, however, need not be contained in one document." *Padilla v. LaFrance*, 907 S.W.2d 454, 460 (Tex. 1995) (citing *Adams v. Abbott*, 254 S.W.2d 78, 80 (Tex. 1952)). The Texas Supreme Court has repeatedly held that multiple writings pertaining to the same transaction will be construed as one contract. *Owen v.Hendricks*, 433 S.W.2d 164 (Tex. 1968); *see also Fort Worth Indep. Sch. Dist. v. City of Fort Worth*, 22 S.W.3d 831, 840 (Tex. 2000).

"Get it in writing" is not just valid folk wisdom, it is Texas law when it comes to the purchase and sale of real property. There are very limited exceptions. A proper contract is best, but even an informal scribbling signed by the parties can be sufficient.

Chapter 13

MORTGAGE LOAN FRAUD

Where There's a Way, There's a Crook

Mortgage loan fraud continues to involve billions in annual losses. The Financial Institution Fraud Unit of the FBI has stepped up its investigation and prosecution of criminal loan fraud, particularly where mortgage industry professionals and insiders are involved. For the fiscal year ending September 30, 2007, the FBI received nearly 50,000 SARs ("suspicious activity reports") of mortgage fraud. As a result, beginning in 2008 the FBI decided to focus on mortgage fraud at the expense of other white-collar crimes. Everyone involved in real estate sales is a potential subject of scrutiny. Prosecutions are not limited to actual mortgage and bank fraud. There are also prosecutions for conspiracy, mail and wire fraud, identity theft, and money laundering.

Additionally, the Residential Mortgage Fraud Act (passed in Texas in 2007) changed the legal landscape at the state level. The Act amended certain sections of the Finance Code, the Government Code, and the Penal Code. It also created a Residential Mortgage Fraud Task Force (Government Code section 402.032) under the direction of the attorney general, which includes a range of state officials—the consumer credit commissioner, the banking commissioner, the credit union commissioner, the commissioner of insurance, the savings and mortgage lending commissioner, the presiding officer of the Texas Real Estate Commission, and the presiding officer of the Texas Appraiser Licensing and Certification Board. The Task Force facilitates the sharing of information and resources in aid of enforcement.

There is also the matter of civil liability. Lenders now file civil suits against perpetrators of mortgage fraud.

What does mortgage fraud look like?

Examples of fraudulent schemes include flipping based on false loan applications and inflated appraisals (this category does *not* include buying property at a bargain price and then selling it for fair market value for a profit, which is entirely legal); nominee loans using the name and credit of straw buyers; equity skimming in "subject to" transactions;

phony second liens to contractors who never perform any work; "silent seconds" that involve concealing the loan of a down payment to a borrower, when the down payment was supposed to come from the borrower's own funds; use of fictitious or stolen identities; and foreclosure schemes that mislead homeowners into paying fees and signing a deed in to an investor allegedly to stop foreclosure. Common to most of these schemes are inflated appraisals that create phantom equity, kickbacks (payments not shown on the closing statement), and falsified loan applications.

One can be reasonably sure that loan fraud has occurred when it is clear that a lender would not have made a particular loan if it had known all the facts, and the lender was prevented from knowing the facts by means of misrepresentation and concealment. Putting it another way: Inducing a lender to make a loan based on false pretenses is fraud.

The FBI uses two categories: "fraud for housing," which occurs when a single borrower misrepresents assets and/or liabilities in order to purchase a home, and "fraud for profit," which occurs when mortgage professionals act collectively to defraud a lender.

Many transactions, while not plainly illegal, fall into a gray area that is increasingly suspect. The popularity of no-money-down investment programs on TV, the Internet, and advanced by seminar gurus has added huge numbers of people to the investment game and resulted in intricate get-rich-quick strategies. The FBI attitude toward these schemes (and to investors generally) is openly disdainful. One official was heard mocking investor entrepreneurs as "entremanures." So if the FBI comes calling, say nothing and contact a criminal defense attorney immediately.

Temptations of the Investment Business

A visit to the courthouse on foreclosure day is akin to watching sharks being fed at the aquarium. The problem, of course, is that it is impossible for *all* fledgling investors to become overnight millionaires. Real success involves hard work over time. Unfortunately, intense competition in the real estate investment business can lead impatient and unethical investors to look for profits in ways that cross the line.

Legitimate investors should avoid investment plans that sound too good to be true, either to the investor or homeowner. Programs that ask a homeowner to sign incomprehensible documents with weird names often involve fraud. If a deal is just too complicated for the average person to understand, it may well involve fraud. If it involves several people signing interests back and forth to one another and not recording anything, it is probably fraud. Payments made off the closing statement are almost certainly fraud.

Some perpetrators believe that giving their documents creative names will exempt them from the law. The problem for con artists who dream up these documents is that courts look to substance over form, and prisons are now offering long-term housing to these clever folks. Juries may not always understand the technicalities of mortgage finance but they intuitively understand fraud. Here are some other tip-offs that you may be dealing with a mortgage loan con artist:

"This is a great investment! You'll make great money with no effort."

"There's no need to talk to a lawyer. These are all standard forms."

"Just sign this blank loan application here. We'll do all the paperwork."

"We put the property in your name. You're totally secure."

"We pay all the costs and you get half the profit! Easy money!"

"We'll pay you a bonus at closing. You'll have cash in your pocket and instant equity."

"We're going to manage and sell the property and then split all the profits with you."

"God has sent us to you to give you abundant wealth."

The Straw Buyer

The straw buyer scenario was more common before the bust, but it still happens. Here's how it works:

1. A crooked investor generally looks for two categories of homes, those owned by distressed sellers who are behind on payments and new-home builders who have unsold inventory that is draining them because of the interest carry.

2. The perpetrator recruits straw purchasers/borrowers who are willing to allow their names and credit to be used in exchange for an up-front, off-the-closing statement kickback (often $10,000 or more) and then buys the property in their names. The note, deed of trust, and other loan documents, including an affidavit of intent

to occupy, are all signed by the straw purchasers at a title company closing that appears legitimate.

3. A real estate broker accomplice may be involved to make this easier and eventually collect a commission from a "client" the broker never met, never obtained a buyer's representation agreement from, and never gave an IABS to.

4. A mortgage broker accomplice submits a fraudulent loan application and supporting documents that show the straw buyer as having significantly higher income than is actually the case.

5. An appraiser accomplice inflates the value of the property, often by $100,000 or more.

6. The amount of the loan applied for exceeds the true market value of the house.

7. A title company may be complicit in this process in order to facilitate a smooth closing with no questions.

8. All the various accomplices and co-conspirators get paid large fees at closing, either on the closing statement for vague and unspecified charges, or off the closing statement altogether.

9. The house is placed on the market but does not sell because its value is grossly inflated.

10. The lender forecloses, taking a loss (part of which is passed on to HUD or a mortgage insurer) and ruining the credit of the straw purchaser. By then, the con artists have left with profits in hand.

Looking closely, it is clear that the whole transaction has been concocted so that the co-conspirators can generate large up-front fees for themselves.

Interestingly, straw buyers often allege that they were wronged. They even file lawsuits. It is difficult to feel sorry for them, however, since they willingly signed blank documents and gladly received an under-the-table payoff at closing. They cooperated in the fraud and benefited from it.

In the past sub-prime lenders were complicit in this process. Eager to make loans and collect fees, many did not supervise the underwriting process as thoroughly as they should.

Applicable Law

In addition to the usual civil statutes that may be violated (statutory fraud, deceptive trade practices, etc.), numerous federal criminal statutes may be involved:

FEDERAL CRIME	LAW	PENALTY
False statement on a HUD loan	18 U.S.C. § 1012	1 year, fine, or both
False statement to obtain credit	18 U.S.C. § 1014	2 years, $5,000, or both
Mail/wire fraud	18 U.S.C. §§ 1341, 1343	5 years, $1,000, or both
Concealment	18 U.S.C. § 1001	5 years, $10,000, or both
Conspiracy	18 U.S.C. § 371	5 years, $10,000, or both
Racketeering	18 U.S.C. §1961	20 years, $25,000, or both
Money laundering	18 U.S.C. § 1956	20 years, $25,000, or both
Aggravated identity theft	18 U.S.C. § 1028	20 years, $25,000, or both

At the state level, the Residential Mortgage Fraud Act amended Texas Penal Code section 32.32(b) to state: "A person commits an offense if he intentionally or knowingly makes a material false or misleading written statement to obtain property or credit, including a mortgage loan." If the value of the property or amount of the loan exceeds $200,000, which is the case with the median-priced family home, then the offense is a first-degree felony punishable by 5 to 99 years in prison and a fine of $10,000.

Also, Finance Code section 343.105 requires that lenders and mortgage brokers give the following notice in 14-point type to residential borrowers at closing:

> **WARNING: INTENTIONALLY OR KNOWINGLY MAKING A MATERIALLY FALSE OR MISLEADING WRITTEN STATEMENT TO OBTAIN PROPERTY OR CREDIT, INCLUDING A MORTGAGE LOAN, IS A VIOLATION OF SECTION 32.32, TEXAS PENAL CODE, AND DEPENDING**

ON THE AMOUNT OF THE LOAN OR VALUE OF THE PROPERTY, IS PUNISHABLE BY IMPRISONMENT FOR A TERM OF 2 YEARS TO 99 YEARS AND FINE NOT TO EXCEED $10,000.

I/WE, THE UNDERSIGNED HOME LOAN APPLICANT(S), REPRESENT THAT I/WE HAVE RECEIVED, READ, AND UNDERSTAND THIS NOTICE OF PENALTIES FOR MAKING A MATERIALLY FALSE OR MISLEADING WRITTEN STATEMENT TO OBTAIN A HOME LOAN.

I/WE REPRESENT THAT ALL STATEMENTS AND REPRESENTATIONS CONTAINED IN MY/OUR WRITTEN HOME LOAN APPLICATION, INCLUDING STATEMENTS OR REPRESENTATIONS REGARDING MY/OUR IDENTITY, EMPLOYMENT, ANNUAL INCOME, AND INTENT TO OCCUPY THE RESIDENTIAL REAL PROPERTY SECURED BY THE HOME LOAN, ARE TRUE AND CORRECT AS OF THE DATE OF LOAN CLOSING.

The borrower must sign this notice. However, "[f]ailure of a lender, mortgage banker, or licensed mortgage broker to provide a notice complying with this section to each applicant for a home loan does not affect the validity of or enforceability of the home loan by any holder of the loan." Tex. Fin. Code § 343.105(d). So the loan is valid without the notice, but it may still constitute fraud.

There are so many definitions of fraud in various statutes that prosecutors have little trouble finding one that can be used against an investor. The Residential Mortgage Fraud Act added another by amending Section 402.031 of the Government Code, which now defines fraud as "any act that constitutes a violation of a penal law and is part of an attempt or scheme to defraud any person." Moreover, this section imposes an affirmative duty to report fraudulent activity to "an authorized governmental agency" if "a person determines or reasonably suspects that fraudulent activity has been committed or is about to be committed." Loan officers, escrow officers, realtors, and attorneys all have this duty. Compliance results in immunity for the reporting individual. Failure to comply makes one a potential coconspirator.

These new laws make sobering reading for anyone involved in the sale, purchase, financing, and closing of residential home transactions. Who is affected? *Any* person (not just the core conspirators) with actual knowledge of the fraud can be indicted for a felony criminal offense, all the way down to the notary. Moreover, culpable mental intent can be inferred from the circumstances, a relatively light burden for prosecutors.

Much of fraud prevention is common sense. If you suspect fraud in a transaction, immediately remove yourself from involvement and report the activity. Do not sign blank documents. Check out the people you're dealing with. Ask questions. Be alert for irregularities. If the answers are overly complex or outright ridiculous, walk away from the deal.

Chapter 14

SAFE ACT AND DODD-FRANK

Federal Efforts to Promote Responsible Lending

The intent of the SAFE Act and the Dodd-Frank law is to achieve better consumer protection by regulating lending practices that were significantly abused in the past. If one wants the big picture of what has happened to the practice of owner finance in Texas over the last decade, then these federal statutes should be considered alongside the 2005 amendments to the Texas Property Code which regulate executory contracts. Collectively, these new laws have combined to forever alter the status of Texas as a haven for residential owner finance.

T-SAFE

The SAFE Act is a federal consumer protection law that each state is required to implement. T-SAFE was passed in 2009 and contains tighter rules than the federal law.

T-SAFE places a licensing requirement on certain types of residential owner financing provided by professional investors. Since traditional owner finance transactions, wraps, and land trusts are all a form of owner finance, the Act applies to these transactions; however, the seller is required to be licensed only if the property is not the seller's homestead and/or the sale is not to a family member. For example, if the subject property is a rental house being sold to a nonfamily member, a strict reading of the law would mean that the seller is required to have a residential mortgage loan origination ("RMLO") license from the Texas Department of Savings and Mortgage Lending in order to complete this transaction.

However, state agencies typically have the power to issue rules and regulations designed to clarify and implement acts of the legislature. In the case of T-SAFE, TDSML has ruled that the Act will not be applied to nonpros—persons who make five or fewer owner-financed loans in a year, thus preserving the so-called "de minimus exemption" under Finance Code section 156.202(a)(3).

Intermediary Agents under T-SAFE

Does T-SAFE effectively shut the door on non-homestead owner finance for persons who do more than five such deals per year? Not necessarily. TDSML has approved the role of an "intermediary agent" who, for a fee ranging from half a point to a point (i.e., 1%) of the loan amount, will step in and satisfy the Act's requirements. The intermediary agent supplies the new form of good faith estimate, the truth-in-lending disclosures, orders an appraisal, gives state-specific disclosures, and the like, and insures that all "cooling periods" are observed in the loan process. So, nonhomestead owner-financed transactions can still be done by professional investors, but only with the assistance of this licensed intermediary—an RMLO. The practical result? Owner financing deals are feasible but at a higher net cost.

There has been a proliferation of RMLOs as a result of T-SAFE. Note that there is an exception to the licensing requirement for attorneys who as part of their drafting duties provide loan terms to the buyer, but most attorneys are steering clear of this loophole because of potential liability. It therefore appears that RMLOs are here to stay. A careful investor /seller is well-advised to utilize an RMLO in every owner-financed transaction both as a means to comply with T-SAFE and to offload potential liability.

Penalties for Violation of T-SAFE

The TDSML may enforce T-SAFE by a variety of measures, including license suspension, a fine of up to $25,000, and an order to make restitution to the buyer. What does restitution mean? Likely a refund of the down payment and all monthly payments that were made.

Dodd-Frank Wall Street Reform and Consumer Protection Act

The Dodd-Frank Wall Street Reform and Consumer Protection Act is a massive piece of legislation passed by Congress in 2010 as part of comprehensive reform of financial regulation. Our focus is Title XIV, entitled "The Mortgage Reform and Anti-Predatory Lending Act," which pertains to residential loans and lending practices. Dodd-Frank seeks to put an end to predatory lending practices, particularly the making of loans to those who cannot afford to pay them back. More lender disclosures and borrower protections are now required.

Dodd-Frank achieves many of its reforms by amendments to TILA (the Truth-in-Lending Act) and RESPA (Real Estate Settlement Procedures Act). The new Consumer Financial Protection Bureau is charged with issuing regulations to implement Dodd-Frank. Regulations and forms, as they are promulgated over the coming years, are likely to present as great a compliance challenge as the Act itself.

Summary of Dodd-Frank

Title XIV subchapter B, section 1411 of Dodd-Frank requires that a seller/lender in a residential owner-financed transaction determine at the time credit is extended that the buyer/borrower has the ability to repay the loan. The seller is obligated to investigate the buyer's credit history, current and expected income, current obligations, debt-to-income ratio, employment status, and the like in order to make this determination, which must be based on verified and documented information. Result? "No doc," "low doc," and other "liar loans" are banned.

The Act provides for a de minimus exception for persons doing not more than three owner-financed transactions per year, so long as the seller/lender is not in the building business.

Loans must be fully amortizing (balloons are not permitted); prepayment penalties are banned; and an owner-financed note must have a fixed rate or, if adjustable, may adjust only after five or more years and be subject to reasonable annual and lifetime limits on interest rate increases. Negative amortization loans (always risky) must be accompanied by disclosure and counseling for first-time buyers.

Mortgage Originators under Dodd-Frank

Dodd-Frank establishes a duty of care for mortgage originators (a broadly defined category under subchapter A section 1401), who are now required to be qualified and licensed. Who is a "mortgage originator?" Anyone who takes a residential mortgage loan application; anyone who offers or negotiates terms of the transaction; and/or anyone who assists a borrower in obtaining or applying for a residential mortgage loan. Real estate brokers and those who perform purely administrative or clerical tasks are expressly excluded. However, real estate lawyers should take heed of this broad definition and make sure their legal documents include a disclaimer that they have not participated in obtaining or negotiating terms of a client's loan.

Mortgage originators are prohibited from steering borrowers to particular mortgage products, and this is backed up by a treble-damages penalty. Additionally, the previous practice by some refinance lenders of encouraging default on an existing loan before extending a new loan is banned. Mandatory arbitration provisions in loan documents (which always, in practice, favor the creditor) are prohibited.

Borrower Defense to Foreclosure

Subchapter B section 1413 of Dodd-Frank permits the borrower to assert a defense to foreclosure if the lender or mortgage originator violated the antisteering or ability-to-repay provisions of the law. This is clearly designed to penalize the formerly widespread practice of putting under-qualified borrowers into loans they could not afford to repay.

The Balloon Problem

Owner-finance notes with balloon provisions are prohibited by Dodd-Frank, a problem for investors who want a quick turn on their investment. So what can be done in lieu of a balloon to provide a borrower with incentive to refinance? Notes may be structured so that the interest rate adjusts upward after, say, the five-year minimum specified in the Act (subchapter B section 1418 requires a six-month notice to the borrower before the rate adjusts). Owner-finance notes may also include a statement on the part of the buyer/borrower that it is his or her goal to refinance the note within a certain period of time. The buyer/borrower may, if appropriate, agree in the note to engage in credit repair by taking part in a credit repair program approved by seller.

It may be true that greater protection of buyers has been achieved by T-SAFE, Dodd-Frank, and revisions to Property Code chapter 5, but these measures have collectively had the effect of raising closing costs, particularly if an RMLO is involved as an intermediary agent. Consult a real estate attorney before entering into an owner-financed sales contract and never use forms off the Internet. Potential liability is now too great to take the risk.

Chapter 15

HIGHER-PRICED MORTGAGE LOANS

Escrow Requirement in Certain Owner-Financed Transactions

Certain home loans have been defined by the Federal Reserve as being "higher-priced mortgage loans" because (in part) the annual percentage rate charged on such loans exceeds the average prime rate by 1.5% for a first lien or 3.5% for a subordinate lien. Rules in this area are particularly important to owner-financed transactions since the APR is often higher than in conventional or FHA financing.

How can you determine if these rules apply to your transaction? If the loan application date is later than April 1, 2010; if the loan will be a first or subordinate lien on a one-to-four family residence; if the property will be owner occupied; and if the APR exceeds the amounts stated above, then such a loan is classified as a higher-priced mortgage loan and the new law applies.

Applicable Law

Applicable law here is Regulation Z, 12 C.F.R. pt. 226, specifically section 226.35. Higher-priced mortgage loan regulations are sometimes referred to as "HPML regs," and such loans are often called "section 35 loans" or "HPML loans." Section 226.35, entitled "Prohibited Acts or Practices in Connection with Higher-Priced Mortgage Loans," became effective October 1, 2009 except for rules requiring collection of an escrow which became effective April 1, 2010.

Laws Impacting Owner Finance

The HPML regs are part of a wave of federal and state regulation designed to curb abuses in owner finance which contributed to the accumulation of bad loans and the subsequent collapse of the market. Among the new laws is Dodd-Frank, which requires that a residential seller/lender in an owner-financed transaction perform affirmative due diligence in order to determine that the buyer/borrower can repay the loan; the federal SAFE Act (T-SAFE in Texas), which requires that a seller/lender of one-to-four family residence in an owner-financed transaction have an RMLO license issued by the TDSML; a Texas requirement that the seller give both the existing lienholder and the buyer a seven-day written notice prior to closing a transaction with an existing loan in place; and burdensome rules relating to contracts for deed and other executory contracts contained in Property Code sections 5.061 et seq. Texas was formerly the wild west of seller financing. Recall the practice of "red flagging" rural lots? Those days are long gone.

HPML Escrow Requirement

The seller in an owner-financed transaction subject to HPML regs *must* establish an escrow account. Title 12 C.F.R. § 226.35(b)(3)(i) states that "a creditor may not extend a loan secured by a first lien on a principal dwelling unless an escrow account is established before consummation for payment of property taxes and premiums for mortgage-related insurance required by the creditor, such as insurance against loss of or damage to property, or against liability arising out of the ownership or use of the property, or insurance protecting the creditor against the consumer's default or other credit loss."

This regulation requires that an escrow account be established before "consummation for payment of property taxes and premiums." When does such consummation occur? The language is unclear, but it is reasonable to interpret "consummation" in this context as the shift to the buyer of the obligation to pay ad valorem taxes and insurance premiums—and this occurs at closing.

A common practice is to provide for an escrow that commences with the first monthly payment. This may not comply with section 226.35(b)(3)(i), however, since the escrow is not established at the closing itself. Since an escrow account cannot be commenced with a zero balance, it may therefore be necessary to open an escrow at closing with a deposit by the buyer of an initial escrow amount, even if that amount is nominal.

What if a buyer wants to terminate the required escrow? This appears to be permissible according to section 226.35(b)(3)(iii), which states that a "creditor or servicer may permit a consumer to cancel the escrow account required in paragraph (b)(3)(i) of this section only in response to a consumer's dated written request to cancel the escrow account that is received no earlier than 365 days after consummation." Must a seller/lender comply with such a request? The statute's use of the word "may" rather "must" suggests that the seller may decline a buyer's request to terminate the escrow.

Escrow and Third-Party Servicers

The traditional Texas owner-financed transaction contemplates that the seller will receive and handle both payments of principal and interest as well as an escrow. There are, however, potential problems with this approach. Will the seller report the amount of interest paid to the IRS? Will the seller have the capability of generating an escrow analysis if required? Does the seller report timely payment history to the credit bureaus? Most individual sellers are neither equipped nor inclined to perform these functions.

There is also the matter of trusting the seller on certain key items—for example, timely payment of taxes and insurance premiums. What if the seller fails to do this and instead mishandles the funds? Another example of trust occurs in wraparound transactions, in which the buyer agrees to make payments to the seller and the seller, in turn, promises to make payments to the first lienholder. What if the seller defaults on this obligation?

A solution to these issues is to engage a third-party servicer who will collect payments from the buyer (including by electronic means) and see to it that any escrow or secondary payments are properly made.

The HPML regs are, along with the SAFE Act and Dodd-Frank, part of a federal trend to impose nationwide regulations upon certain lending practices as they relate to owner finance. Texas, once the haven for easy money, now finds itself in the same highly-regulated environment as everyone else.

CREATIVE TRANSACTIONS

Chapter 16

LEASE-OPTIONS, LEASE-PURCHASES, AND RIGHTS OF FIRST REFUSAL

Are They Still Useful in Texas?

Lease-Options

Lease-options have always been a favorite tool of Texas real estate investors—one of the "Big Three" alongside contracts for deed and lease-purchases—all of which are creative devices for getting under-qualified buyers into a home immediately. However, the Property Code now defines residential lease-options for longer than 180 days as executory contracts subject to strict regulation and penalties if not done exactly right. *Exactly right.* Specific requirements must be observed and the burden is entirely on the seller to do so. Violation incurs not only penalties under the Property Code (return of *all* payments made by the buyer including monthly payments) but potential liability under the dreaded DTPA, which can involve treble damages plus attorney's fees. The risk to the seller of using lease-options (or any other executory contract) is now significant, and investors should therefore use them, if at all, with caution.

Why are lease-options executory contracts?

Executory contracts include any transaction that defers some material action by either party that pertains to real property ownership or possession into the future. So why do lease-options fall within this definition? Because the Property Code says so. Section 5.062(a)(2) states: "An option to purchase real property that includes or is combined or executed concurrently with a residential lease agreement, together with the lease, is considered an executory contract for conveyance of real property." There is an exception for lease-options for 180 days or less under section 5.062(c)—otherwise, the TREC 1-4 contract would violate this provision when combined with a short-term lease. Commercial lease-options are not affected.

Executory Contracts: Requirements

Just for the record, one can *still* do a long-term lease-option—but consider the requirements. The landlord/seller must provide the Buyer with a recent survey or a current plat; copies of liens, restrictive covenants, and easements; a Seller's Disclosure of Property Condition; a disclosure for nonsubdivision properties stating utilities may not be available until the subdivision is recorded; tax certificates; a copy of the insurance policy showing the name of the insurer and insured along with a description of the insured property and the policy amount; a seven-day notice letter; and an annual accounting that includes amounts paid, amounts owed, payments remaining, taxes paid, and the amount paid for insurance premiums plus an accounting for any insurance proceeds.

Additionally, it is required that sales advertisements disclose the availability of water, sewer, and electric service. The seller must provide a thorough disclosure of the financial terms of the transaction, including the interest rate, amount of interest charged for the term of the contract, the total amount of principal and interest to be paid, and the nonexistence of a prepayment penalty. Excessive late fees and prepayment penalties are banned.

Even if all the foregoing statutory requirements are met, the buyer may *still* cancel an executory contract for *any reason* within 14 days of signing.

The Short-Term Lease-Option

It is nonetheless true that lease-options may be useful if the term is 180 days or less *or* if the property is paid for (meaning a lender's consent will not be needed). Accordingly, an investor should not avoid utilizing a 180-day (or less) lease-option if it is appropriate under the circumstances, particularly if there is a possibility that the option may be exercised during that period. Also, if the parties decide in good-faith to renew the option for another short term, they should not hesitate to do so. We recommend using a 179-day option term just to avoid any issue about whether or not the statute has been violated, since it is never a good idea to cut matters too close when dealing with legal limits or deadlines.

A Month-to-Month Lease Combined with an Option

What if the lease is "month-to-month?" If it includes an option to purchase, do the requirements and penalties of Property Code sections 5.062 et seq. apply? The answer is yes, so long as the term of the option fails to be expressly limited to 180 days or less. Since the lease can easily extend for longer than 180 days, the option can as well. This arrangement is therefore an executory contract.

Potential Solution: Stacking Short-Term Options

What about the possibility of stacking six-month option contracts—i.e., allowing the option to expire and then renewing it again and again? This would appear to be a loophole, making stacking a possible way for a very aggressive investor to still do a lengthy lease-option without complying with the executory contract rules, although at some risk. If challenged by the tenant/buyer, a judge may examine the totality of the circumstances, including the intent of the parties, and declare that the arrangement is a de facto executory contract. It all comes down to whether or not the tenant/buyer becomes disgruntled and decides to (1) challenge the transaction with a lawsuit, or (2) resist an eviction based on an executory contract defense. No challenge, no issue. There are no executory contract police. Having said that, lease-option arrangements that endure in the aggregate for longer than 180 days are perilous. The legislature clearly intended to discourage their use in residential transactions and deliberately imposed significant liability on landlord/sellers for doing them improperly.

Lease-Purchases

A lease-purchase is conceptually different from a lease-option. In a lease-purchase or rent-to-own, a portion of each monthly rent payment is set aside and credited toward the tenant/buyer's down payment. It is common, but not universal, for a lease-purchase to provide that after a certain amount is paid in, the tenant is able either (1) to convert the transaction from a lease to an owner-financed sales transaction in which the tenant gets a warranty deed and gives back a note and deed of trust to the seller, or (2) the seller agrees that the tenant/buyer may show the accumulated down payment on a loan application to a third-party lender and thereby qualify for financing.

Are lease-purchases executory contracts? Yes, since fulfillment of a material term is deferred into the future.

Lease-Purchase-Option Hybrids

Lease-purchases may provide that once a sufficient down payment is paid, the tenant/buyer will have an option to purchase the property at a certain price. Result? The lease-purchase becomes tangled up with a lease-option. It becomes become a hybrid "lease-purchase-option." What if the lease-purchase provides that payments will continue over a number of years until the property is paid for? In such a case it may not be a lease-purchase at all but an old-fashioned contract for deed.

Two points are worth noting. The first is that each of these devices—lease-options, lease-purchases, and contracts for deed—can, if only slightly modified, become hybridized with something else, sinking the transaction deeper into the executory contract hole. The second point is that regardless of the ultimate form such hybrid contracts take, they remain executory contracts for purposes of the rules and penalties of Property Code sections 5.061 et seq.

Recording Requirement

All residential executory contracts must now be recorded. Property Code section 5.076 states that "the seller shall record the executory contract, including the attached disclosure statement . . . on or before the 30th day after the date the contract is executed." Additionally, any instrument that terminates the contract must also be recorded.

Lease-Purchases in the Real World

Residential lease-purchases for longer than 180 days are no longer a feasible strategy for investors because of the multitude of requirements and the potential liability for doing them improperly. There is really no way to use a stacking technique here. Add the fact that the Property Code declares open season on the investor/seller whenever a tenant/buyer becomes disgruntled with an executory contract, and there are more reasons to avoid lease-purchases than there are to do them—especially since loss of an executory contract lawsuit could present an extinction event for a small investor.

The Right of First Refusal ("ROFR")

A right of first refusal ("ROFR") is a preemptive right to purchase specific real property at some future time upon defined terms and conditions. *ROFRs do not specify a price.* Circumstances vary, and therefore the language of a ROFR clause may vary as well. For example, a ROFR may be triggered by an offer received by the owner from a third party; in such a case, the owner is obligated to first offer the property for sale to the holder of the ROFR at the same price and upon the same terms. Another scenario may occur if the owner makes the decision to sell the property but does not yet have a buyer; the ROFR may obligate the owner to first offer the property to the holder of the ROFR.

The principal benefit to a ROFR is that it is not an executory contract, even when combined with a lease. Caution: As soon as a specific price is included, it is likely that a ROFR will be transformed into an option and become an executory contract. ROFR's are therefore not an effective tool for the investor/seller who wants to preset an above-market price in order to lock in a long-term profit.

ROFR versus Options

Certain characteristics are shared by ROFRs and options. Both are exercisable in the future. The validity of both can be limited to certain time periods or terms, i.e., either may expire before it is exercised. They can occur in both residential and commercial situations. Also both ROFRs and options grant the holder the *power* but not the *obligation* to act. There is generally no breach or liability for damages if the holder of an option chooses to do nothing.

However, a ROFR differs from an option in that it is conditional, not fixed, and does not specify a dollar price. An option to purchase, on the other hand, is a unilateral contract which gives the holder the right to compel sale of property at a certain price within a certain option term. When an owner gives notice of intent to sell, the ROFR matures or ripens and then becomes enforceable.

The terms of an option consist of the contractual provisions granting the option along with the terms and conditions of any third-party offer. Once the property owner has given the holder notice of his intent to sell, the terms of the option cannot be changed for as long as the option is binding on the owner. *City of Brownsville v. Golden Spread Elec. Coop., Inc.*, 192 S.W.3d 876 (Tex. App.—Dallas 2006, pet. denied).

What if an investor/seller gets creative with document wording and deletes the word "option" from the document, substitutes ROFR language in its place, and then goes on to specify a dollar price? Under the *Brownsville* case, once price is specified, it is likely that the ROFR becomes an option and therefore an executory device. Further, courts are more likely to interpret a contract clause in light of what it *actually is* rather than what it *pretends to be* (the "quacks like a duck" rule). The result could be a finding that executory contract rules have been violated, or worse, that fraud has been committed by the investor.

Drafting ROFR Language

All of this presents an interesting challenge when attempting to draft a ROFR. Here is one example:

> In the event Owner offers the Property for sale, then Holder shall have the right (but not the obligation) to purchase the Property under the following terms and conditions: (1) Once Owner has established an asking or

> listing price for the Property, Owner shall first notify Holder in writing of Owner's intent to sell and shall then offer the Property for sale to Holder at this price. Holder shall have 10 days from receipt of such notice to consider this offer, and if Holder accepts, Holder shall have 45 days to close. Consideration may be cash or third-party financing or, if agreed between Owner and Holder, by assumption, wraparound, or owner finance. (2) If Holder shall decline or fail to purchase the Property at the listing or asking price, Owner shall be free to offer the Property for sale to others. However, if a bona fide offer is received from a third-party prospective buyer, then Owner shall again notify Holder in writing and offer the Property to Holder at the price and upon the same or better terms as named by the prospective buyer. Holder shall have 10 days from receipt of such notice to consider this offer, and if Holder accepts, Holder shall have 45 days to close. Holder may shorten or eliminate any applicable time periods in this paragraph by waiving or declining in writing to exercise Holder's right of first refusal. The right of first refusal described in this section shall expire on
>
> ___________.

The advantage of the foregoing method is that the ROFR sales price is ultimately set by a third-party buyer. However, what if the ROFR as drafted merely gives the holder a general right? Some method has to be found to establish price. In the following instance, value is determined by reference to prevailing fair market value:

> In the event Owner intends to offer the Property for sale, Owner must first offer the Property for sale to Holder at a price equivalent to prevailing fair market value. Terms of sale shall be cash or third-party finance, and closing shall be within 45 days.
>
> If the parties cannot agree on what constitutes fair market value, then two appraisers shall be promptly selected, one by Owner and another by Holder. The two appraisers selected shall proceed to promptly determine the fair market value of the Property, taking into consideration its condition, comparables, and any outstanding indebtedness, liabilities, liens, and obligations relating to the Property. The appraisers shall deliver their

> respective reports within thirty (30) days. If the two appraisers arrive at different valuations, then these two valuations shall be averaged in order to produce a final valuation. The final valuation shall be binding on both parties. Each party waives the right to contest the final valuation in court. The costs of the appraisals shall be split equally between Owner and Holder.

The ROFR is a useful tool which stops short of being an executory device, but only so long as one does not try to stretch the language in order to make it an option by a different name.

Other Preferential Rights

There are similar but lesser preferential rights that also falls within this general category. One is a right of first negotiation ("ROFN") which means exactly what the title suggests and no more. There is no mention of price and no obligation to conclude a deal. Another is a right of first offer ("ROFO") which obligates the seller to notify a buyer of his intention to sell, and the buyer will then have the right to make an offer, the terms of which are not specified in advance. ROFRs, ROFNs, and ROFOs are potentially useful substitutes for a lease-purchase, but they must be carefully structured and worded so as not to fall into the executory conveyance trap.

Caution to Investors: Avoid the Courtroom

Lease-options, lease-purchases, and other executory contracts present the same worrisome prospect of litigation with limited or no defenses for the investor, who is seldom the most admired person in the courtroom. Even if executory contract rules are inapplicable, a court can still look to DTPA section 17.50(a)(3) which prohibits "any unconscionable action or course of action by any person"—a multi-edged weapon to say the least. Investors should find a good real estate lawyer, one with courtroom experience, and pay attention to what he or she says about how a judge or jury may react to a proposed deal and the documents that underlie it, particularly if there are executory contract implications. A good lawyer knows that real estate documents should always be drafted as if one will someday have to defend them in court.

Chapter 17

WRAPAROUND TRANSACTIONS

A Form of Owner Finance Leaving Existing Loan(s) in Place

A wraparound transaction is a form of creative seller-financing that leaves the original loan and lien in place when a property is sold. The buyer usually makes a down payment, gets a warranty deed, and signs a new note to the seller (the "wraparound note") for the balance of the sales price. This wrap note, secured by a new deed of trust (the "wraparound deed of trust"), becomes a junior lien on the property behind the existing first lien. The buyer makes monthly payments to the seller on the wrap note and the seller in turn makes payments to the first-lien lender. The original lender's note is referred to as the "wrapped note" and it remains secured by the existing "wrapped deed of trust." It is possible to wrap more than one prior note (e.g., an 80/20).

Often the principal of the wrap note to the seller exceeds the amount of the payoff on the wrapped note. This is seller profit. Alternatively, the buyer may make a cash payment to the seller for the seller's equity, and the wrap note payment will then be structured to correspond closely to the amount of the payment on the wrapped note (a mirror wrap).

Specific wrap terms can vary, but the principle remains the same. Wraps may be done on both residential and commercial properties. Wrap paperwork begins with the earnest money contract, which should include an addendum setting forth the terms of the wrap. At closing, details of the wrap should be summarized in a comprehensive wraparound agreement.

Alternatively, if the parties are clear on terms and ready to move forward immediately, they can skip the contract phase and request that an attorney prepare wrap documents for immediate closing.

If and when the buyer gets a refinance loan, the wrapped loan is paid and released, and the seller keeps any cash that exceeds the payoff amount of this first lien. The main difference between a wrap and a conventional sale is that the seller must wait until the wrap note matures or is paid in order to receive the full sales proceeds.

Wraparound financing is sometimes referred to as subordinate lien financing.

Wraparound Documentation

Wrap documents should, at minimum, include:

1. a wrap note signed by the buyer;
2. a wrap deed of trust securing payment of the wrap note;
3. a warranty deed with vendor's lien conveying title to the buyer; and
4. a wraparound agreement covering miscellaneous details.

The interest rate on the wrap note is often higher than that on the wrapped note since seller financing usually carries a rate slightly higher than market. The wrap note is often amortized over 15 or 30 years. In the past, most wrap notes were ballooned in 3 to 7 years, giving the investor a reasonably short time horizon for realizing a profit; however, Dodd-Frank now prohibits balloons in owner-financing.

Other Forms of Seller Financing

Wraps are a form of seller financing. There is no disputing it. Dodd-Frank and the SAFE Act apply.

As noted in the previous chapter, residential lease-options and contracts for deed were both restricted by executory contract provisions incorporated into the Texas Property Code in 2005. Because there are now severe penalties on sellers if strict, burdensome rules are not followed, investors have moved away from lease-options and contracts for deed. Only a few types of residential owner financing remain practicable and reasonably low-risk: traditional owner finance, used when residential property is paid for; exit land trusts, which involve temporarily deeding the property into a trust until a credit-impaired buyer can obtain financing; and wraparounds.

How is a wrap different from a contract for deed?

A wraparound is not an executory contract. It is an "executed" (complete) transaction as opposed to an "executory" (incomplete or unfinished) transaction. The buyer gets a deed to the property at closing, not at some future time, so the executory contract rules in Property Code sections 5.061 et seq. do not apply. In the event of default, the seller must foreclose in order to get the property back. This is usually not an undue hardship since Texas has one of the fastest nonjudicial foreclosure statutes in the country.

What about doing a wrap but delaying delivery of the deed to the buyer?

Some wraparound arrangements provide that the deed to the buyer will be held in escrow (perhaps by a lawyer) as security for a period of time—until the buyer pays in the full down payment, for instance. The wrap paperwork then states that the buyer is only leasing until the deed is delivered out of escrow. This is a bad idea. A material item of the transaction—the *most* material term, in fact—is unexecuted. Since the deal is unfinished, it qualifies as an executory contract and is subject to Property Code requirements and penalties, along with a nasty tie-in provision that makes violations of section 5.061 et seq. also violations of the DTPA.

There is another version of this practice, the "security deed" technique. A security deed is a deed back from the buyer to the seller that is intended to be filed by the seller only if the buyer defaults—i.e., in lieu of going through foreclosure. This is risky since a future court may disapprove of deliberately avoiding foreclosure procedures. Remember, real estate investors are not the most beloved of persons in the hallowed halls of justice. The common perception is that investors are greedy predators exploiting the unfortunate. Juries are often happy to award treble damages and attorney's fees against investors, so caution is in order.

Isn't a wrap the same thing as an assumption?

No. In an assumption, the buyer formally assumes the legal responsebility for paying one or more existing notes. Sometimes this is done with the approval of the seller's lender, paying an assumption fee, and signing onto the debt; more often, the promise to assume the existing debt is made directly (and only) to the seller by means of an assumption deed. Either way, it is expressly stated that the buyer is taking on the legal obligation of paying the first-lien note. This is not the case in a wrap, which is a kind of "subject to" transaction. The wrapped first-lien note is the exclusive responsibility of the seller.

In a wrap, therefore, the first-lien note and the deed of trust securing it remain undisturbed. A new note (the wrap note) secured by a new wrap deed of trust is created. In other words, there are two separate and independent sets of payment obligations. The seller is obligated on the wrapped first-lien note until it is paid and released; and the buyer is obligated to the seller on a new wrap note and wrap deed of trust. These obligations coexist.

How can I be sure a wrap is legitimate?

Wrap transactions *are* legitimate, primarily because there is nothing that says they are not. There are numerous Texas cases in which wraparound transactions have been upheld. Even the State Bar of Texas, in its Real Estate Forms Manual, publishes suggested forms for wrap documents.

Are there recent laws affecting wraparounds?

There are recent laws affecting *all* forms of owner-financed transactions. These laws include the SAFE Act, or T-SAFE as implemented in Texas, and Dodd-Frank.

The SAFE Act imposes a licensing requirement on certain types of owner financing extended by persons who are regularly engaged in selling owner-financed residences. A seller is required to be licensed as an RMLO if the property is not the seller's homestead and/or if the sale is not to a family member. So, if the property is a rental house being sold to a nonfamily member, then the seller *is* required to have an RMLO license, which requires training, a background check, and an exam. Note that the licensing rule applies only to residential wraps and is not applied to persons making five or fewer owner-financed loans in a year.

Dodd-Frank overlaps the SAFE Act in regulatory intent and effect. It requires that a seller/lender in a residential owner-financed transaction (including wraps) determine at the time credit is extended that the buyer/borrower has the ability to repay the loan. The seller is obligated to investigate the buyer's credit history, current and expected income, financial obligations, debt-to-income ratio, employment status, and the like in order to make this determination. Dodd-Frank provides for a de minimus exception for persons doing no more than three owner-financed transactions per year (so long as the seller/lender is not in the building business)—but (1) balloon notes are not permitted; (2) the seller must determine that the buyer has the ability to repay; and (3) the note must have a fixed rate or, if adjustable, may adjust only after five or more years and be subject to reasonable annual and lifetime caps.

What if there is more than one existing lien?

It is not uncommon to wrap more than one note and lien (e.g., a first and a second). The prior liens may even be to different lenders. The principle is the same: The buyer pays the seller on the wraparound note, and the seller then pays both prior notes. The lien securing the wraparound note is subordinate to both of the prior liens.

Example of a Wrap

Consider the example of 123 Oak Street which is valued at $100,000 but has been slow to move. There is a first lien in the amount of $50,000 to Apple Bank and a second lien in the amount of $25,000 to Orange Bank which, taken together, result in $25,000 equity. In the usual case, a purchaser would make a down payment and obtain third-party institutional financing, allowing the seller to receive his equity at closing and go happily on his way. But what if the buyer is unable to get traditional financing? The solution is a seller-financed wrap note that may be in a premium amount—say $110,000—which is subordinate to the notes due Apple and Orange Banks. The wrap note will likely bear a higher than market rate of interest. It will be secured by a wrap deed of trust that enables the seller to foreclose if the buyer defaults on the wrap note.

Is a wrap a device to get subprime buyers into homes?

Perhaps, but prudent investors will require the buyer/borrower to have a substantial down payment. The seller/lender should evaluate and approve the buyer's qualifications just as any other lender would. In fact, Dodd-Frank requires this. The wraparound should be viewed as a legitimate device to sell property to reasonably qualified buyers who have money to put down and can afford the monthly payments. For less qualified buyers, a land trust may be the better option.

Can wraps be used in conjunction with land trusts?

Yes. There may be circumstances where it may be a good idea to first transfer the property into a land trust and then do a wrap, but this requires more complex documentation since a trust agreement will also have to be prepared.

Are wraps just for homes?

No. Both residential and commercial wraps are possible. Commercial deeds of trust are more likely, however, to contain provisions that actually prohibit any transfer of title without prior lender consent. In all cases, but especially in commercial cases, one should carefully review the deed of trust securing an existing loan before proceeding with a wrap.

Why would a seller do a wrap?

The wrap seller can unload property at full market price (or even higher)—property that might otherwise have to be discounted or sit idly on the market. The seller gets at least some cash today (the down payment) which either goes into the seller's pocket or is used to reduce principal on the wrapped note (or a negotiable combination of both). The seller is then out from under the payment burden, although he or she must continue to be involved by collecting and forwarding payments to the first lienholder—unless a third-party servicer is used. The seller also gets the benefit of any spread between the interest rate on the wrapped note and wraparound note.

Why would a buyer do a wrap?

That is an easy question. The buyer does not have to apply and qualify for a new loan, at least not immediately. The buyer gets title to the property and immediate possession without lengthy delays, expensive loan fees, and closing costs.

Why would a broker encourage a wrap transaction?

Aside from meeting objectives of the broker's client, the buyer's down payment supplies cash for the broker's commission to be paid at closing, just as with any other transaction.

Is title insurance available?

Yes, but availability is limited. Some title companies are more inclined to insure wraps than others. Certain underwriters are not comfortable with the wraparound process for reasons of their own. It may be necessary to shop title companies until a wrap-friendly title company is found.

If a title company is issuing insurance, then closing will be held at the title company. However, most wraps are closed without title insurance in a lawyer's office based on an informal title search or a title report.

Isn't a wrap a breach of contract with the lender? What about the due-on-sale clause?

A wrap transaction is neither a breach of contract nor a violation of due-on-sale. The usual due-on-sale clause merely gives the lender an option to take action if it chooses. Look closely at paragraph 18 of the FNMA deed of trust: It says that a lender *may* (not must) accelerate.

Isn't there some kind of notice requirement before doing a wrap transaction?

Yes. Property Code section 5.016 requires that the seller (1) give seven days' notice to the buyer before closing that an existing loan that will remain in place; (2) inform the buyer that buyer has this same seven-day period in which to rescind the earnest money contract without penalty; and (3) also provide a seven-day notice to the lender. These notices are all the obligation of the seller and must be in the form prescribed by the statute. Actual lender consent, however, is *not* required, which makes this a rather odd law. Lender notices, often sent to the loan servicer, generally produce no response.

Note that the buyer's opportunity to cancel is an exclusively preclosing remedy. There is no right of rescission after closing has occurred.

Property Code section 5.016(c)(10) provides an exception to the notice requirement when "the purchaser obtains a title insurance policy insuring the transfer of title to the real property." Thus if you are able to get a title company to insure your wrap, you may dispense with seven-day notices.

This is a law that has no teeth to speak of. As a consequence, it is widely disregarded. For now, it has not had a significant restraining effect on owner-financed transactions.

What kind of down payment should the seller get on a wrap?

Down payments are an underwriting issue. In the case of a wrap, the seller is also the lender and (like any lender) should carefully consider the risks inherent in the transaction as well as the creditworthiness of the borrower before determining the amount of down payment and what interest rate to charge. Dodd-Frank requires such due diligence. It is likely that a down payment of less than 10% falls within the risky category.

Can part of the down payment be financed? Yes. There is no prohibition against it. Typically, the buyer would pay part of the down payment at closing and then promise to pay the balance within a short period—say 30 to 90 days—utilizing a second wrap note (a "down payment note"). Again, this is an underwriting issue for the seller but it is a common enough practice.

What if both notes are due on the first of the month?

The timing of payments is an issue and should be addressed in the wraparound agreement. It is a good idea to schedule payments on a wrap note seven to ten days before payments are due on the wrapped note, to allow time for the seller to collect payments from the buyer and then forward them on to the wrapped lender in a timely manner.

What about casualty insurance on the property?

Sellers in wrap transactions nearly always want to cancel their casualty insurance policy. This is inadvisable. The wrapped lender, which usually collects an escrow for taxes and insurance or at the very least is named as additional insured, will be notified of the cancellation. The seller will then get a default letter from the wrapped lender who will likely "force place" another policy (usually a more expensive one) at the seller's expense. The existing policy should therefore be left alone *and* the buyer should obtain his own policy. This is an imperfection in the wrap process.

There is also an issue relating to insurable interest. What happens if there is a loss? Collecting on the seller's insurance policy can be problematic after a wrap since title to the property has changed hands. Even if the seller agrees to make a claim on behalf of the buyer, the insurer may refuse to pay it, asserting that the seller no longer owns the property. Worse, this could potentially be construed as insurance fraud. Therefore the buyer should procure separate casualty and contents insurance, and claims should be made pursuant to the buyer's policy. It is unfortunate that this results in two policies, but there may be no reliable way around it. Insurance issues should be thoroughly addressed in the wraparound agreement.

If there is no escrow for insurance being collected by the wrapped lender, then it is in the seller's best interest to collect one from the buyer.

What about "double wraps"?

So long as the wrap deed of trust permits it, a wrapped loan can be wrapped and wrapped again, although the documentation can become prolific. This permits an investor to purchase property on a wrap and then sell it the same way (at a higher price and interest rate, of course), collecting a down payment (the investor's front-end profit) from a new buyer in the process. Usually, this new buyer commits to go through credit repair with the goal, but not the requirement, of paying off the wrap note early. The investor then gets his back-end profit.

Substitution of Collateral Clauses

An additional, advanced trick: some investor/buyers include a "substitution of collateral" clause in their wrap notes that allows the property to be freed from the wrap lien so long as property of reasonably equivalent value is substituted in its place. If the buyer is an investor with multiple properties this could be a useful strategy.

What if the buyer defaults on the wrap note?

Let's review: The seller receives a wrap deed of trust that enables the seller to foreclose if the buyer defaults in paying the wrap note. The seller can also seek and obtain a deficiency judgment if the sales price at foreclosure is insufficient to discharge the wrap note plus accrued interest and fees. Accordingly, the seller has the same ability to enforce the wrap note and lien as does any other lender. The foreclosure of a wrap is no different from foreclosing on any other ordinary lien.

Texas is fortunate to have an expedited nonjudicial foreclosure process. Property Code section 51.002 requires that a homeowner be given at least a 20-day notice of default and intent to accelerate the note if the default is not timely cured. If the deed of trust is on the FNMA form (which would be unusual for a wrap) then a 30-day notice and opportunity to cure is required. The default notice must be followed by a second letter stating that since the default was not cured, the note is accelerated and the property is being posted for foreclosure. This second notice must be given at least 21 days before the first Tuesday of the month in which the foreclosure will be held. So most Texas foreclosures take a minimum of 41 days—51 days if a FNMA deed of trust is involved—although, to repeat what we have said elsewhere, one should avoid cutting it close when it comes to legal notices. It is prudent to allow a cushion.

What if the seller defaults by not paying the wrapped lender?

The wrap agreement should provide that if the seller fails to make payments to the wrapped lender, the buyer may do so and receive credit against the wrapped note. The buyer should also have the power to request documentary proof from the seller that the wrapped note is current.

Two related situations are of interest: What happens if the seller (1) files bankruptcy and seeks discharge of the wrapped debt, or (2) dies leaving the wrapped debt unpaid? In either case, the buyer could be forced to refinance the debt on short notice, which may be challenging. In the case of seller bankruptcy, the seller should agree in the wrap agreement to execute a reaffirmation agreement on the wrapped debt rather than surrendering the property to the lender. As for premature death, the buyer should check to see if the seller has or can add term life protection (payoff insurance). If not, the buyer might consider obtaining a term life insurance policy on the seller in the amount of the balance on the wrapped debt.

What about the interest deduction?

The seller continues to be able to deduct interest paid on the wrapped loan. Nothing has changed there. As to interest on the wrap note, interest received by the seller must be reported as income, and interest paid by the buyer is deductible.

What are the disadvantages of a wrap?

There are shortcomings to a wrap. The seller has to wait until the wrap note matures in order to receive the full proceeds of the sale. Also, the wrapped loan is frozen in place and cannot be refinanced for the duration of the wrap. The seller has to collect and remit payments, which requires ongoing involvement. If the wrap borrower defaults, the seller must foreclose. In the unlikely event a loan is accelerated, the buyer may have to quickly secure traditional financing, so the wraparound agreement should specify the amount of time in which this must be done. The parties may also be carrying duplicate casualty insurance policies. Wraps are useful devices, but they are not perfect.

What about cost?

A properly drafted wraparound transaction will include a warranty deed, a wraparound deed of trust, a wrap note, and a wraparound agreement to address details. There may also be a down payment note involved. These are sophisticated, customized documents. Only an attorney experienced in preparing wrap documents should draft this paperwork. There are no standard forms available from any source that are adequate to the task. Also, because there is no wrap addendum promulgated by TREC or TAR, an addendum needs to be prepared and attached to the TREC 1-4 contract. Accordingly, attorney fees for wrap documentation may be somewhat more expensive than for the average closing.

Chapter 18

"SUBJECT TO" TRANSACTIONS

Buying Property without Accepting the Obligation to Pay the Debt

In order to understand "subject to" transactions, one must separate the concept of title from the concept of debt. They are divisible. A deed is a signed written document that conveys legal title to real property. A note is a signed written document promising to repay a debt. The two *can* be split and frequently are. Transferring title to real property without transferring the obligation to pay the debt associated with it is a "subject to" transaction.

Mechanics of a Sub 2

In a sub 2, an investor/buyer takes title but makes no promises about assuming the existing debt. In fact, a properly worded sub 2 deed expressly states that the buyer is *not* assuming any such responsibility. Sub 2s are often used by investor-buyers in order to buy, fix, and flip for a short-term profit. This is a sample sub 2 clause:

> This conveyance is made subject to any and all indebtedness of Grantor and liens against the Property, including but not limited to that certain indebtedness and liens securing same evidenced by a note in the original principal amount of $___, dated ___, executed by Grantor and payable to the order of ___, which note is secured by a vendor's lien retained in deed of even date recorded at Clerk's File No. ___in the Official Records of Real Property of ___ County, Texas, and is additionally secured by a deed of trust of even date to ___, Trustee, recorded at Clerk's File No. ___ in the Official Records of Real Property of ___ County, Texas. Grantee does not assume payment of this or any other indebtedness of Grantor.

Form of Sub 2 Deeds

There is no standard form for a sub 2 deed although Texas does have certain rules that apply if any deed is to be valid. Must the buyer sign a sub 2 deed? Usually not. Most often, the investor-buyer is accepting title and making no promises or agreements at all, so there is no reason for a signature.

The sub 2 deed need not show the actual price by the investor-buyer (presumably a buyout of the seller's equity, if any). It is customary for confidentiality reasons to recite that consideration paid is "ten dollars and other valuable consideration" although the actual amount paid can be shown if the parties so desire.

Recording

As with any other deed, there is no requirement that a sub 2 deed be recorded in the county clerk's real property records in order to be valid—only that execution occur before a notary followed by delivery to the grantee. When this is done, the title transfer is effective between the parties. It is nonetheless in the buyer's interest to record a deed, not just to preserve the record chain of title but to avoid the possibility that the grantor may sell the property twice.

General Warranty Deeds versus Special Warranty Deeds

The term "warranty deed" is loosely used to refer to a deed that contains both express and implied warranties. There is also a deed without warranties. A general warranty deed is the preferred form of deed for a buyer because it expressly warrants the *entire* chain of title, whereas a special warranty deed warrants title *only* from the grantor. Although special warranty deeds are more common in commercial transactions, receiving a sub 2 deed with special warranty should not trouble an investor, particularly since the last transaction involving the property likely encumbered it with a purchase-money lien and a title policy therefore issued at that time. In any case, sophisticated investors should know how to access the real property records and do quick title checks of their own.

Sub 2 versus Quitclaims

Some investors consider it adequate to acquire a quitclaim from a seller rather than a sub 2 deed with either general or special warranties. This is not the best practice. Why? A quitclaim is the weakest form of transfer and title companies often decline to insure a chain of title containing a quitclaim. Expect that a title company may ask that a deed with general or special warranties be obtained to replace the quitclaim. If a grantor is unable or unwilling to provide any warranties then a deed without warranties should be used.

Due-on-Sale Issues

As emphasized elsewhere in this book, there is no such thing as breaching or violating the usual due-on-sale clause. Due-on-sale merely enables the lender to choose to act—if the borrower transfers title then the lender *may* demand immediate payment in full. Transferring title without prior consent does not constitute an offense—moral, civil, or criminal. Experience shows that the risk of acceleration is small so long as the loan remains current.

Resale of Sub 2s

A sub 2 may be resold several different ways. First, having put a property under contract, an investor may simply assign the contract to a new buyer. For this reason, the sub 2 contract should be expressly made assignable. Another method is for the investor to close and then flip the property for a sum of cash, transferring the property on a sub 2 basis to the new buyer. A third option is for the investor to close and then resell the property by means of selling financing, i.e., collecting a down payment and transferring the property utilizing a warranty deed, promissory note, and deed of trust. The latter option obviously involves a long-term commitment by the investor.

Contract Note

Generally speaking, the TREC 1-4 contract should be used for acquiring sub 2s, but it should be accompanied by a "Subject To Addendum." Since neither TREC nor TAR offer such an addendum, a custom addendum will be needed.

A sub 2 deed is a useful device that should be part of any investor's tool kit, ready to be deployed when the opportunity arises. Sub 2 documents, like other creative real estate documents, are not created equal. Consult a real estate attorney. Never use forms from other states or off the Internet.

Chapter 19

ASSUMPTIONS

Picking up the Note

The essential features of an assumption are that the buyer (1) takes title to property by assumption deed (usually with a vendor's lien), containing either general or special warranties; and (2) promises to pay the balance of the indebtedness being assumed, a promise that may or may not be secured by a deed of trust to secure assumption. Additional documents such as an assumption agreement may also be needed.

An assumption may be accomplished with or without consent of the lender, although a small due-on-sale risk may exist if title to property is transferred without lender consent. Nonetheless, the vast majority of assumptions occur unofficially without consent. In the usual case, the buyer becomes obligated to pay the assumed indebtedness but this promise is made to the seller, not the lender. The only way one becomes obligated to a lender is to sign a note to that lender. Similarly, the only way one is released from a payment obligation is for the lender to cancel the note and sign a release of lien.

What is the difference between an assumable and a nonassumable loan?

Most all loans today are referred to as nonassumable. This is meant to be contrasted with certain loans in years past that could be assumed merely by paying an assumption fee and notifying the lender of the new owner.

But is the term "nonassumable" accurate? Not really. As stated earlier in this book, the concept of title is separate from the concept of debt. An owner of property is almost always entitled to transfer title whenever and to whomever he or she wishes. Doing so, however, does not relieve the seller from responsibility to pay the note (since the seller signed it), nor does it automatically obligate the buyer to pay it (since the buyer did not sign it). A deed transfers title—that's all.

The assumability issue is relevant in determining whether or not the lender will allow substitution of one obligor on the note for another. In other words, will the lender let the seller off the hook for the debt and replace him under the note with the borrower? The answer is almost always *no*. Lenders want the buyer to apply, qualify, pay fees, and get a new loan. That is, after all, their business.

What about due-on-sale?

If an owner transfers title without consent, has an illegal act been committed? Has the owner breached the covenants of the deed of trust? Not usually, at least not under the commonly-used FannieMae deed of trust. Lenders would, of course, prefer to be notified if a loan is going to be assumed by a third party (so they can impose costs and conditions) but they have no absolute right to that. They have only the post-transfer option to accelerate, and this rarely happens when payments are kept up to date.

Is an assumption the same thing as a wrap?

No. In a wrap, a new debtor-creditor relationship between seller and buyer is created. The buyer becomes obligated to the seller on a new wrap note secured by a new wrap deed of trust. As to the existing note (which is "wrapped"), the seller remains obligated to continue monthly payments until it is paid and released. The wrap and the wrapped obligations coexist. By contrast, in an assumption, the buyer expressly assumes responsibility for paying the existing note. There is no new note.

What is the difference between an assumption and a "subject to" transaction?"

In an assumption, the buyer promises to pay the existing debt. By contrast, in a "subject to" deal, the buyer takes title but expressly disclaims any obligation to pay the seller's debt, even though that debt is secured by a lien on the property. The buyer might make payments or might not. This is a typical assumption clause:

> As further consideration, Grantee promises to keep and perform all of the covenants and obligations of the Grantor contained in the Assumed Note and the Deed of Trust and (subject to any non-recourse provisions that may apply) to indemnify, defend, and hold Grantor harmless from any loss, attorney's fees, expenses, or claims attributable to a breach or default of any provision of this assumption by Grantee. Grantee shall commence payments on the Assumed Note on or before the next regular due date under the Assumed Note.

This is a typical "subject to" clause:

> This conveyance is made subject to any and all indebtedness of Grantor and liens against the Property, including but not limited to that certain indebtedness and liens securing same evidenced by a note in the original principal amount of $_______, dated _____, executed by Grantor and payable to the order of ________, which note is secured by a vendor's lien retained in deed of even date recorded at Clerk's File No. ______________in the Real Property Records of ______ County, Texas, and is additionally secured by a deed of trust of even date to ________, Trustee, recorded at Clerk's File No. __________ in the Real Property Records of ___ County, Texas. Grantee does not assume payment of this or any other indebtedness of Grantor. Grantor indemnifies and holds Grantee harmless from any and all liens, liabilities, debts, causes of action, damages, or claims of any kind that exist or may arise against the Property.

See the difference?

Assumptions are appropriate for those who intend to hold a property for a while. "Subject to" transactions, however, are usually entered into by investors who want to flip to a new buyer, perhaps after doing some rehab work first, without incurring any responsibility for the existing note in the process.

Can title insurance be obtained on an assumption transaction for which lender approval was not obtained?

Usually not. Title companies are conservative institutions that avoid potential liability, so most assumptions will need to be closed in the office of an attorney familiar with creative transactions. If a buyer is curious about the status of title, and an investor-buyer should be, then a title report (much cheaper than title insurance) can always be obtained.

What if there is more than one existing loan—an 80-20 for example?

It is not uncommon for a buyer to assume more than one note (e.g., a first and second lien). The notes may even be payable to different lenders. The principle is the same.

Can an investor-buyer make a limited agreement to pay the note until the house is flipped?

Yes. This is an interesting hybrid, not a true assumption but not a true "subject to" either. An investor-buyer may (either in the deed from the seller or in a side agreement) contractually agree with the seller to make loan payments for a limited time—say, a year, or perhaps until the property is resold to a third party. The wording might look like this: "Although buyer does not formally assume any legal obligation to pay the existing indebtedness, it is agreed between buyer and seller that buyer will commence making monthly payments directly to the lender on ____, 201_ and continue timely making such monthly payments for a period of 12 months."

What documents are involved in an assumption?

There are two options here: the first is seller-oriented, since it includes security for the seller, namely the right to foreclose upon the buyer and take the property back if the buyer does not comply with the assumption terms. Documents required are a warranty deed with vendor's lien and a deed of trust to secure assumption. Additional documents—a separate assumption agreement, a property management letter sent to the lender, and a power of attorney in favor of the buyer—may be included. These supplementary documents are advisable, if for no other reason than in the future it may be necessary for the buyer to inquire about payoff, and without legal authority (i.e., a document signed and acknowledged by the original borrower) a lender will not supply this confidential information.

The second, simpler option is more favorable to an investor-buyer. It is used when the seller does not require, or perhaps even care about, taking security for the assumption. This might be true if the seller's credit is already in poor shape. The seller may just want to sign the property over to an investor and never hear another word about it. For this, one document—an assumption deed—is sufficient to complete the transaction. Again, however, a property management letter or power of attorney is advisable if it is anticipated that payoff information will be needed in the future.

What if the buyer defaults on the assumption?

If the seller received a deed of trust to secure assumption at closing, then the seller may foreclose if the buyer defaults. Texas has an expedited non-judicial foreclosure process. Property Code section 51.002 requires that a homeowner be given at least a 20-day notice of default and intent to accelerate the note if the default is not timely cured. If the seller merely signed an assumption deed without a vendor's lien and without a deed of trust to secure assumption, then the seller is out of luck. Even if the seller did not get a deed of trust to secure assumption for the buyer, the seller may foreclose on the vendor's lien retained in the deed—but this is a judicial process (a lawsuit), not something that can be accomplished on the courthouse steps.

Chapter 20

DUE-ON-SALE

"There is no due-on-sale jail"—Attorney Bill Bronchick

We have touched upon due-on-sale in previous chapters, but it is now time to look at this subject in detail. There are a variety of contractual and statutory factors that need to be considered. However, the fundamental fact is this: If a transaction involves a title transfer without prior consent of the lender, then the risk of acceleration (however small) is present if the lender's deed of trust contains a due-on-sale clause. And nearly all of them do.

Due-on-sale has become a more important consideration since lease-options, long a mainstay of residential investor portfolios, are now defined as executory contracts subject to burdensome restrictions and requirements. Especially problematic is Prop. Code section 5.085-(b)(3)(C) which requires that "the lienholder consents to verify the status of the loan on request of the purchaser and to accept payment directly from the purchaser if the seller defaults on the loan." This means that the lienholder must be informed of *and* consent to an executory transaction, which is unlikely to ever occur as a practical matter. Accordingly, residential executory contracts longer than 180 days, to the extent that they are feasible at all, are effectively limited to paid-for properties. Residential investors owning property subject to a lien now tend to look to other alternatives—wraparounds, land trusts, or leases with a right of first refusal—all of which require consideration of due-on-sale.

Historically, mortgage lenders are not interested in foreclosing upon a performing loan merely because the borrower has transferred title. However, some will send irate letters demanding that the new owner apply and qualify to assume the loan, threatening that otherwise the property will be posted for foreclosure. Whether or not that threat is real or just a bluff is a calculated gamble. It is nonetheless clear that acceleration *can* happen. So can lawsuits by a party who alleges that he or she was not properly advised on the implications of due-on-sale and claims damages as a result. Accordingly, attention must be paid to due-on-sale issues when drafting documents for creative transactions.

The Seven-Day Notice Requirement

Property Code section 5.016 attempts to deal with the issue of due-on-sale by (1) requiring seven days' notice to the buyer before closing that an existing loan is in place; (2) giving the buyer this same seven-day period in which to rescind the contract to purchase; and also (3) requiring that a seven-day notice be sent to the lender, theoretically giving the lender an opportunity to accelerate and call the loan due. Clearly, the statute is designed to discourage transaction structures that separate title from debt and result in the lender losing control over a loan. Still, there is nothing illegal or even unethical about doing this. It happens often, most notably in "subject to" and wraparound transactions.

Section 5.016(c) lists 11 express exceptions to the seven-day notice rule:

> **(c) This section does not apply to a transfer:**
>
> **(1) under a court order or foreclosure sale;**
>
> **(2) by a trustee in bankruptcy;**
>
> **(3) to a mortgagee by a mortgagor or successor in interest or to a beneficiary of a deed of trust by a trustor or successor in interest;**
>
> **(4) by a mortgagee or a beneficiary under a deed of trust who has acquired the real property at a sale conducted under a power of sale under a deed of trust or a sale under a court-ordered foreclosure or has acquired the real property by a deed in lieu of foreclosure;**
>
> **(5) by a fiduciary in the course of the administration of a decedent's estate, guardianship, conservatorship, or trust;**
>
> **(6) from one co-owner to one or more other co-owners;**
>
> **(7) to a spouse or to a person or persons in the lineal line of consanguinity of one or more of the transferors;**

> **(8) between spouses resulting from a decree of dissolution of marriage or a decree of legal separation or from a property settlement agreement incidental to one of those decrees;**
>
> **(9) to or from a governmental entity;**
>
> **(10) where the purchaser obtains a title insurance policy insuring the transfer of title to the real property;**
>
> **(11) to a person who has purchased, conveyed, or entered into contracts to purchase or convey an interest in real property four or more times in the preceding 12 months.**

The most obvious available exception between non-family members is item (10)—a transaction where title insurance is issued (an odd exception, actually, since it was never the purchaser's *title* that was in doubt).

Transfers into a trust do *not* constitute an exception, although transfers by an existing trustee are excepted. So creating a land trust is not a means around the seven-day notice requirement.

No time period is specified during which a lender must act on the notice, if at all. The actual effect of this relatively recent statute remains to be seen, particularly since the only sanction provided is to allow a prospective purchaser to back out of the sales contract before closing (not after).

Effect of the Mortgage Fraud Act on Seven-Day Notices

The Texas Residential Mortgage Fraud Act requires virtually anyone connected with a real estate transaction (including real estate brokers, mortgage brokers, escrow officers, attorneys, etc.) to report to an authorized government agency suspicious activity that may involve real estate fraud. Tex. Gov't Code § 402.031. Question: Is failure to give the seven-day notice required "suspicious?" Future cases could answer this question in the affirmative. While Property Code section 5.016 may be largely toothless, fraud sanctions can be severe. Accordingly, the seven-day notice should be given unless there is a specific exception is available.

The Wording of Due-on-Sale

Even if seven-day notice must be given, it is not necessarily true that a lender *will* accelerate and foreclose; nor is true that a lender always *may* take such action. Take a close look at the language of the Fannie Mae/Freddie Mac Uniform Deed of Trust, which is nearly universally used to secure institutional residential loans. It contains the following due-on-sale clause:

> 18. Transfer of the Property or a Beneficial Interest in Borrower. As used in this section 18, "Interest in the Property" means any legal or beneficial interest in the Property, including, but not limited to, those beneficial interests transferred in a bond for deed, contract for deed, installment sales contract or escrow agreement, the intent of which is the transfer of title by Borrower at a future date to a purchaser.
>
> If all or any part of the Property or any Interest in the Property is sold or transferred (or if Borrower is not a natural person and a beneficial interest in Borrower is sold or transferred) without Lender's prior written consent, Lender may require immediate payment in full of all sums secured by this Security Instrument. However, this option shall not be exercised by Lender if such exercise is prohibited by Applicable Law.

Conveying title without lender consent is not a crime or even a "violation" of this clause. Secondly, paragraph 18 expressly states that a lender may not act if such action is "prohibited by Applicable Law." What is that?

Exceptions Provided by "Applicable Law"

The federal Garn-St. Germain Depository Institutions Act, 12 U.S.C. § 1701j-3, is among the applicable law that limits lenders' ability to act in matters of due-on-sale:

> **(d) Exemption of specified transfers or dispositions**
>
> **With respect to a real property loan secured by a lien on residential real property containing less than five dwelling units, including a lien on the stock allocated**

to a dwelling unit in a cooperative housing corporation, or on a residential manufactured home, a lender may not exercise its option pursuant to a due-on-sale clause upon—

> **(1) the creation of a lien or other encumbrance subordinate to the lender's security instrument which does not relate to a transfer of rights of occupancy in the property;**
>
> **(2) the creation of a purchase money security interest for household appliances;**
>
> **(3) a transfer by devise, descent, or operation of law on the death of a joint tenant or tenant by the entirety;**
>
> **(4) the granting of a leasehold interest of three years or less not containing an option to purchase;**
>
> **(5) a transfer to a relative resulting from the death of a borrower;**
>
> **(6) a transfer where the spouse or children of the borrower become an owner of the property;**
>
> **(7) a transfer resulting from a decree of a dissolution of marriage, legal separation agreement, or from an incidental property settlement agreement, by which the spouse of the borrower becomes an owner of the property;**
>
> **(8) a transfer into an inter vivos trust in which the borrower is and remains a beneficiary and which does not relate to a transfer of rights of occupancy in the property; or**

(9) any other transfer or disposition described in regulations prescribed by the Federal Home Loan Bank Board.

Subsection (8)—the living trust exception—gets the most attention. This exception was intended to allow individuals to create family trusts for estate planning purposes, especially probate-avoidance, without worries about due-on-sale.

Are land trusts a solution to due-on-sale risk?

Subsection (8) is also the exception relied upon by many investors who use land trusts with the intention of avoiding the applicability and enforceability of due-on-sale. As stated above, this was not the purpose of the exception; however, setting that point aside, there remain an obvious pitfall to this approach: such trusts make use of a lease, lease-option, or other document allowing the buyer/beneficiary to move into the property immediately—which clearly "relates to a transfer of rights of occupancy." So while land trusts may in the right circumstances be effective creative vehicles, it cannot be claimed that they are a method of dodging due-on-sale under Garn-St. Germain.

Other applicable law exists. For instance, the FDIC has promulgated 12 C.F.R. § 591.5(b)(1), which is unfortunately even more restrictive than Garn-St. Germain. It requires that in order for a land trust to avoid enforcement of a due-on-sale clause, the property must continue to be owner-occupied—something which is almost never true in the typical investment scenario. This rule reads:

§ 591.5 Limitation on exercise of due-on-sale clauses.

(b)(1) A lender shall not (except with regard to a reverse mortgage) exercise its option pursuant to a due-on-sale clause upon:

(vi) A transfer into an inter vivos trust in which the borrower is and remains the beneficiary and occupant of the property, unless, as a condition precedent to such transfer, the borrower refuses to provide the lender with reasonable means acceptable to the

> **lender by which the lender will be assured of timely notice of any subsequent transfer of the beneficial interest or change in occupancy.**

Investor and seminar gurus often make extravagant claims that their complex and expensive forms provide immunity from due-on-sale issues, ironclad asset protection, expedited eviction in event of default, and other proprietary strategies that will lead an investor along the gold brick road to prosperity. Such claims are usually false. Few of these packages are customized for Texas, nor do they take into account the executory contract rules, violations of which are defined to be deceptive trade practices. Seminar guru forms can now get investors in real trouble.

Note on Earnest Money Contracts

Consideration of due-on-sale begins with the earnest money contract, although TREC promulgated forms may be less than adequate in dealing with the subject. It is a good idea to consult a real estate attorney to obtain a suitable special provisions addendum that addresses the non-standard nature of any creative transaction, including but not limited to due-on-sale issues.

Chapter 21

LAND TRUSTS

A Form of Creative Owner Finance

There are many kinds of trusts and most of them can be adapted to hold real estate, whether investment property or the homestead. The difference between types of trusts revolves around their intended purpose, so one needs to be clear about goals before setting out to utilize a land trust. This chapter focuses on two groups of land trusts: transactional trusts (our term) used as short-term devices to acquire or transfer property, and holding trusts (our term again) the purpose of which is to acquire property (either anonymously or otherwise) and hold an asset for a longer term.

The scope of this chapter is limited to trusts which are formed during the lifetimes of the participants for the purpose of holding investment or homestead real estate. Testamentary trusts, which take effect upon death, are part of the estate planning process and can be substantially different, often because of tax issues, so consult an appropriate expert for advice on those. Living trusts for the homestead are addressed in the next chapter.

Types of Land Trusts

Transactional trusts include:

entry trusts, used by an investor to acquire a property to be flipped using an assignment of beneficial interest; and

exit trusts, used by an investor to "sell" property to a buyer who is working to restore credit and obtain traditional financing.

Holding trusts include:

anonymity trusts, which hold an asset under the trust's name with no reference to a trustee or underlying ownership; and

living trusts for the homestead, a probate-avoidance device.

Clients often ask attorneys for a "standard" trust (or worse, a fill-in-the-blank form they can use themselves) neither of which exists at any acceptable level of quality. There is no substitute for the analysis and drafting expertise of a competent professional in this complex area. Because trust agreements can be written in so many different ways, the challenge for the attorney is to discover what the client is trying to achieve and then tailor a document to suit specific needs.

Trust Basics

While land trusts can be used flexibly, there are certain structural items that do not change:

(1) The *trustor* (or grantor) is the current title-holder to the property. The trustor is therefore the person /entity who transfers property into the trust.
(2) The *trust corpus* (or *trust estate*) is the real property or other asset that is conveyed into the trust.
(3) The *trustee* (which cannot be an LLC) is the manager/administrator of the trust with authority to manage, maintain, lease, and sell the trust property.
(4) The *successor trustee* serves if the trustee dies, resigns, or cannot otherwise serve.
(5) The *beneficiary* is the true party in interest, the one with "ownership" to use that term loosely. An LLC can be a beneficiary.
(6) The *contingent beneficiary* acquires the beneficial interest if the primary beneficiary dies (note that there would be no contingent beneficiary if the beneficiary originally named is an LLC).

The same person cannot serve as trustor, trustee, and beneficiary or the trust disappears as a matter of law (the doctrine of merger). In order for an attorney to draft a land trust, the client needs to specify which persons or entities will be acting in each role.

There are two parts to the land trust process: (1) creating the trust, and (2) conveying the property or asset into the trust by means of a warranty deed (realty) and/or bill of sale (non-realty).

The Entry Trust (Investor Acquisition of Property in Preparation for a Flip)

There are two types of transactional land trusts available to real estate investors: (1) an entry trust used as a tool to acquire and then transfer real estate by means of an assignment of beneficial interest, and (2) an exit trust designed to hold title to real estate while an under-qualified buyer does credit repair until able to obtain a third-party loan. Both are popular.

In the case of entry trust, an investor coaxes a distressed seller into transferring property by recorded deed into a trust, after which the seller then executes an unrecorded assignment of beneficial interest to the investor. This is usually done in anticipation of a foreclosure. Entry trusts have the benefit of a certain measure of anonymity. However, these trusts do not delay or stop foreclosure unless the investor is willing to reinstate the loan and continue payments until the property is sold.

Drafting the entry trust is critical. Certain types of trusts allow the original seller to retain a beneficial interest (always a bad idea) that allows the original seller to a share of the profits when the property is flipped. Others permit the original seller to have a power of direction over the trustee (an even worse idea).

A significant risk, from the investor's point of view, is that the original seller may still transfer the property to someone else in defiance of the unrecorded assignment of beneficial interest that has been given to the investor. For this reason, depending on the circumstances, a "subject to" deed may be a simpler and better solution for investors than an entry trust. For asset protection purposes, the grantee on the "subject to" deed should be the investor's LLC.

The Exit Trust (Transfer to a Trust Pending Credit Repair)

Exit trusts can be a bit complicated. Basically, the trustor (the investor) is the "seller." A credit-impaired "buyer" is designated as a majority beneficiary of the trust. "Seller" and "buyer" are loosely-used terms in this context since there is no deed being executed into the end user at closing. Title is placed in the trust.

The property is conveyed into trust by general warranty deed and the buyer takes immediate possession. The trust acts as a temporary parking place for title to the property while the buyer works to obtain financing in order to purchase the property outright at a specified price. Sound similar to a lease-option? It is, except that beneficial interests in a trust are personal property, not real property, and therefore one can plausibly argue that they do not fall under executory contract provisions of the Property Code.

Structurally, an exit trust might work like this: the trust names a minority (10%) beneficiary, who is the trustor/investor/seller; and a majority (90%) beneficiary/buyer who acquires an option to purchase the minority beneficiary/seller's 10% interest at a fixed option price. The option is exercisable within a specified term so long as the majority beneficiary/buyer is not in default.

As noted, there is no deed, recorded or unrecorded, into the name of the buyer, since he or she is *not* acquiring actual title to the property at the time the trust is created—only the option to buy a personal-property beneficial interest. Ultimate transfer of title to an end user is deferred until credit repair and third-party financing are completed. For the time being, the only warranty deed being executed is the deed into the trust.

Creation of an exit trust is a private transaction except for the recording of the warranty deed. The trust agreement is not recorded. In order to achieve maximum anonymity, the name of the trust should be generic.

Use of an LLC in Combination with an Exit Trust

Trust law in Texas falls under the Property Code, whereas the law of business entities (LLCs and corporations) falls under the Business Organizations Code. That gives us a clue as to the respective function of these entities. Trusts can hold property, of course, but there is no liability barrier against lawsuits as is the true with entities formed under the BOC. Even if property is held in an anonymity trust, the trust—including the trustee as well as other participants in the trust—are still individually and personally exposed, an undesirable result given the propensity of plaintiffs' attorneys to sue every name they can find that is connected to the transaction.

Which leads us to the question: How may an exit trust be combined with the liability barrier of an LLC? One possibility: The trustor/investor first conveys the property into an LLC, which is followed by a transfer from the LLC into the trust. Including the LLC in this structure adds significant asset protection since, as stated, a trust alone has no liability barrier.

Trusts combined with LLCs can present significant hurdles to a troublemaking plaintiff who seeks to find and sue the property owner. A series LLC, which allows assets and liabilities to be held in separate and insulated compartments, is recommended to enhance asset protection.

Exit Trusts Are a Form of Seller Financing

The executory contract rules of Property Code sections 5.061 et seq., the SAFE Act, and the Dodd/Frank law have combined to make seller financing of residential real estate a challenge for investors. The subject of seller financing is mentioned here because clients occasionally ask if use of a trust (an exit trust for example) constitutes seller financing. The answer is *yes*, it does.

Exit Trusts as an Alternative to Lease-Options

A well-drafted land trust may provide an alternative to lease-options, which are expressly defined to be executory contracts. And generally speaking, executory contracts in residential transactions are difficult (if not almost impossible as a practical matter), just as the legislature intended. However, one can argue to a judge with a straight face that a land trust falls outside executory contract rules so long as the trust agreement provides for an option to purchase a *beneficial interest* in the trust (which is personal not real property), rather than an option to purchase the real property itself.

The Anonymity Trust

An anonymity trust is executed along with a warranty deed conveying real property into the trust. The traditional way for a trust to hold property is by expressly stating the name of the trustee, e.g., "John Jones, Trustee;" however, it is possible to list the grantee as the trust—e.g., the "123 Oak Street Trust." It is untrue that one must name the trustee in the deed for purposes of recording, since county clerks will record such deeds so long as they are property executed and acknowledged. Anyone seeking to know who the principals are and what assets they have has their work cut out for them.

Users of anonymity trusts should anticipate future objections from a title company and be prepared to re-execute and re-record a deed which names the trustee.

The Title Company and the Trust Agreement

When trust property is sold, it is likely that the title company will want to see the trust agreement. A written trust agreement must therefore exist. It must also be properly drafted so that the title company will accept it as valid. Otherwise, the title company may ignore the trust altogether and require signatures from all persons having an actual or potential interest in the property or, in the alternative, a judicial determination of heirship—either of which defeats the purpose of creating the trust in the first place.

Due-on-Sale

It is widely advertised by seminar gurus that land trusts prevent a lender from exercising due-on-sale. However, Garn-St. Germain (the federal living trust exception) was intended to create an exception for transfers of property to family living trusts designed to avoid probate. It was not intended to provide a safe haven for investors seeking to use trusts as part of their business plan. *The truth is that a land trust does not defeat due-on-sale because a land trust invariably contemplates a transfer of rights of occupancy—so due-on-sale provisions remain effective and enforceable.* Nonetheless, so long as monthly payments remain current, the discussion may be academic since lenders are generally loathe to foreclose on performing loans.

Not all land trusts are created equal. There are a myriad of trusts available on the Internet that purport to be good in all fifty states. *This is a false.* A principal defect of trusts marketed over the Internet is failure to consider or comply with Property Code section 5.061 et seq. pertaining to executory contracts. Some attempt to create liens that are unenforceable in Texas. Many involve complex, exotically-named transactional documentation with "fill-in-the-blank" forms, a sure indicator that they are junk. The place to get a valid Texas land trust is from an experienced Texas asset protection lawyer who knows what he or she is doing in this area.

Chapter 22

LIVING TRUSTS FOR THE HOMESTEAD

Avoiding Probate

The living trust is a tried and true means of avoiding probate of the homestead. A trust of this type should be distinguished from other kinds of land trusts—for example, a pure anonymity/asset protection trust that has no probate objectives, or an investor trust that contemplates short-term acquisition of investment property or a transfer of underlying ownership by means of an assignment of beneficial interest (described in the previous chapter as entry trusts and exit trusts, respectively).

Suitable Uses for a Living Trust

A living trust that includes the homestead should be considered, along with a pour-over will, as part any middle class estate plan. Note that the emphasis here is on probate avoidance and not asset protection. Why? Because homesteads are already protected in Texas from forced sale to satisfy judgments. *See* Tex. Const. art. XVI, § 50; Tex. Prop. Code chs. 41, 42. So it is useful to generally distinguish between homestead-exempt assets (protected by statute) and investment assets (which are un-protected).

Should living trusts be used for the long-term holding of investment properties? Probably not, because trusts have no liability barrier as do LLCs. An LLC, in particular the series LLC, is better suited to holding investments.

On the other hand, it is possible to create a living trust which not only owns the homestead but acts as the sole member and manager of an investor's LLC. This advanced structure is most suitable for use with a holding company in a two-company asset protection plan.

Creating the Trust

There are three possible parts to the living trust process: (1) establishing the trust with a signed trust agreement; (2) executing and filing a warranty deed conveying the home into trust; and (3) executing a pour-over will to move miscellaneous assets into the trust upon death.

As with other trusts, a trustor establishes the trust and conveys property into it. A trustee (or cotrustees if husband and wife) is appointed to direct trust affairs on behalf of the beneficiaries (again, usually the spouses) and, upon the death of the last beneficiary, on behalf of one or more contingent beneficiaries (usually the children). Since title remains in the trust, and the trust does not die, the surviving beneficiaries "inherit" the trust property but without probate or other involvement by courts or lawyers. All that changes are the percentage beneficial interests in the trust, and this occurs automatically.

The trust agreement should state the trust's purpose in general terms along the following lines: "to hold, preserve, maintain, and distribute the Trust Property for the benefit of the Beneficiaries, including but not limited to payment of expenses for their respective health, education, maintenance, and support as the Trustee, acting in his or her sole discretion, deems reasonable, prudent, and necessary." The trustee is charged with management of the trust. Texas law confers wide powers upon a trustee including selling and purchasing trust property.

The trustor should reserve the right to revoke or amend the trust. The terms of the trust are therefore not finally fixed until the trustor dies (or, in the case of husband and wife cotrustees, when the surviving spouse dies) at which time the trust becomes irrevocable and the contingent beneficiaries succeed to the entire beneficial interest. No deed or probate is required at that time. Even though Texas has an expedited probate process, the result may be a considerable saving of time, effort, attorney's fees, and court costs.

The trust agreement, unlike the warranty deed that follows it, should not be recorded. It is a private and confidential document, the terms of which need not even be disclosed to the contingent beneficiaries. A brief "Summary of Trust Terms" or "Memorandum of Trust" is occasionally prepared to provide to third parties if deemed necessary by the trustee.

A spendthrift clause should be included that prohibits a beneficiary from assigning his or her interest in the trust to creditors.

Trust Property

Trust property may be of any type, whether personal or real, tangible or intangible, and wherever located. Additional property may be transferred into trust at a later date after the trust is established.

The trust need not formally assume existing liabilities on trust property in order for the transfer to be effective. Property can be taken "subject to" existing indebtedness (i.e., without the trustee taking any liability for the debt), or the debt can be wrapped. "Subject to" is more common.

Real property is conveyed into trust by general or special warranty deed recorded in the county clerk's real property records. The deed should make certain specific recitals concerning the homestead nature of the property. *Conveying the property by deed into the living trust is an essential part of the process since the trust agreement, by itself, does not transfer title.*

Transferring property into a revocable living trust does not reduce a trustor's assets for Medicaid purposes. Trust property is still counted by Medicaid as belonging to the trustor.

Preserving the Homestead Tax Exemption

The trust agreement should contain language that preserves (1) homestead protections available to the trustor pursuant to Texas Constitution article XVI, section 50 and Property Code chapters 41 and 42; and (2) any available homestead tax exemption whether currently on file or not. It is prudent to make these recitals in the trust agreement even though Property Code section 41.0021 states that transfer of a residence into a "qualifying trust" retains the homestead character of the property. Similar language should also be recited in the deed into trust so as to make it clear to the local taxing authorities that a living trust has been established for the homestead.

Mixing Anonymity Techniques with Living Trusts

It is not advisable to utilize anonymity techniques when deeding property into a living trust for the homestead. Why? Because such matters are likely to become an issue only after the trustor/trustee is deceased and therefore unavailable to sign any curative deed that a title company may demand. Accordingly, a trustee should always be named in any deed associated with a living trust.

Due-on-Sale

Unlike investment land trusts, federal law creates a living trust exception to the enforcement of due-on-sale clauses on homesteads that remain owner-occupied. Garn-St. Germain Depository Institutions Act, 12 U.S.C. § 1701j-3. Due-on-sale is therefore not a factor.

Pour-Over Will

It is good practice for the trustor to execute a last will and testament that contains pour-over provisions designed to convey into the trust any property that was not previously designated. In this way, the trust and the will work together as part of an overall strategy. It is also possible to have life insurance paid directly to the living trust. This may be advantageous for purposes of paying off liens on the homestead.

The Title Company

If and when the property is sold out of the trust, a title company will probably want to see the trust agreement. What if the trustor used a junk form from the Internet? It is possible that the title company will ignore the trust altogether and either require a deed from all heirs or a judicial determination of heirship—either of which can defeat the purpose of creating the living trust in the first place.

To facilitate a title company's cooperation, the trust agreement should include release and indemnity language that a title company may rely upon in issuing title insurance. In rare cases, if all of the foregoing measures have been unsuccessful in obtaining a title company's cooperation, it may be necessary to change title companies.

Drafting and Maintaining the Trust

The purpose of a living trust is serious business and should never be relegated to fill-in-the-blank or Internet forms, most of which are not specifically designed to comply with Texas law. Additionally, it may be necessary to make amendments to the trust agreement over the years, especially if one homestead is exchanged for another or if the names of beneficiaries change. Trust maintenance can be as important as trust formation.

Chapter 23

ADVERSE POSSESSION

Is This a Creative Investment Strategy?

Legitimate adverse possession claims are rare. Rather than happening as a singular event, they tend to accrue incrementally over the years without notice or fanfare. Classic adverse possession claims include the family that gradually takes over the empty lot next door to their home, or the rancher who has fenced in an adjoining tract and pastured his cattle there for a decade.

Adverse possession refers to circumstances under which one may lawfully lay claim to ownership of property not originally one's own. The statute governing adverse possession is Civil Practices & Remedies Code sections 16.021et seq. It defines adverse possession as "an actual and visible appropriation of real property, commenced and continued under a claim of right that is inconsistent with and is hostile to the claim of another person." Case law adds that it must be true that the possessor of the property *actually does* openly possess it (the belief of entitlement to possess is insufficient), has possessed it *continuously* for the statutory period (sporadic possession is insufficient), and that the possessor *peaceably* asserts a claim of right *adverse* to and *exclusive* of all others (possession shared with an owner is insufficient). All of these are fact issues for a court to decide. *Kinder Morgan N. Tex. Pipeline, L.P. v. Justiss II*, 202 S.W.3d 427, 438 (Tex. App.—Texarkana 2006, no pet.).

It is not enough to be merely caring for property temporarily, or even paying the taxes on it, until the owner reappears. One can pay taxes on someone else's property for years, but if other adverse possession requirements are not met, then those payments are nothing more than a gift to the owner.

Property Description

So you want to make an express adverse possession claim to the "West 40 acres north of the railroad tracks?" Not good enough, at least not if you will be utilizing an affidavit. The location and boundaries of land claimed must be determinable with reasonably certainty, and that means there must be a proper legal description (lot and block or metes and bounds).

This may necessitate a survey, especially in the case of rural property. One alternative is to obtain such a survey first and then file an affidavit of adverse possession with the survey attached as an exhibit; another option—if it is urgent to put an instrument on record immediately—is to file the affidavit with the property description as it is currently available and then later amend the affidavit to include the full metes and bounds.

Strict Rules Apply

Adverse possession rules are specific for a reason. As the Texas Supreme Court has stated, the adverse possession "doctrine itself is a harsh one, taking real estate from a record owner without express consent or compensation." *Tran v. Macha*, 213 W.W.3d 913, 914 (Tex. 2006). The statute sets forth rules and conditions under which the doctrine applies, and these must be conclusively met. Close enough is not good enough. In the event adverse possession is litigated, all issues become questions of fact to be decided by the court.

The statute is structured in such a way as to require an affirmative act by the original owner to reclaim the property within certain periods of time, referred to as statutes of limitation. If the original owner is prevented from taking the property back by means of peaceable self-help, then he or she must file a trespass to try title suit to establish legal ownership and reclaim possession. If the original owner does not act, then his or her claim is barred and the adverse possessor prevails. The doctrine of adverse possession does not apply to public lands or against a government entity.

The Various Statutes of Limitation

Adverse possession law is based on notice along with the opportunity to respond to that notice. The legitimacy of an adverse possession claim is established when circumstances are such that it is visible to others—meaning others are or should be on actual notice that the possessor is asserting a claim of right to the property which is actual, open, notorious, exclusive, adverse, hostile, continuous, and uninterrupted for the applicable statutory period.

The burden here is on the record owner. Once an owner discovers the presence of a potential adverse possessor or is otherwise put on notice of an adverse possession claim, he or she *must* act to defeat the possessor's claim within the period prescribed by one of three statutes of limitation—or lose title.

Tex. Civ. Prac. & Rem. Code § 16.024 (Three-Year Statute):

> **A person [i.e., the original owner] must bring suit to recover real property held by another in peaceable and adverse possession under title or color of title not later than three years after the day the cause of action accrues.**

Under this section, the possessor must actually have title (i.e., a deed as part of a regular chain of title) or at least "color of title," which refers to a claim of title that has a reasonable basis but for some legitimate reason does not fit within the usual chain of title. So, the possessor must be able to produce conveyance or title paperwork to support the claim if it is to be successfully asserted under the three-year statute.

Tex. Civ. Prac. & Rem. Code § 16.025 (Five-Year Statute):

> **(a) A person [i.e., the original owner] must bring suit not later than five years after the day the cause of action accrues to recover real property held in peaceable and adverse possession by another who:**
>
> **(1) cultivates, uses, or enjoys the property;**
>
> **(2) pays applicable taxes on the property; and**
>
> **(3) claims the property under a duly registered deed.**
>
> **(b) This section does not apply to a claim based on a forged deed or a deed executed under a forged power of attorney.**

This is self-explanatory. Note that under this five-year statute, some sort of deed of record is still required.

Tex. Civ. Prac. & Rem. Code § 16.026 (Ten-Year Statute ["Bare Possession Statute"]):

> **(a) A person must bring suit not later than 10 years after the day the cause of action accrues to recover real property held in peaceable and adverse**

possession by another who cultivates, uses, or enjoys the property.

(b) Without a title instrument, peaceable and adverse possession is limited in this section to 160 acres, including improvements, unless the number of acres actually enclosed exceeds 160. If the number of enclosed acres exceeds 160 acres, peaceable and adverse possession extends to the real property actually enclosed.

(c) Peaceable possession of real property held under a duly registered deed or other memorandum of title that fixes the boundaries of the possessor's claim extends to the boundaries specified in the instrument.

The 10-year provision is the catch all. A deed or other memorandum of title is not necessary so long as the elements of adverse possession are met. However, such documentation may be useful to establish the boundaries of the claimed tract; otherwise the key to determining boundaries may be that which is fenced in as a "designed enclosure"—not just a "casual fence." *Rhodes v. Cahill*, 802 S.W.2d 643, 646 (Tex. 1990).

Two other sections, section 16.027 and section 16.028, are less commonly applied. The first provides a 25-year limitation "regardless of whether the person is or has been under a legal disability." The second allows a 25-year limitation based on a title instrument, even if that instrument is void on its face or in fact.

Statutes of limitation do not include any periods of disability (minority, insanity, or service in the armed forces) on the part of the original owner.

Statutes of limitation may be tacked or combined by various successive possessors of the property so long as there exists "privity of estate" (a direct legal connection) between these persons.

What sort of action should the owner take to defeat a claim of adverse possession? The most obvious option is to physically displace the interloper, if that can be accomplished peaceably, or file a suit for forcible detainer. If neither is effective, or if the adverse possessor asserts a title claim, then the owner's remedy is litigation in the form of a trespass to try title action and request for a declaratory judgment.

Litigation by the Adverse Possessor

Alternatively, an adverse possessor may be the one to file suit to establish title. To do so, the possessor must prove (1) a visible appropriation and possession of the land, sufficient to give notice to the record titleholder (2) that is peaceable, (3) under a claim of right hostile to the title holder's claim, and (4) that continues for the duration specified in the applicable statute. What is a "visible appropriation?" The possessor must "visibly appropriate the property as to give notice to any other person that they claim a right to the property." *Perkins v. McGehee*, 133 S.W.3d 291, 292 (Tex. App.—Forth Worth 2004, no pet.). Many people accomplish this by fencing the property and otherwise asserting clear dominion over it.

Section 16.034 provides that the prevailing party in a suit for possession of real property may receive an award of costs and reasonable attorney's fees.

Creative Approaches: The Affidavit of Adverse Possession

What should an adverse possessor do who believes that one of the above statutes of limitation allows him to claim ownership? The first and best option is to file a trespass to try title action. However, if a lawsuit is not affordable, a second choice is to file an affidavit of adverse possession in the county real property records which contains specific wording asserting the various elements of an adverse possession claim. Such an affidavit acts as a marker that commences notice, thereby providing a fixed point for the running of applicable statutes of limitation. As the affidavit matures over time it gradually acquires increased credibility.

Note that it is possible to file an affidavit before the applicable statute of limitation has fully run. The affidavit may assert a date when adverse possession commenced (which may be a date years in the past) and state that should current circumstances continue and should the entire limitations period expire, then the claimant will become the fee simple owner.

Title Research

It is a good idea to research title to determine if there are known owners who can be located. Title companies will issue a relatively inexpensive title report or an online service can be used. The title report can provide useful information in drafting the affidavit. If the title report reveals owners of record that can be located, a potential adverse possession claimant may be better advised to contact them and attempt a deal that preserves the existing chain of title. Unfortunately, this will likely involve payment of money for their interests.

Hybrid Affidavits

If heirs exist (whether they can be found or not), then an affidavit of adverse possession may be combined with an affidavit of heirship—entitled "Affidavit of Heirship and Adverse Possession." The heirship portion of the hybrid affidavit should include a recitation of family circumstances along with a statement of who the heirs are believed to be, in light of Probate Code section 52. The adverse possession section would make the usual assertions as to actual and peaceable possession, etc. At least two disinterested witnesses should sign. Three is better.

Adverse Possession in the Case of Cotenant Heirs

It makes for an interesting case when a possessor intends to stake an adverse possession claim against family members in an heirship situation—for example, a son wants to claim the family farm after his parents died without wills and his siblings have long since disappeared. Senate Bill 473 (introduced in 2011) would have added Civil Practice & Remedies Code section 16.0265 to address the situation of adverse possession against a "cotenant heir." Although SB 473 passed in the Senate, it did not pass in the House. So for now, adverse possession against cotenant heirs is accomplished in the same manner as against any other persons.

Co-Owners

Generally, a cotenant (legal term for co-owner) may not adversely possess against another cotenant unless the claimant clearly repudiates the title and claims to be holding adversely to that title. *Dyer v. Cotton*, 333 S.W.3d 703 (Tex. App.—Houston [1st Dist.] 2010, no pet.). Also, an affidavit of adverse possession, or a deed based on adverse possession, puts cotenants on notice of an adverse possession claim only if that instrument is recorded prior to the other cotenants acquiring their interest.

Paying Taxes

Clients routinely inquire about payment of back taxes on land they want to adversely possess. "Should we pay the taxes?" they ask. Well, yes; otherwise the taxing authorities will eventually conduct a tax sale and title will be acquired by someone else. Clients also ask "Can you guarantee that if I pay the taxes I won't lose my money?" The answer is of course *no*. Firstly, lawyers never guarantee anything. Secondly, it is always possible that the true owner of the property will appear and demand possession. If that occurs, then the client has made a gift to that person by paying back taxes.

The affidavit of adverse possession is a creative device that is inexpensive and often effective. The process is not, however, without a measure of risk and uncertainty.

Creating a New Chain of Title

As an additional creative step, the affidavit of adverse possession may be followed by a deed to the property out of the adverse possessor (a third-party trustee, for instance) and then another deed back into the name of the adverse possessor. The objective is to give the adverse possessor an actual recorded deed in his or her own name, in order to create a new chain of title. Such deeds should contain specific and appropriate language pertinent to adverse possession with the ultimate goal of passing muster with a title company.

This approach is designed to allow the adverse possessor to obtain credibility of title over a period of time. Using this method does not usually produce instant results and therefore is *not* suited for investors who want to adversely acquire property and then flip it.

Do-it-yourselfers beware. These transactions should be handled only by a capable real estate attorney in order to avoid doing more damage than benefit when it comes to the adverse possession claim.

Remedies for the Record Owner

What should an owner do who is put on notice that someone else is making a claim of adverse possession? There are a couple of options, but it is important to observe that *doing nothing is not one of them,* since the statute of limitations will eventually run and the claimant will succeed in acquiring legal title. One possibility is to file an opposing affidavit in the real property records expressly rejecting the adverse possessor's claim; in certain circumstances this may be enough to end the matter. Otherwise, the only safe course of action is for the owner to file suit.

What does the attorney need from the client?

Circumstances vary, of course, so the client should be prepared to explain the nature of his or her adverse possession of the subject property. Have they fenced it? Erected a structure? Do they mow and maintain it? Pay taxes on it? The client should also be prepared with a proper legal description of the property (lot and block or metes and bounds). A copy of the last recorded warranty deed is useful in this respect. It does little good to make an adverse possession claim if the boundaries of the property are uncertain. In many cases, the client is best advised to get a survey before proceeding. Finally, if the case involves potential heirs, and the likely strategy will be the filing of a hybrid affidavit, then the client will need to do some research on who the heirs are and where they can be found. Obtaining a title report from a title company is a good idea.

A Note on Illegality

Real estate lawyers are regularly approached by persons who wish to undertake a campaign of asserting adverse possession as to properties (sometimes dozens of them) that they perceive to have been "abandoned." These are often foreclosed houses owned by lenders that are currently sitting idle. The statute does not contemplate or condone the use of the adverse possession rules as a business plan for aggressive investors. In fact, such a strategy expressly involves breaking and entering, filing false instruments, slander of title, and fraud. Accordingly, district attorneys in Texas have begun prosecuting such offenses. No reputable attorney will assist a client in taking such actions.

ASSET PROTECTION STRUCTURING

Chapter 24

LLC FORMATION

A Basic Step in Asset Protection

This chapter discusses forming traditional and series LLCs, although our preference is clearly for the series LLC which provides significant benefits to real estate investors. We favor LLC formation in Texas and Nevada, which have similar statutes and are both among the best states for asset protection.

Why form an LLC?

There are lots of good reasons to form an LLC including (1) using the liability barrier to minimize personal exposure and maximize asset protection; (2) organizing and managing one or more businesses; (3) tax benefits including pass-through taxation; (4) achieving a measure of anonymity; (5) investor credibility in marketing and doing creative transactions; and (6) in the case of a series company, compartmentalization and insulation of assets and liabilities within separate series.

Separation of Business from Personal Affairs

An LLC is a useful device in separating business from personal affairs. Failing to do this is a common mistake of novice investors. Running business income and expenses through one's personal account may not be illegal, but it can complicate your defense if you are sued. It will be alleged that you "commingled funds" which may arouse the suspicions of the judge and jury and result in your failing the "smell test." This sort of error can result in an investor being held personally liable for damages.

Why risk it? Set up an operating account in the name of your LLC in which all income and related expenses are clearly shown, coded separately for each series or property. In the case of investors who are landlords, a separate account for tenant security deposits is always the best practice. If suit is filed it is likely that a plaintiff will demand an accounting and production of bank statements. Be prepared to show a sound business structure that functions with integrity. This is an essential part of any investor's asset protection strategy.

Anonymity

Anonymity, at least in a certain amount, is a key aspect of asset protection and a primary reason for forming an LLC. Ideally, your personal name should *never* appear on any deeds or leases, and a tenant should *never* write a check to you personally. There is an old rule that people tend to sue whomever they write their checks to. Make sure that is never you.

It has been reported that a new lawsuit is filed every 1.3 seconds. Literally millions of lawsuits will be filed this year. At least some courts will award huge damages for such things as serving coffee that is too hot. In this legal environment, asset protection is a serious matter, and an LLC is an excellent tool for achieving it.

Asset Protection

Although there is no such thing as a bulletproof plan to avoid personal liability or protect assets, one can get close. An LLC is an important step in getting there.

Asset protection is like a cross-country horse race: the more fences a plaintiff and his attorney have to jump, and the more effort and money they have to spend in order to get to you personally, the better protected you are. One way or another, plaintiffs have to pay their lawyers, and that means either cash or contingent fee—and few good lawyers will take a real estate fraud case on a contingent fee if they know they will have to penetrate a bona fide LLC before getting to any real assets.

Setting up an LLC

In forming a Texas LLC, one of the first things to consider is a company name, including whether or not it is available. The easy names tend to be taken, so one needs to be creative. Name availability information is available by calling the Texas Secretary of State at (512) 463-5555. In any case, do not be distressed if a favorite name is unavailable, since the better strategy is to use an assumed name ("DBA") for day-to-day company operations. Also, avoid using one's personal name for the company—"John Jones Investments LLC," for instance. Why make it easier for potential plaintiffs to know who owns the company? Better to use a generic LLC name and seek out preferred DBAs for everyday use.

After determining that a name is available, let your attorney know who the original members are going to be and what percentage of ownership each will have. Generally, LLCs have a managing member or comanaging members (common for husband and wife teams), although it is also possible to hire a manager who is not a member. An LLC may also have officers if the company agreement so provides. Who will be serving in these capacities? The client will also need to choose a registered agent with a physical street address in Texas, which can include a suite number but *not* a reference to a P.O. Box, PMB, Box, or other obvious indication that the address is not a physical office or residence. The Secretary of State occasionally googles a submitted address and may reject it if they think it is a POB.

The registered agent will receive and forward official company mail from the Secretary of State, the Comptroller, and anyone who is putting the company on formal legal notice. The RA is also the person who is served with process by the constable if the company is sued. For privacy reasons, listing the home address as the registered address is not recommended. Use of a physical office address is a better alternative. Note that the Certificate of Formation in Texas also requires listing the initial managers and their addresses. These addresses *may* (and should) be a POB rather than a home address.

All LLCs Are Not Created Equal

All LLCs are not created equal. Basic one pager, no-frill filings do *not* contain key asset protection provisions and should never be used by a serious investor. One's goal should not be to merely "set up an LLC" and consider the job done. *The goal should be to establish an LLC that includes sophisticated asset protection provisions beginning with the very first documents filed with the state* (the Certificate of Formation in Texas or the Articles of Organization in Nevada). The need for quality documentation continues with the company agreement, the minutes of the first meeting, and so forth. These documents work together to build a wall against lawsuits and creditors. The company should also have a formal record book with a seal and membership certificates that are dated and issued.

Clients often report that "I already have an LLC." Often, they mean that the minimum initial paperwork has been filed (often by an Internet service), the filing fee paid, and nothing else done. In Texas, this may not be sufficient to maintain the company's liability barrier if the LLC is challenged in court. If the LLC is not sufficiently independent and fully established, a court could potentially "pierce the corporate veil" and hold individual members personally liable, despite Texas's rather tough rules on the issue of piercing.

Clients will go on to say the following about the formation of their LLCs: "Oh, I just filled out and filed the standard forms." That is the point. *There are no "standard forms" for establishing and properly documenting an LLC,* regardless of what Internet services may say or imply in promotion of their highly simplistic products. Even the very basic forms that are available at the Secretary of State's website are of minimal use—

they will get you a file number, minimal legal status, and that is about all. Will they get you real asset protection? Do not count on it.

Internet Services

Use of an Internet service to form an LLC should never be considered by any serious investor or business person. If it is worth setting up an LLC in the first place, then it should be done with maximum effectiveness relative to the company's purpose and the desire of its members for asset protection. As for Internet legal forms services, an entire article could be written on how they often do more harm than good. Here is what Internet services do not provide:

> NO comprehensive advice on how to structure business and investments to achieve an overall asset protection plan;
>
> NO attorney to serve as organizer, initial member, and/or registered agent in order to maximize anonymity;
>
> NO sophisticated company agreement that deters creditors from taking control of your company;
>
> NO advice on how to move property into the LLC after it is formed;
>
> NO advice on how to use the LLC in conjunction with a land trust;
>
> NO advice on how to set up and arrange the LLC's finances, including LLC accounts, injecting capital, or loaning money to the LLC;
>
> NO advice on how to maintain the LLC liability barrier to prevent a plaintiff from "piercing the veil," and
>
> NO follow-up questions answered by a lawyer after the LLC is formed.

The documents provided by such services are so simplistic as to be barely above the level of junk. Business lawyers spend a fair percentage of their time cleaning up inadequacies in companies formed this way and offering asset protection advice that the client should have received from the beginning.

The Series LLC

The series LLC allows an investor to hold assets and liabilities within separate compartments or series which effectively operate as subcompanies. It shares characteristics with the traditional Texas LLC, including the benefit of informal management, an effective liability shield, and pass-through taxation; but the series format also adds the unique ability to segregate assets and insulate them from liability arising from other assets within the same company.

Alternative Business Structures

Clients occasionally ask if they should form a corporation instead of an LLC. While the corporate format is still available, it has been declining in use, something that can be verified by examining the filings at the Secretary of State's office. The LLC combines the best of a corporation and a partnership. Generally, a corporation should be considered only if an investor has significant net income that needs to be retained in the corporation at lower tax rates (Nevada is a good place for this since there is no corporate income tax).

General partnerships, including a variation called "tenants in common," are also the subject of inquiry by clients. So are trusts. These may be useful structures in the right circumstances, but should be generally be used in conjunction with an LLC. Why? Because an LLC has a liability barrier. General partnerships, TICs, and trusts do not.

Limited partnerships (with a corporation or LLC as a general partner) have a liability shield but are more complex structures suitable for large commercial transactions—acquiring shopping centers, apartment buildings, and the like—rather than residential flips or rentals.

Separating Assets from Activities: The Two-Company Structure

If an investor has (or intends to acquire) five to ten properties or more, a two-company structure is recommended. This should consist of a shell management company to interact with the public and a separate, stand-alone holding company to own hard assets. The fact that the holding company exists quietly in the background and does not enter into contracts or business dealings makes it nearly impossible to sue successfully. Few investors or business persons need anything more exotic than this.

Company Documents

It is critical that your attorney draft LLC governing documents so that they discourage creditors from even contemplating going after your membership interest. Asset protection provisions should be included from the outset in the Certificate of Formation and then extensively set out in the company agreement. *See* Part V, ch. 25: *LLC Governing Documents*.

Classes of Members

The owners of an LLC are referred to as members rather than shareholders or partners. We suggest establishing two classes of members and announcing this fact in the company's Certificate of Formation. Class A members are "regular" members who have full ownership and voting rights; Class B members are those who acquire their membership interest by some unfriendly or coercive means, including debt collection. They cannot vote and are not entitled to distributions except with the unanimous approval of the Class A members. How better to deter adversaries than to make it clear from the outset that any interest they obtain (or obtain influence over) will be essentially worthless?

Company Maintenance

In order to maintain the company as a separate legal entity that provides a liability barrier for its members, a certain amount of maintenance is advisable. The members should meet at least once a year. The first meeting of members (also called the organizational meeting) should include approval of the details of the Certificate of Formation and the Company Agreement. Annual meetings in successive years should review and ratify the preceding year's actions, recognize unusual events or circumstances, and elect new managers. It is also a good idea to hold special meetings to approve major decisions, the purchase or sale of real property, a loan to the company, or acceptance of new members and the associated realignment of percentage interests.

An LLC, like a corporation, is a distinct legal entity with its own rights, duties, and remedies. It has its own employee identification number ("EIN"), although the LLC's tax return is combined with the members' personal return (similar to a partnership). However, an LLC requires continued respect for its independence in order to maintain its separate status. It may be *your* company, but it should still be treated at arm's length for legal purposes. This is important if one wishes to avoid personal liability for the actions of the company or its agents and employees. Unless the company pays its state and federal taxes, maintains a bank account, conducts regular meetings, keeps records, and the like, then in the event of a lawsuit, a court could possibly decide an LLC defendant is not a "real" company—and allow the plaintiff to proceed directly against the members/owners personally. It will be alleged that the company is a sham and nothing but the personal alter ego of its owners, designed to shield them from the consequences of wrongful conduct. Needless to say, this could be a disaster and entirely defeats the purpose of forming an LLC in the first place.

Remember, plaintiffs' lawyers are looking for deep pockets and hard assets wherever they can be found. If there is a hole in your company's liability shield, an aggressive lawyer will likely find it.

What if you have a company but are still sued personally?

Even if one has a properly constituted and operating LLC, it is still possible to be sued in a personal capacity. In fact, this happens alarmingly often in spite of the Texas bias against piercing. Unless one has personally guaranteed indebtedness of the company, this is a form of lawsuit abuse—yet plaintiffs' lawyers do it anyway. The defense attorney should respond by sending out written discovery (including interrogatories and requests for production) to find out if the other side has any basis for insisting on personal liability. If no basis can be shown, a motion for partial summary judgment should be filed to have any personal names removed as defendants. The LLC's attorney should also ask for fees and costs for having to go through this process. If the LLC has been properly maintained and there is no evidence of fraud, then the motion should be successful. If not, this defense can be reasserted at trial.

Moving Property into the LLC

Any and all investment property acquired or currently held in a personal name should be moved into the LLC by means of general or special warranty deed without delay. It is not advisable to transfer a Texas homestead into an LLC since the homestead is already protected by the Property Code and Texas Constitution. Keep in mind the general rule: Personal and homestead-exempt assets should be kept separate from investment assets, and an LLC is a good mechanism for doing this.

Chapter 25

LLC GOVERNING DOCUMENTS

Building a Solid Foundation for Asset Protection

Asset protection lawyers hear such questions as "What documents should be included or created when forming a new LLC?" or "Why is it necessary to do anything more than file a bare minimum Certificate of Formation?"

Clients asking such questions are usually motivated by a desire to keep things both simple and inexpensive. They suspect that lawyers want to over-complicate projects with lengthy documents in order to collect higher fees. After all, in Merry Old England (from whence much of our law is derived), lawyers were actually paid by the word—this is true—and solicitors of the day were rewarded for creating long doc-uments full of obscure verbiage.

Properly documenting an LLC has nothing to do with this dubious history. First, there are organizational, management, and accounting issues to be dealt with. Secondly, when involved in litigation relating to an LLC, one of the first things a plaintiff's attorney will demand to see is the company book with all relevant documentation. If this documentation does not exist, or is inadequate, the plaintiff may seek to pierce the company's liability barrier. This occurs with exasperating regularity in spite of Texas' actual fraud rule. *See* Part V, ch. 28: *Piercing the Veil of an LLC.*

LLC Documents

It is not just the quantity of LLC documentation that matters but its quality and sophistication. LLC documents should contain asset protection clauses and provisions *from the very beginning of the formation process*. Formation documents can be several pages long and include reference to such matters as series specifications, notice of restrictions on sale or transfer or membership interests, and division of membership interests into Class A and Class B. Since the Certificate of Formation is a filed document and public record, creditors are put on notice from the outset that this particular company is the real thing. LLC documents should include:

(1) the Certificate of Formation ("COF");
(2) a comprehensive company agreement;
(3) the minutes of the first meeting of members (organizational meeting);
(4) signed and issued membership certificate(s);
(5) signed consent by the registered agent; and
(6) warranty deeds and bills of sale conveying assets into the LLC or its individual series.

All of the foregoing documents should be organized and kept in a company book with labeled tabs. The company seal should also be kept with the company book. Although the seal has no true legal effect in Texas, it adds ceremonial and decorative value to official company documents and be should applied to membership certificates in the space provided.

The Certificate of Formation

The COF supplies the essential information required by the Business Organizations Code and Secretary of State in order to establish a traditional or series LLC. It may also contain such additional information concerning the business and operations of the company as the initial members may wish to make public. For confidentiality and anonymity reasons, however, the COF should include no more information than is prudent or advisable to maximize asset protection.

Every company must have a registered agent. This person's name and physical address (not a post office box) must be specified in the COF. The COF must also disclose the name and address of the company's initial manager. Note that the manager's address *may* be a post office box. In fact, we recommend a post office box or office address rather than disclosing one's home address. The third name is that of the organizer, often an attorney who (like any other organizer) must be an authorized representative of the company.

If the company is to be a series LLC then the Business Organizations Code requires that the COF contain a "notice of limitation on series liability." It is recommended that the COF go into considerable detail on this, clearly stating that each series is independent and is not responsible for the debts and liabilities of other series or the company at large.

The Company Agreement

The company agreement governs internal operations. It should be designed to maximize asset protection and will be one of the first documents produced in discovery if the company is sued, since it is not recorded with the Secretary of State or anywhere else. The plaintiff will want to see, first, if one exists and second, if it contains any provisions that may be an impediment to recovery.

The company agreement should not be confused with the organizational meeting of members. Although the content of these two documents may occasionally overlap, they are conceptually different and are designed to address separate items and issues.

Company agreements are fairly lengthy and should be customized to fit the circumstances. However, all company agreements contain certain key provisions including but not limited to:

> *Series LLC provisions.* Designation of the company as a series LLC and a description of series characteristics, operations, membership, and management.
>
> *Voting of percentage interests.* A quorum should be defined. Most decisions should made by majority vote, but major decisions may require either a supermajority or unanimous vote.
>
> *Two classes of membership.* These are Class A ("regular" members) and Class B members who are defined to be any persons who gain membership or influence by means of a court judgment, execution upon a judgment, assignment of a membership interest in satisfaction of a debt, charging order, or contested divorce. Class B members have very few rights in the company—basically the right to receive notices and be present at meetings. They cannot vote. This structure assures that members do not wind up in a disastrous partnership with other members' creditors or ex-spouses, since these persons are usually seeking to dissolve the company or sell off its assets for cash.
>
> *Restrictions on sale or transfer of membership interests.* Language to the following effect should be included: "No Member may assign, convey, sell, encumber or in any way alienate all or any part of that Member's Membership

Interest without the prior written unanimous consent of all the other Members, which consent may be given or withheld, conditioned or delayed, as the remaining Members may determine in their sole discretion, without any requirement that such consent not be unreasonably withheld." Including a provision of this kind is critical to the successful operation of a small company. Basically, each member has a right of first refusal to purchase the interest of every other member. If there are multiple members, then the membership interest to be sold will be divided *pro rata* among members choosing to exercise this right.

Dispute resolution. The members should agree to mediate unresolved disputes prior to resorting to litigation or the filing of a complaint with any government agency.

The First Meeting of Members

The organizational meeting should address a whole array of items pertaining to the company's start-up. Important elements include:

Persons present. The initial paragraphs of the minutes recite the date and location of the meeting as well as persons present. The attorney who drafted the company's formation documents is often listed as present and being the one who prepares the minutes.

COF. The members approve the details of the COF and the various expenses incurred in forming the company.

Company purpose. A general purpose statement is preferred, e.g., "any and all lawful purposes for which a limited liability company may be organized under the Texas Business Organizations Code." The minutes may go on to state that the company will focus its attention upon a particular business such as investing in real property.

Initial members and percentages. The initial members, their respective initial contributions (whether in the form of capital or services rendered), and their respective percentage interests in the company should be specified.

Approval of company agreement. The company agreement should be reviewed and approved.

Election of managing members. A managing member or comanaging members are designated with the operational authority to manage day-to-day operations.

Official seal. The company seal should be affixed and approved.

Membership certificates. The form and issuance of membership certificates should be approved.

Organizational expenses. Expenses incurred incident to forming and establishing the LLC should be approved and ratified. Reimbursement for company organizational expenses should be approved.

Appointment of registered agent. The registered agent and registered address should be recited and approved.

Assumed names. These are often recited and approved.

Series LLC provisions. Provisions establishing the company as a series LLC are included, along with approval of conveyance of assets into individual series.

Banking and bookkeeping. This section should approve obtaining an EIN, opening an operating account, and check-writing authority.

Conclusion. The concluding paragraphs of the minutes should resolve that the company may commence business, state that members waive notice of the meeting, and approve the minutes. All members sign.

Annual and Special Meetings

For company maintenance purposes, the company should have at least one formal meeting per year—"formal" in the sense that it is reduced to writing and included in the company record book. The basic elements of the annual meeting are review and ratification of the preceding year's actions by the company, its managing members, and officers; specific approval of any major decisions; recognition of any unusual events or circumstances not in the company's ordinary course of business; and election of new managers and officers who will serve in the forthcoming year.

It is also advisable to hold special meetings to approve any major decision, approve the purchase or sale of real property, approve a loan to the company, or accept new members. Special meetings addressing such issues may be held anytime.

LLC documents contain common elements that should be addressed in the case of every new company. However, enterprises vary. Their purposes and members are different. The formation and organizational documents should be carefully drafted to reflect these differences. They should also provide tough protection from creditors and plaintiffs who may seek to pierce the veil and hold individual members liable for debts and actions of the company. Ongoing annual and special meetings should be held to preserve to maintain records and the independent legal character of the company. All relevant documents should be organized and contained in the company record book.

Chapter 26

THE SERIES LLC

A Preferred Vehicle for Real Estate Investors

The traditional Texas LLC has long been a favorite of real estate investors and others, especially after limited partnerships were made subject to the Texas franchise tax January 1, 2007. Investors who formerly created investment structures based on limited partnerships (with a corporation as general partner) then shifted their focus to LLCs, which are cheaper to file and less complicated to manage and maintain. New filings at the Secretary of State reflect that formation of other types of entities is down significantly, while LLCs compose the majority of new filings. It is not an exaggeration to declare that for most smaller-scale real estate investors the LP and the corporation are all but dead, and the LLC has taken their place.

Recently, a new type of LLC—the series LLC—has become available in Texas. It is an excellent way for real estate investors to own multiple properties and businesses, allowing investors to acquire multiple assets and sort them into separate cells.

This chapter discusses structural and operational details of a series LLC as they relate to an asset management and protection program. Note that it is not necessary to implement the series aspect of a series company unless and until one is ready to do so; until then the company operates exactly the same as a traditional LLC. Accordingly, there is no downside to electing to form a series LLC rather than a traditional LLC, even if there is no immediate intention to create series.

Series LLCs began in Delaware in 1996 and are now available in a number of states. Our preference is for Texas and Nevada, which have similar statutes.

What is a series company?

A series LLC allows an investor to hold assets and liabilities within separate cells or series which effectively operate as subcompanies. However, the series are *not* stand-alone legal entities in their own right—at least not technically (Tex. Bus. & Com. Code §101.622)—but in many respects they act as if they were. An individual series is statutorily empowered to enter into contracts, file and defend lawsuits, buy and sell property, and "exercise any power or privilege as necessary or appropriate to the conduct, promotion, or attainment of the business, purposes, or activities of the series." Tex. Bus. & Com. Code §101.605(5). A series can obtain its own EIN if it chooses and be treated separately for federal tax purposes. A series may (but is not required) to have its own bank account. A series can (and should) operate under its own assumed name. Given all of these characteristics, declaring that a series is not technically a stand-alone legal entity may be a distinction without a difference, at least most of the time.

Note that the Texas Comptroller, for its purposes, states that a "series LLC is treated as a single legal entity. It pays one filing fee and registers as one entity with the Texas Secretary of State. It files one franchise tax report as a single entity, not as a combined group, under its Texas taxpayer identification number."

The series LLC shares characteristics with the traditional LLC, including the benefit of informal management, an effective liability shield, and pass-through taxation; but a series LLC also has the ability to segregate and compartmentalize assets and liabilities within individual series. This offers significant protection and operational flexibility.

How does a series LLC differ from a traditional LLC? The answer is found in one word: *exposure*. In the case of a judgment against a traditional company, *all* assets of the LLC are available for purposes of satisfying that judgment. Not so with a series LLC. If a series is sued, liability is contained within that series and does not spill over to other series or the company at large.

Is the series LLC risky because it is a new vehicle? Not at all. The series LLC is now available in at least eight states and is accumulating a solid, court-tested track record. It is an idea whose time has come, particularly for real estate investors who can acquire multiple properties while avoiding complex structures with multiple entities.

Legal Authority

The Texas series LLC (like traditional Texas LLC's, corporations, and limited partnerships) is governed by Business Organizations Code title 2, chapter 101. Changes to the BOC made by the 81st legislature in 2009 (including authorization of the series LLC) along with minor improvements made by the 83rd legislature in 2013 have made it a model of progressive legislation and improved Texas's already deserved reputation as an excellent place to do business *and* engage in asset protection. There is no longer any good reason to go to another state to form an LLC unless one is specifically looking for an extra layer of protection by virtue of physical and jurisdictional distance.

BOC sections 101.601 and 101.602 read:

§ 101.601. Series of Members, Managers, Membership Interests, or Assets

> **(a) A company agreement may establish or provide for the establishment of one or more designated series of members, managers, membership interests, or assets that:**
>
> > **(1) has separate rights, powers, or duties with respect to specified property or obligations of the limited liability company or profits and losses associated with specified property or obligations; or**
> >
> > **(2) has a separate business purpose or investment objective.**
>
> **(b) A series established in accordance with Subsection (a) may carry on any business, purpose, or activity, whether or not for profit, that is not prohibited by section 2.003.**

§ 101.602. Enforceability of Obligations and Expenses of Series Against Assets

> **(a) Notwithstanding any other provision of this chapter or any other law, but subject to Subsection (b) and any other provision of this subchapter:**
>
> **(1) the debts, liabilities, obligations, and expenses incurred, contracted for, or otherwise existing with respect to a particular series shall be enforceable against the assets of that series only, and shall not be enforceable against the assets**

of the limited liability company generally or any other series; and

(2) none of the debts, liabilities, obligetions, and expenses incurred, contracted for, or otherwise existing with respect to the limited liability company generally or any other series shall be enforceable against the assets of a particular series.

(a) Subsection (a) applies only if:

(1) the records maintained for that particular series account for the assets associated with that series separately from the other assets of the company or any other series;

(2) the company agreement contains a statement to the effect of the limitations provided in Subsection (a); and

(3) the company's certificate of formation contains a notice of the limitations provided in Subsection (a).

Added by Acts 2009, 81st Leg., R.S., Ch. 84, section 45, eff. September 1, 2009.

Benefits of Simplicity and Economy

Lawyers are frequently asked "How many LLCs do I need, and how many properties can I safely hold in one LLC?" The series LLC eliminates these issues, at least up to a point. Our answer to the first question is most often "One LLC or perhaps two if you choose a two-company structure." Our response to the second question is "No more than 20 or 25 properties should be held in a single LLC, even a series LLC." This is our arbitrary, but informed, opinion. The statute permits an infinite number of series, but prudence suggests that even a series company should have some limit on the number of properties it owns. When an investor has established Series A through Series Z—that's 26 properties—it is time to consider establishing another holding entity. Asset protection is a cautious enterprise.

What if an investor has only one property or business to put into the company? Should he or she still consider a series LLC? Perhaps the question should be "Why not?" since there are no significant additional up-front costs and one can delay implementation of series until an appropriate time. *Until series are created, the company behaves exactly the same as a traditional LLC.* It is not necessary that one already have multiple properties or businesses in order to form a series LLC.

If real estate investment is in one's future, it may be wise to go ahead and establish a series structure early. As investment properties are acquired, additional series can be easily created for them and no state filings or legal fees are necessary. To facilitate this, the company agreement should provide that a series is automatically created when it receives title to a property or asset—for example, in the name "ABC LLC—Series A"—without necessity for amending the company agreement or other formality. Of course, a special meeting can always be held to document the establishment of a series (or any other significant LLC event) if the members consider it prudent to do so.

Those averse to the idea of multiple series may elect to form a traditional LLC, which continues to be useful for a single investment or business purpose. A traditional LLC is also suitable to act as a management company.

Series LLC Formation and Conversion of Traditional LLCs

In order to establish a series LLC, BOC section 101.604 requires that specific wording be included in the Certificate of Formation. The filing of the COF is an excellent opportunity to put the public on notice that the company has a serious asset protection firewall in place. Accordingly, minimalist filings, in particular Internet forms, should be avoided. These are seldom adequate for any serious purpose, and they certainly fall short in the context of a series LLC.

It is possible to convert an existing traditional LLC to a series LLC by means of a Certificate of Amendment. Unfortunately, nearly all of the company documentation of the traditional company (organizational minutes, company agreement, etc.) will need to be replaced so there is little in the way of cost savings, except for a lower filing fee. Note that this approach is not recommended unless the existing traditional company is free of baggage such as debts, tax liabilities, contractual obligations, pending or threatened litigation, and the like.

Insulation of Each Series

A series LLC contains individual series in which properties or businesses can be held separately and distinctly from the assets held by other series and by the company at large. In other words, each series may contain a separate rental property (a common arrangement); or, alternatively, by way of example, Series A could contain a rental fourplex; Series B could contain a strip center; Series C could contain a business that buys and sells real estate notes; series D could contain a general contracting business; and so on. The important point is that each series is insulated from the other as well as from assets and liabilities held by the company at large.

A point of clarification here: A series LLC can still own property without a series designation, as an asset of the company at large. For example, property transferred into "ABC LLC" would become a general company asset, even if the company is a series LLC, because no specific series is named in the transfer.

Let's return to the main distinction between a traditional LLC and a series LLC. Suppose there is a foreclosure on a property contained in Series A, and there is a deficiency at the foreclosure sale (i.e., the property sold for less than the amount owed the lender). The lender then sues and obtains a deficiency judgment. Assuming that the series company and its transactions were properly structured, the judgment would be enforceable *only* against Series A assets, *not* against the assets of Series B, Series C, or the assets of the company at large. This is not true of a traditional LLC which holds its properties in a collectively vulnerable pool. All by itself, this is a compelling reason to establish a series LLC rather than a traditional LLC.

Record Keeping

Good record keeping is important. In fact, series insulation is preserved only so long as "records maintained for that particular series account for the assets associated with that series separated from the other assets of the company or any other series." Tex. Bus. Orgs. Code § 101.601(b)(1). In other words, records must be maintained "in a manner so that the assets of the series can be reasonably identified by specific listing, category, type, quantity, or computational or allocational formula or procedure." Tex. Bus. Orgs. Code § 101.603(b). Implicit in the statute is the idea that assets and liabilities of a series can and should be separate both from the assets and liabilities of other series *and* those of the company at large. Commingling among these categories should be avoided.

Series record keeping is not as daunting as it may sound. A simple coding system for company assets and expenditures (all within a single checking account) would satisfy the statutory requirement of reasonableness. It is *not* necessary to establish a bank account for each series in order to comply with section 101.603(b)—although a real estate investor may decide to take this step if the properties held by each series are significantly and substantively different, either operationally or in terms of tax treatment.

As always, records should be kept in anticipation of litigation, particularly litigation that includes piercing allegations, since such allegations (abusive though they may be) are nearly automatic in contemporary business litigation. Internal documents that reasonably identify the activities of each series are therefore very important.

Series Assets

An investor should think carefully before mixing and matching entirely different businesses within the same company. Generally speaking, one should not place an asset or enterprise in one series that:

(1) creates a much higher level of liability or potential for legal action than businesses in other series;
(2) has a significantly different debt structure (involving development loans, personal guarantees, and the like) than that in other series;
(3) receives significantly different tax treatment from other series or is involved in a payment plan with the IRS;
(4) serves as a management entity with exposure to the public (tenants, vendors, contractors, and the like) since this function is better placed in a separate LLC altogether.

Entities with any of the foregoing characteristics should be placed in separate, stand-alone LLCs (either traditional or series), referred to among asset protection advisors as "single purpose entities" or "SPEs." Examples are restaurants, retail stores, and apartment complexes. Merely because the BOC permits entirely different enterprises to be contained within the same entity does not mean that one actually should do so.

Title Insurance and Assumed Names

Both title companies and lenders are new to transactions involving specific series, so this is an evolving area at the level of practice. For instance, title companies typically require a certificate of good standing for an LLC, whether traditional or series. Title companies can be obsessive about this. We have even encountered title companies that demand a certificate of good standing for specific series. This reflects a misunderstanding of the law and the series concept. Since series are created privately, without necessity for public notice or state filing, no official method exists for establishing that a series (as opposed to the company at large) is in good standing. Some lawyers argue that the statute should be amended to provide for registration of series and therefore the ability of the state to determine if a particular series is in good standing or not. We oppose this idea on anonymity and asset protection grounds. As much company activity as possible, including the creation of series, should be kept out of the public records. Amending the statute to require series registration and good standing would only serve to make Texas a less attractive asset protection destination.

One should also expect that a title company will require that an assumed name certificate be filed indicating that the company is doing business by and through one of its series—e.g., "ABC LLC DBA Series A." *See* Part VI, ch. 33: *Assumed Names*.

Anticipate that a title company will also require a company resolution evidencing both the creation of a series and its authority to enter into the subject transaction. This is not a problem. It may also be necessary to educate the title company (and possibly its attorney) as to the fact that individual series are empowered by statute to hold title to real property and grant liens. Tex. Bus. Orgs. Code § 101.605(3), (4). Title companies often demand a copy of the company agreement, a demand we resist whenever feasible. Company agreements are private, proprietary documents that are not usually the business of anyone but members of the company.

Separating Assets from Activities: The Two-Company Structure

Our recommended asset protection structure for serious, long-term real estate investors involves two LLCs, a management company and a holding company. The fact that the holding company (formed in either Texas or Nevada) does not enter into contracts or business dealings makes its assets beyond reach in most cases. Few investors or business persons need anything more complex than a two-company structure, although there may be good reasons to vary or customize this model as circumstances require.

Chapter 27

LLCs: A BRIEF TAX INTRODUCTION

Every Investor Should Have a Good CPA

Obtaining an EIN

The quickest way to secure an EIN is from the IRS website (www.irs.gov). Alternatively, one may complete the IRS hard-copy SS-4 form and mail or fax it to Internal Revenue Service, Attn: EIN Operations, Cincinnati, OH 45999 (fax number 859-669-5760). An EIN may be also be obtained by calling (800) 829-4933 between 7:00 a.m. and 10:00 p.m. Monday through Friday. Note that the EIN application requests that the applicant list a "responsible party" along with that party's social security number.

Each series of a Texas series LLC is permitted (but not required) to have its own EIN, assumed name, and bank account. Texas banks are new to series entities and an investor may have to explain to the bank officer what he or she is doing. If the bank is hesitant, direct them to Business Organizations Code section 101.601(20)(b): "A series established in accordance with Subsection (a) may carry on any business, purpose, or activity, whether or not for profit, that is not prohibited by section 2.003."

Federal Tax Returns

The LLC will have to file its own annual federal income tax return unless the company and its series are treated for federal income tax purposes as a "disregarded entity." A "disregarded entity" is disregarded as an entity that is separate from its owner for federal income tax purposes. Under the IRS default rules for entity classification, IRS Reg. § 301.7701-3(b), a single-member LLC is automatically disregarded and a multi-member LLC is automatically taxed as a partnership. In a case where a natural person (Form 1040 filer) is the only LLC member, the activities of the disregarded entity are reported on the taxpayer's Form 1040—Schedule C. In a community property state (Texas), a husband and wife who wholly own an LLC as community property have the option of either receiving disregarded or partnership treatment. IRS Rev. Proc. 2002-69.

Alternatively, your CPA may assist you in filing the entity classification election to receive tax treatment other than that provided by the default rules (accomplished by means of Form 8832). The other option for a single-member LLC is being classified as an association taxable as a "C" corporation (in which case the entity would file Form 1120—a "U.S. Corporation Income Tax Return"); or an "S" corporation (in which case the entity would file Form 1120S—a "U.S. Corporation Income Tax Return for an S Corporation"). A multimember LLC may also elect to be classified as an association taxable as a "C" or an "S" Corporation. Unless there is a compelling business reason to elect "C" corporation status that is well researched, this status should not be elected. In general, according to IRS regulations, once an entity has made its tax election, an election may not be changed for 60 months.

So should your entity make an S Corporation election rather than stick with the default position of a disregarded entity? It depends. Dallas CPA Angie Sebeniecher advises as follows: "If the IRS considers the client as dealer (doing this business for their livelihood), then their business income is subject to self-employment tax. The S Corporation election can be used to minimize that. If classified as a dealer, none of the gains are considered capital gains. It's all considered ordinary income, subject to the tax rate the individual is in, plus self-employment tax. I usually recommend this for people flipping property on a regular basis." Consult your CPA for advice relating to your specific circumstances.

Series IRS Returns

Should a series file its own tax return? Not usually, but it may. If a series has its own EIN, activities that are different from other series, and/or a different membership structure, a separate annual federal income tax return may be best. Let your CPA know that the U.S. Treasury Department has proposed regulations, 26 C.F.R. pt. 301 (Sept. 14, 2010), which state that the IRS will treat individual series as separate entities—each of which may elect "pass through" tax treatment if the established criteria are met. The *Journal of Accountancy* states that "the tax treatment of the series will then be governed by the check-the-box regulations (Treas. Reg. §§ 301.7701-1 through 301.7701-3). . . . The IRS decided that the factors supporting separate entity status for series outweigh the factors in favor of disregarding series as entities. . . . They specifically looked at the fact that the rights, duties, and powers of members associated with a series are direct and specifically identified. They also noted that individual series may have separate business purposes and investment objectives. The IRS concluded that these factors are sufficient to treat domestic series as entities formed under local law." Among other things, this means that individual series will have their own K-1 (www.journalofaccountancy.com/Web/20103328.html).

The IRS offers a helpful online tax workshop for new businesses designed to help small business owners learn their tax rights and responsibilities.

Texas Franchise Taxes

As for Texas franchise tax, the Comptroller of Public Accounts sends a notice to new filers of the date on which the first state franchise tax report is due (May 15th). It will also show the LLC's state taxpayer number (which is different from the file number at the Secretary of State's office). The letter will also ask that you "please complete an online Franchise Tax Accountability Questionnaire within 30 days."

A Texas franchise tax return must be filed with the Comptroller even if the company has no income. It is due by May 15th of the year following formation. Many new companies are eligible to file the No Tax Due Information Report (Form 05-163) if the LLC is a passive entity as defined in Tax Code section 171.0003; if it has annualized income less than the statutory threshold ($600,000); if the company has zero Texas gross receipts; or if the company is a real estate investment trust ("REIT") as defined by Tax Code section 171.0001(c)(4). If your company does not fall into one of these categories, one will likely be filing the EZ Computation Report (Form 05-169).

For owners of more than one Texas registered entity, it will likely be necessary to include an Affiliate Schedule (Form 05-166). This is an unsettled area. The Comptroller is inclined to take the self-serving view that all real estate ventures with common ownership are "affiliated" for purposes of assessing franchise tax. Investors with multiple, varied interests know this is nonsense.

The Comptroller's Public Information Report (PIR)

The annual filing of a Texas Franchise Tax Public Information Report (the "PIR" found on Form 05-102) is required by the Comptroller. It is due by May 15th of the year following formation. It is a simple form. The PIR requires disclosure of the names of each current "officer, director, or member" of the LLC. This is different from the Certificate of Formation which called for the names of the initial managers, not members. Since LLCs do not have directors, that is not an issue; however, one needs to supply the name of any person or entity who is a member, a managing member, or a nonmember manager. This of course has implications for any anonymity strategy an investor may have.

Visit the Comptroller's website at www.window.state.tx.us. to view resources available. Their phone number is (800) 252-1381.

Failure to Pay Franchise Taxes

Failure to pay Texas franchise tax will result in the company's right to transact business, as well as the right to sue and defend itself in Texas courts, being forfeited. If the company's right to transact business is lost, then the company's officers, directors, partners, members or owners may become liable for debts of the entity, including taxes, penalties and interest, which are incurred after the due date of the report and/or payment. *See* Tex. Tax Code §§ 171.251, 171.2515, 171.252, 171.256. For future reference, to determine if the company is in good standing with the Texas Comptroller, call (800) 252-1281 or go to www.ecpa.cpa.state.tx.us/coa/index.html.

There is no annual filing required at the Secretary of State's office.

Banking with a Series LLC

Lawyers hear lots of questions, comments, and complaints in this area. Firstly, the series concept is new to most Texas banks; and secondly, lenders generally have become so difficult to work with that it is nearly impossible to know with certainty what they will require, either for purposes of opening an account or obtaining a loan. A physician client of ours was even asked for a copy of his medical school diploma.

This chapter has been intentionally brief. Even though basic tax information has been presented, it is not a substitute for ongoing advice and guidance from a good CPA who is a regular member of the investor's team. All new LLC owners should consult a CPA concerning the best way to handle their new company for federal and state tax purposes. Certain tax benefits may be available but are not automatic.

Chapter 28

PIERCING THE VEIL OF AN LLC

An Avoidable Catastrophe

This chapter addresses "piercing the corporate veil," which refers to the limited circumstances under which the liability shield of a registered legal entity may be pierced and the individuals behind that entity held personally accountable. Knowing when this might or not occur is an important factor in asset protection since a piercing event defeats the central purpose of forming an LLC in the first place.

Piercing the veil is an equitable remedy the applicability of which depends on the specific facts at hand; nonetheless, the liability barrier of a registered entity may be pierced only in exceptional circumstances. *See Wilson v. Davis*, 305 S.W.3d 57, 59, 69 (Tex. App.—Houston [1st Dist.] 2009, no pet).

Evolution of the Law

Traditional Texas law in this area is summarized by *Rimade Ltd. v. Hubbard Enterprises*, 388 F.3d 138 (5th Cir. 2004), which drew upon case law and statutes beginning with the foundational Texas Supreme Court case of *Castleberry v. Branscum*, 721 S.W.2d 270 (Tex. 1986). The *Rimade* court stated, "Under Texas law, there are three broad categories in which a court may pierce the corporate veil: (1) the corporation is the alter ego of its owners and/or shareholders; (2) the corporation is used for illegal purposes; and (3) the corporation is used a sham to perpetrate a fraud." 388 F.3d at 143. Two years after *Rimade*, and partially in reaction to it, the legislature enacted Business Organizations Code section 101.114, which sought to further limit piercing by codifying the law in this area:

> **§ 101.114. Liability for Obligations**
>
> **Except as and to the extent the company agreement specifically provides otherwise, a member or manager is not liable for a debt, obligation, or liability of a limited liability company, including a debt, obligation,**

or liability under a judgment, decree, or order of a court.

Section 21.223 further defines and limits the exposure of shareholders and members:

§ 21.223. Limitation of Liability for Obligations

(a) A holder of shares, an owner of any beneficial interest in shares, or a subscriber for shares whose subscription has been accepted, or any affiliate of such a holder, owner, or subscriber of the corporation, may not be held liable to the corporation or its obligees with respect to:

(1) the shares, other than the obligation to pay to the corporation the full amount of consideration, fixed in compliance with sections 21.157-21.162, for which the shares were or are to be issued;

(2) any contractual obligation of the corporation or any matter relating to or arising from the obligation on the basis that the holder, beneficial owner, subscriber, or affiliate is or was the alter ego of the corporation or on the basis of actual or constructive fraud, a sham to perpetrate a fraud, or other similar theory; or

(3) any obligation of the corporation on the basis of the failure of the corporation to observe any corporate formality, including the failure to:

(A) comply with this code or the articles of incorporation or bylaws of the corporation; or

> **(B) observe any requirement prescribed by this code or the articles of incorporation or bylaws of the corporation for acts to be taken by the corporation or its directors or shareholders.**

> **(b) Subsection (a)(2) does not prevent or limit the liability of a holder, beneficial owner, subscriber, or affiliate if the obligee demonstrates that the holder, beneficial owner, subscriber, or affiliate caused the corporation to be used for the purpose of perpetrating and did perpetrate an actual fraud on the obligee primarily for the direct personal benefit of the holder, beneficial owner, subscriber, or affiliate.**

Did you notice that language? That a defendant must "perpetrate an actual fraud on the obligee primarily for the direct personal benefit of the holder, beneficial owner, subscriber, or affiliate?" Strong stuff. Actual fraud committed primarily for the "direct personal benefit" of the shareholder or member is required for piercing in Texas, at least for contract-type claims. This is Texas's actual fraud rule: "To determine if the [members of an LLC] are liable under the asserted veil-piercing theories, the Court must analyze both the question of whether the facts satisfy any of the asserted veil-piercing strands and the question of whether any of the [members] caused [the LLC] to be used for the purpose of perpetrating and did perpetrate an actual fraud on [the plaintiff] primarily for the direct personal benefit of the considered defendant." *In re JNC Aviation, LLC,* 376 B.R. 500, 527 (Bankr. N.D. Tex. 2007), *aff'd,* 418 B.R. 898 (Bankr. N.D. Tex.2009).

Accordingly, merely alleging "alter ego" (commonly and carelessly done by plaintiffs' attorneys) is by itself insufficient *as a matter of law.* Texas courts recognize the "strict restrictions on a contract claimant's ability to pierce the corporate veil." *Ocram, Inc. v. Bartosh,* No. 01-11-00793-CV2012, WL 4740859, at *2-3 (Tex. App.—Houston [1st Dist.] 2012, no pet.).

Corporate Rules Applied to Limited liability Companies

The reader may note that the foregoing statute refers specifically to corporations. What about LLCs? Business Organizations section 101.002 provides the answer by importing the piercing provisions of section 21.223 into the realm of LLCs. In other words, the same standards apply to both corporations and LLCs even though provisions of the statute may refer to a corporation rather than an LLC and to shareholders rather than members. Accordingly, LLC members can expect to receive the same treatment as shareholders of a corporation, no more, no less. *See Penhollow Custom Homes, LLC v. Kim,* 320 S.W.3d 366 (Tex. App.—El Paso 2010, no pet.).

In *SSP Partners v. Gladstrong Investment (USA) Corp.*, 275 S.W.3d 444, 451-52 (Tex. 2008), the Texas Supreme Court stated that the limitation on entity liability may be ignored only when the corporate form has been used as part of an unfair device to achieve an inequitable result. Continuing this line of thought, also in 2008, the Houston Court of Appeals (1st District), in *Tryco Enterprises, Inc. v. Robinson*, 390 S.W.3d 497 (Tex. App.—Houston [1st Dist.] 2012, no pet.), stated that in order "[t]o pierce the corporate veil and impose liability under an alter ego theory of liability pursuant to *SSP Partners*, a plaintiff must show: (1) that the persons or entities on whom he seeks to impose liability are alter egos of the debtor, and (2) that the corporate fiction was used for an illegitimate purpose, in satisfaction of . . . BOC section 21.223(a) and (b)." *Id.* at 508. What factors are important? The Court of Appeals in *Tryco* listed the following:

> (1) whether the entities shared a common business name, common offices, common employees, or centralized accounting;
> (2) whether one entity paid the wages of the other entity's employees;
> (3) whether one entity's employees rendered services on behalf of the other entity;
> (4) whether one entity made undocumented transfers of funds to the other entity; and
> (5) whether the allocation of profits and losses between the entities is unclear.

Any and all of the above should be considered red flags in a piercing case. From an asset protection perspective, all can be avoided by sound planning and documentation.

Liability of Company Officers and Managers

The signature by a corporate officer or LLC manager does not, by itself, make that individual personally liable for company obligations, even if the signature line fails to specify that the signer is acting solely in his or her capacity as an officer or authorized representative. *Neel v. Tenet HealthSys. Hosps. Dallas, Inc.*, 378 S.W.3d 597, 604-04 (Tex. App.—Dallas 2012, pet. filed). This rule tracks a central tenet of agency law: An agent is not liable on contracts made on behalf of a principal whose identity has been disclosed. Nonetheless, it is always the better practice to make sure that the signer on a contract fully discloses the capacity and authority to act on behalf of the entity for which he or she signs.

Directors and officers face full personal exposure, however, if the entity fails to pay its taxes. Tex. Tax Code § 171.255. If a registered entity's status is forfeited for nonpayment of taxes, then each director, officer, or manager may be held liable for debts of the entity from the date on which the tax was due up to the time the entity is reinstated. *In re Trammel*, 246 S.W.3d 821 (Tex. App.—Dallas 2008, no pet.).

Litigation and Discovery

During the discovery phase of a lawsuit involving a corporation or LLC, a plaintiff's attorney will likely request production of the company book and all relevant company documentation. Purpose? If the company has no company book or documentation other than a Certificate of Filing, the plaintiff's attorney may then amend his pleadings to include an allegation that the LLC is merely the alter ego of the individuals behind it, and therefore the liability shield should be pierced to hold members personally responsible for company wrongdoing. But what does "alter ego" mean? "Under the alter ego theory, courts disregard the corporate entity when there exists such unity between the corporation and individual that the corporation ceases to be separate and when holding only the corporation liable would promote injustice." *Mancorp, Inc. v. Culpepper*, 802 S.W.2d 226, 228 (Tex. 1990). In other words, the company failed in its mission to become and maintain itself as a legal entity independent of its owner. While Business Organizations Code section 21.223(a)(2) eliminates the alter-ego theory *as a basis* for veil piercing, it cannot be eliminated *as a factor* in a case where actual fraud is present, particularly since piercing in Texas has always been linked to values of fairness and justice.

Single-Member LLCs

Clients often worry whether or not the LLC liability shield will hold up if there is only one member. This is not a concern in Texas. Since Business

Organizations Code section 101.002 makes it clear that rules in this area relating to corporations also apply to LLCs, then (subject to the piercing rules outlined above) an LLC's liability shield remains intact even though there is only one member.

Implications for Series LLCs

A series LLC (as opposed to a traditional LLC) allows for different compartments or series that are insulated from the assets and liabilities of other series within the company. While not technically separate legal entities, these individual series nonetheless behave as subcompanies capable of doing business independently of the company at large, entering into contracts, and holding title to property. There is not yet Texas case law on this subject, although extensive precedent exists from other jurisdictions to which a Texas court may look for guidance in the series context. It is our view that even if a particular series is pierced, the other series within the company will remain intact.

Company Documentation

Many business persons utilize online services or otherwise engage in no-frill LLC filings involving a one-page COF and the payment of a filing fee—and then believe they are safe from lawsuits. This may not be so if the company fails to follow up with a company agreement, issuance of membership certificates, minutes of meetings, and the like. While section 21.223(a)(3) expressly eliminates the failure to observe corporate formalities as a basis for piercing, such failure may well be subtly considered by a real-world court in determining whether or not an actual fraud was perpetrated. Add an inflamed jury, one that is outraged at a perceived injustice, and the risk that a court will pierce the veil grows more likely. The law is not a machine. One cannot underestimate the human factor. It is more prudent to be safe than sorry when it comes to company documentation and other formalities.

What if documentation for an LLC or other entity has not been attended to for years? Fortunately, it is legal to go back in time and document a company's activities, so long as this is not linked to actual fraud. Such documents are signed by the members as of a retroactive effective date, regardless of the date of actual signature. For more detail on the content of principal LLC documents, read the chapter *LLC Governing Documents.*

Paying Franchise Taxes

Failing to pay Texas franchise tax and subsequent loss of the company's charter can be disastrous for asset protection. Note the following from the Tax Code:

> **§ 171.255. Liability of Directors and Officers**
>
> **(a) If the corporate privileges of a corporation are forfeited for the failure to file a report or pay a tax or penalty, each director or officer of the corporation is liable for each debt of the corporation that is created or incurred in this state after the date on which the report, tax, or penalty is due and before the corporate privileges are revived. The liability includes liability for any tax or penalty imposed by this chapter on the corporation that becomes due and payable after the date of the forfeiture.**
>
> **(b) The liability of a director or officer is in the same manner and to the same extent as if the director or officer were a partner and the corporation were a partnership.**
>
> **(c) A director or officer is not liable for a debt of the corporation if the director or officer shows that the debt was created or incurred:**
>
> > **(1) over the director's objection; or**
> >
> > **(2) without the director's knowledge and that the exercise of reasonable diligence to become acquainted with the affairs of the corporation would not have revealed the intention to create the debt.**
>
> **(d) If a corporation's charter or certificate of authority and its corporate privileges are forfeited and revived under this chapter, the liability under this section of a director or officer of the**

corporation is not affected by the revival of the charter or certificate and the corporate privileges.

Trusts and Piercing Rules

Trusts—whether created for the purpose of anonymity, facilitating land transactions, or for probate avoidance—can be an important element in an overall asset protection structure. However, a trust is not a legal entity in the same sense as a corporation or LLC. Trust agreements are not filed anywhere and have no state registration or approval. Accordingly, there is no liability barrier and piercing rules do not apply. The participants in a trust—the trustor/grantor, the trustee, and the beneficiaries—are *automatically* exposed to lawsuits in their personal and individual capacities. For this reason, investment trusts are most effectively used in conjunction with an LLC. The exception is a stand-alone living trust for the homestead since the homestead and related assets are already protected by Texas Constitution article XVI, section 50 and Property Code chapters 41 and 42.

The law applicable to LLCs in this area continues to evolve at the level of the courts. In particular, the *Tryco* case, on appeal to the Texas Supreme Court, may be influential. The safest practice is to establish and maintain an LLC with thorough and ongoing documentation. It is also sound business practice to periodically document the activities and events affecting one's company.

Chapter 29

JOINT VENTURES

Partnering with another Investor on a Specific Project

It is always useful to begin a discussion by defining terms. So what is a joint venture? And how does it differ from other investment vehicles such as general partnerships, limited partnerships, and tenant-in-common ("TIC") arrangements?

A joint venture differs from a general partnership in its narrower scope. General partnerships are usually created for the long term for a broad range of business purposes. They may contemplate engaging in various enterprises with the intention that the partnership will endure from one transaction to the next into the indefinite future. Joint ventures, by contrast, generally have a specific task or time frame. They perform that task, net profits are distributed, and they are done. One example would be investors pooling resources and efforts in order to buy, rehab, and re-sell either a residential house or a commercial project—a flip, in other words. Another example would be investors acquiring raw land to hold for a couple of years and then sell.

Applicable Law

All Texas partnerships, including joint ventures, are subject to the Texas Revised Partnership Act, Tex. Rev. Civ. Stat. art. 6132b-1 et seq. In the context of real estate joint ventures, it is also important to have a working knowledge of the Texas Property Code. Professional investors keep a paperback copy of the Property Code on their desks.

It is worth noting that a joint-venture agreement dealing with real estate does not, by itself, represent an interest in property or act as a transfer of that property. For that, a deed is required. *Sewing v. Bowman*, 371 S.W.3d 321 (Tex. App. —Houston [1st Dist.] 2012, pet. filed].

Limited Partnerships

Limited partnerships, in which a general partner (usually a corporation or LLC) is the only member to assume unrestricted liability, are more often used by sophisticated investors engaging in large commercial transactions. All of the partners are usually corporations or LLCs and the members have knowledgeable attorneys who have crafted lengthy, clever documents. This chapter will bypass further discussion of limited partnerships and instead focus on smaller-scale real estate joint ventures.

Tenant-in-Common Arrangements

What about TICs? How are these different from joint ventures? Our explanation will reveal our bias against these arrangements.

TICs are written up as general partnerships but are nonetheless focused on a specific deal, often a larger project such as an apartment complex or a strip center. Promoters seek out investors, usually affluent novices, who are packaged together in their personal capacities. In other words, these newbie investors do not form an LLC or corporation to act on their behalf in the deal; they sign the TIC agreement individually and then go on to personally guarantee a seven-figure note to a bank. If the value of the investment (often inflated to begin with) declines, the results are almost uniformly awful. Only the promoters—who have since taken their profits and moved on to other schemes—win.

Real estate lawyers are accustomed to counseling TIC investors who have awakened to find that a lender suddenly seeks to hold them individually liable for a very large sum. Few consulted an attorney before signing up with the TIC. Many are otherwise smart and successful professionals who should have known better.

Intelligent Structuring

No contract or transaction should ever be entered into without a consideration of asset protection ramifications if the deal fails. It is often the attorney who must counsel a starry-eyed, in-a-rush client that a proposed transaction could fail as well as succeed. In the event of failure, what is the exit strategy? Which of the client's assets will be exposed and how can that exposure be limited?

Lawyers can often see disaster looming, not because they are prescient but because they have seen this film before. In certain cases, when a happily oblivious client is determined to self-destruct, a lawyer may find it necessary to decline the representation.

Intelligent structuring implies an awareness not only of the mechanics of a proposed transaction but also of potential outcomes and their consequences. A willingness to look down the road, so to speak, where it may fork one way or another. Clients are astonishingly reluctant to this, accusing the attorney of trying to "kill the deal"—an unjust charge in most cases. An attorney's job is to make the deal work, ideally in the client's best interest, which brings us back to structuring issues.

Knowledgeable investors will have an entity, perhaps a management company, that (acting through an assumed name) is utilized for business with tenants, vendors, contractors, brokers, and other persons who might one day get riled up and file a lawsuit. The management company is a shell that contains employees, rental furniture, and leased vehicles. It is an equity-free dead-end for creditors. Hard assets reside in a separate holding company that does business with no one. The public does not even know that the holding company exists. In any case, prudent investors never sign contracts, leases, and the like in their personal name. All decisions that may have liability implications are made with an eye toward asset protection.

In the context of a joint venture, it is therefore preferable for the investor to choose an existing entity (or perhaps form a new entity) in order to participate in the deal, *making the joint venture a partnership of entities*. This provides the best protection. And when it comes to personal signatures and guarantees, the solution is often to *just say no*.

The Menace of Family and Friends

The title of this section is only partially intended to be humorous. All lawyers can tell stories of clients who propose doing a transaction with a brother-in-law, or perhaps borrowing money from parents, and declare that no written agreement is necessary because the other party is family or a close friend. In fact, the reverse is true. *In transactions involving family and friends it is more important to reduce the agreement to a signed writing, not less so.* Anyone who has witnessed the agony of intra-family litigation knows this to be true.

Minimal Contents of a Joint Venture Agreement

When it comes to drafting contracts and agreements, joint ventures included, we prefer that the effective date, the name and contact information of the parties, and the subject property all be plainly visible on the first page. The agreement should go on to address the following:

> What are the respective percentage interests of the partners?
>
> How will the joint venture be managed? By majority vote? Will some issues require unanimous vote? Will there be a managing partner? What are the limits of his authority?

What are the specific actions and duties required of each partner?

What about the investment property/project itself? Are there parameters for its rehabilitation and resale that need to be stated?

What will be the term (length) of the agreement? Presumably it will end when the project is finished and net proceeds are distributed, but this needs to be spelled out.

How will funds be handled? Who will sign checks? What about additional, future contributions if necessary?

Will there be loans as well as capital contributions by the partners? What about loans made by banks or hard money lenders? Promissory notes will need to be authorized and executed.

What about meetings of the partners? What constitutes a quorum? Who controls the agenda?

Suppose a partner wants to sell his interest or cash in? Suppose a partner dies? Will remaining partners have a right of first refusal to buy the decedent's interest? On what terms?

What happens if a partner's spouse files for divorce? Will remaining partners unwillingly wind up in business with the ex?

Every contract or agreement should have a default paragraph. What constitutes a default by a partner? If default occurs, what is the procedure for expelling a defaulting partner?

What about disputes among the partners? Will mediation be required?

Finally, never underestimate the "miscellaneous" paragraph at the end of a contract. It deals with such issues as amending the agreement, which law applies and where venue will be located if a suit is filed, and so forth.

A complete joint venture agreement will address all of these items and more, which is not to say that joint venture agreements need to be unduly complex, long, or intimidating. Consult an attorney knowledgeable in the field in order to draft a joint venture agreement and before signing one. Never use forms off the Internet for this purpose.

Chapter 30

BUYING OR SELLING YOUR LLC

Query: Convey the Company or its Assets?

This chapter discusses the elements of buying or selling a small business LLC in Texas, whether the business is focused on real estate investment or otherwise. The heart of the transaction is the purchase and sale agreement, which resembles an earnest money contract to sell real estate. In fact, if the business owns real property, then the agreement may also serve as a contract to convey that property.

There is a consistent rule of thumb relating to the sale of a business: *The transaction is never as simple or inexpensive as the seller and buyer would like it to be.* The complexity, due diligence burden, and professional expense (lawyer, CPA, business broker, appraiser, etc.) incurred by both sides in such transactions often substantially exceeds that which would accompany a comparably-sized sale of real estate alone.

The Purchase and Sale Agreement

The purchase and sale agreement will, at the very least, identify parties and the business to be sold; state whether the sale is a transfer of a company as an entity or of assets only, and then list those assets; specify the sales price and how it will be paid; provide for earnest money; include an inspection period for the buyer's due diligence; contain representations and warranties by both seller and buyer; provide protections for confidential information; specify conditions precedent that must be met for the transaction to close; and provide remedies in the event either party defaults. Various exhibits and attachments (deeds, an inventory of personal property, a list of liabilities, a copy of the office lease, copies of employee agreements, etc.) should accompany the purchase and sale agreement.

At closing, additional documents may be required, for example: a deed of real property to the new owner; if an asset sale, a bill of sale for inventory as well as furniture, fixtures, and equipment; a promissory note and security agreement if there is seller financing; a deed of trust if realty is involved; an approval by the landlord for the buyer to assume an existing lease; a customer or client list; various assignments; notice letters to customers and vendors; UCC forms; and other documents necessary to create a smooth and secure transition to new ownership.

The Parties

The first step is to ascertain the identity of seller and buyer. Is the seller a sole proprietorship? A corporation? An LLC? A determination needs to be made as to who actually owns the enterprise that is being transferred, who has authority to speak for and convey the business, and whose consent must be obtained (this may include spouses). If the selling entity is a corporation or an LLC, then that entity will need to be in good standing with the Secretary of State and Comptroller and have proper, up-to-date records that the buyer should carefully examine as part of the due diligence process.

Similarly, will the buyer be an LLC? An individual or a partnership of individuals? It is often advisable to establish an LLC to take title to and operate a newly acquired business. This is done for reasons of liability protection as well as convenient allocation of percentage interests among persons participating. If the buying entity is as yet unformed or unknown, the buyer should be listed by name in the agreement plus the phrase "and/or his assigns," thereby providing an opportunity to get an entity formed prior to closing of the sale.

Sale of Assets or Entity?

In buying a business, the buyer can acquire either the assets of the enterprise or the entity that owns those assets. In an asset sale, the assets transferred are specifically listed, as are the assets that are excluded. Ownership of the entity remains with the seller, as do the entity's debts and liabilities, unless specific exceptions are made. In the sale of a corporation or LLC, the seller's stock or membership interest is assigned and transferred to the buyer. Since ownership of assets remains with the entity, a bill of sale is not usually required.

Buyers' counsel generally prefer an asset purchase because it comes without the potential for hidden or undisclosed liabilities. On the other hand, acquiring the seller's entity may be accompanied by advantages such as an existing credit rating, established vendor accounts, or lines of credit. However, buying an entity may significantly increase the amount of due diligence that must be performed by the buyer.

The Sales Price

As with any transaction, the sales price can be paid in cash, partly in cash and partly by bank or SBA financing, or by means of cash plus seller financing. Existing indebtedness may also be wrapped or taken "subject to." In the case of third-party financing, the buyer will want closing to be contingent upon obtaining financing approval. If the deal is seller-financed, the seller will want to evaluate and qualify the buyer before giving final approval for closing. If either contingency fails, then earnest money is usually refunded, less any independent consideration paid for the inspection period.

How the sales price is divided up—between inventory, furniture, fixtures, and equipment, goodwill, and the like—is less a matter of legal principle than old-fashioned common sense. Caution to buyers: *Do not overpay for goodwill.* Often the single most valuable assets of a business (a service business in particular) are its employees and its lease, or what remains of it.

It is generally in the seller's best interest to provide that if the business is subsequently transferred, any outstanding seller financing must be paid in full (a due-on-sale clause). The seller should also reserve the right to inspect the business and its records to assure continued compliance with the purchase and sale agreement.

Due Diligence and the Inspection Period

Nothing is more critical for the buyer than effective use of the inspection period to perform prudent due diligence. What kind? The following is a basic list excerpted from a purchase and sale contract:

> (a) physical inspections, including inspections of the business premises, inventory, furniture, fixtures, and equipment; (b) economic and financial evaluations including but not limited to a detailed examination of the books and records of the business; annual and quarterly tax returns as well as ad valorem tax records; records of utilities usage; any agreements with contractors and/or employees; financial statement of the business; (c) current credit report; (d) marketing evaluation, including examination of the customer/client list, receivables history, and related files; and (e) any appropriate environmental assessment or engineering study including performance of tests such as soil tests, phase I or II environmentals, materials tests, equipment tests, and air sampling.

Depending on the nature and circumstances of the business to be sold, one could easily come up with additional items for scrutiny.

The important point for the buyer is to be able to terminate, prior to expiration of the inspection period, if the business is unsuitable for the buyer's intended purpose, is not in satisfactory physical or financial condition, or is otherwise unacceptable for any reason. Timely termination allows the buyer to receive the return of the earnest money less the inspection consideration. If the results of the buyer's inspections are satisfactory, it is common for additional earnest money to be due at that point. In fact, investors should generally want to structure payment of earnest money in two parts, even in purchases of rental houses: a modest initial amount followed by payment of additional earnest money after due diligence is completed.

Paradoxically, or so it would seem, the seller *wants* the buyer to have a right to terminate. Why would the seller of a business want a reluctant buyer, particularly if the seller is going to finance him?

Attempting to cut corners in the area of due diligence can have calamitous consequences. Buyers and sellers seeking to avoid legal fees may use some sort of contract off the Internet, not even knowing if it is valid in Texas, and when one party defaults, make the unpleasant discovery that litigation costs far exceed the expense of having properly documented the transaction in the first place.

Representations and Warranties

Both seller and buyer make representations and warranties ("reps and warranties"), breach of which is a default or at least a basis for terminating the agreement. Reps and warranties can be made to survive closing, survive closing for a limited time, or not survive closing at all. Buyers want the seller's reps and warranties to be broad and extensive in time and scope; sellers naturally want to limit their ongoing liability, preferring that reps and warranties expire at closing and merge into the closing documents, thereby putting a period on liability.

Examples of typical seller's reps and warranties include an assurance of authority to enter into the transaction; good and marketable title to the assets; full disclosure of liens and liabilities; no litigation pending or threatened; and the like. A buyer's focus is on full disclosure. A seller often wants to eliminate reps and warranties entirely and convey the business "as is"—something only foolish buyers go for. The result is usually a compromise.

For their part, buyers need to assure the seller of sufficient expertise and financial soundness to fund operations and pay liabilities as they arise. No seller wants to have to take a business back and sell it a second time.

Confidential Information

Confidential information about the business will likely be revealed during the course of the buyer's due diligence, and the seller has a right to demand that this remain permanently confidential. In addition to proprietary information about products, services, marketing strategies, and so forth, the seller is also in possession of sensitive information about employees and co-owners. As a result, the purchase and sale agreement should include a strict covenant on the part of the buyer, enforceable by injunction if necessary, not to reveal confidential information at any time to third parties. This covenant should apply whether or not the deal eventually closes. It should also prohibit the buyer from utilizing the information in order to compete with the seller in the future.

Seller's Covenant Not to Compete

If the transaction closes, a legitimate concern of the buyer is that the seller may set up shop nearby and continue in the same line of work. Accordingly, the purchase and sale agreement should contain a covenant by the seller not to compete with the buyer. Courts have upheld noncompetes so long as they are reasonable in duration and in geographical scope. What is reasonable? Like so much in the law, it depends. In the Houston area, for example, there are three large counties (Harris, Fort Bend, and Montgomery) that vie for the metropolitan area's business. Therefore, any meaningful covenant not to compete would include these three counties.

The seller should also be prohibited from soliciting the buyer's customers and employees. This can happen in subtle ways so the agreement needs to be carefully drafted to encompass both direct and indirect action of this sort.

The Closing

At some point the deal must close or the sale fails, so there should be a date certain for closing. Certain items (ad valorem taxes, receivables, and current rent, for instance) may need to be prorated. If real property is involved, the buyer should weigh the need for title insurance versus obtaining a title report or abstract of title. If title insurance is not required, closing at an attorney's office is just as effective as closing at a title company and it may be a lot faster.

When closing at a title company, *never* allow the title company attorneys to prepare documents for the sale of a business. There are two reasons for this: first, they represent the title company, not the buyer or seller, and have no incentive to draft documents in anyone's best interest other than that of the title company; and second, sales of businesses are not usually their expertise.

Default

Every contract should specify what happens in the event one party fails to perform. Typically, the seller will want to provide for minimal liability if he defaults—the buyer gets to keep the earnest money as liquidated damages and the agreement terminates. Similarly, if the buyer defaults, the seller should be content with keeping the earnest money and moving on to the next buyer. The remedy of specific performance is not usually a practical or effective remedy against buyers, so it is of no great importance if the seller waives it.

A buyer wants more. After all, a buyer is expending more than just earnest money. The cost of effective due diligence can be many thousands of dollars and if the seller changes his mind about selling then the buyer can be substantially out-of-pocket. The agreement should therefore provide that the buyer can recover these expenses from a defaulting seller. The buyer will also want to reserve the right to sue for specific performance, a meaningful remedy for the buyer.

If a buyer defaults postclosing (usually for not paying a seller-financed note), the seller's remedies are contained in the note and security agreement and, if real estate is involved, in a deed of trust (or a combined deed of trust and security agreement). Essentially, the seller's remedy is to take the business and property back. This is usually a disaster since inventory is depleted, equipment missing, the lease is in arrears, and customer goodwill is down the drain. It is therefore critical that a seller choose the right buyer to begin with and get a solid down payment.

Get a Good Business Attorney

Both buyer and seller should get an experienced business transactions lawyer and listen to his or her advice. Clients are often driven by emotions—the desperate desire to get rid of a business or an irrational determination to acquire one. Since the lawyer does not usually receive a commission, he or she has no stake in the transaction and may be the only person providing factual and objective advice.

ASSET PROTECTION STRATEGIES

Chapter 31

ASSET PROTECTION IN TEXAS

Strategy, Planning, and Execution

Keys to Asset Protection

Strategies

- advance, preemptive planning before lawsuits and creditor action
- creating a legal barrier to personal liability with the appropriate entity
- separating assets (properties) from activities (contracts, leases, etc.)
- maximizing anonymity in the public records
- utilizing homestead and income protections afforded by the Texas Constitution and Property Code
- asset spreading and compartmentalization (series LLC)
- equity stripping—maximizing one's (apparent) debt in the public records
- generally exhausting an opponent's resolve and resources

Tools

- shell management LLC to do business with the public, tenants, vendors, etc.
- holding company for assets (TX or NV series LLC) that stays in the background
- anonymity LLC formation
- anonymous land trusts
- assumed name certificates (DBAs)—state and county
- attorney-client privilege (use of attorney as registered agent)
- living trust for the homestead to achieve probate avoidance

The History

Texas has an established history of being a haven for debtors. For over a hundred years there has been a saying "So-and-so has gone to Texas." Sometimes this meant the person had physically relocated to Texas; just as often it implied that he had left town to beat his creditors. This grand, if ethically sketchy, tradition continues. The Texas Constitution, the Business Organizations Code, and the Property Code make it possible for individuals and businesses to establish fortress-like operating structures *and* shield substantial income and assets from execution upon a judgment. Together, these Texas laws make the Lone Star State a nearly ideal venue for asset protection.

Homestead Protections for Individuals in Texas

Texas offers unique protections for residents that should be integrated into any asset protection plan. These "homestead protections" are contained principally in the Texas Constitution article XVI, section 50 and in Texas Property Code chapters 41 and 42. They apply to both income and assets. In other states, execution on a judgment can strip you of your possessions and put you on the street, but that is usually not true in Texas. If a lawsuit is anticipated, or if a judgment creditor is expected to attempt collection, then it is wise to review and maximize these protections well in advance of litigation. It is even wiser to formulate an asset protection strategy long before adverse events occur.

The homestead is the crown jewel of exemptions. It is protected from forced sale for purposes of paying debts and judgments *except* in cases of purchase money, taxes (both ad valorem and federal tax liens against both spouses), owelty of partition (divorce), home improvement loans, home equity loans, reverse mortgages, liens pre-dating the establishment of homestead, refinance loans, or the conversion or refinance of a lien on a mobile home that is attached to the homestead. Other liens are void. No matter how much the home is worth, an ordinary judgment creditor cannot force its sale in the absence of fraud. *See In re McCombs*, 659 F.3d 503, 507 (5th Cir. 2011). Texas homestead laws are liberally construed by the courts. *London v. London*, 342 S.W.3d 768, 776 (Tex. App.—Houston [14th Dist.] 2011, no pet.). Furthermore, an attempt by a creditor to place or enforce a lien against the homestead can be defeated using the procedure in Property Code section 53.160. *See* Part VI, ch. 35: *Lien Removal.*

It is also possible to move safely from one homestead to another. Property Code section 41.001(5)(c) states: "The homestead claimant's proceeds of a sale of a homestead are not subject to seizure for a creditor's claim for six months after the date of sale." This expressly permits homestead equity to be rolled over. *Taylor v. Mosty Bros. Nursery, Inc.*, 777 S.W.2d 568, 570 (Tex. App.—San Antonio 1989, no writ). However, beware of the propensity of title companies to collect judgments upon sale of the homestead in disregard of section 41.001(5)(c). Some title companies have a reflex reaction requiring that all judgments on Schedule C of the title commitment be paid or released. If that occurs, and if the property is homestead, then the seller should aggressively assert section 41.001(5)(c). If the title company continues to insist that the judgment be paid, then the remedy may be to change title companies.

The homestead must be rooted in real estate. A yacht, for instance, is not homestead but moveable chattel. *Norris v. Thompson*, 215 S.W.3d 851 (Tex. 2007).

Section 28 of the Texas Constitution prohibits garnishment of wages, which protects the income of a person who receives a salary or wages. A creditor cannot touch either one, at least not while they are on their way to the debtor.

Considerable personal property is also exempt from execution. Property Code sections 42.001 et seq. specifically list the amount and types of exempt personal property, including a vehicle for each licensed driver in the household; home furnishings; and the debtor's IRA or 401(k). In keeping with Texas' frontier spirit, you can even keep two horses if you wish.

Also exempted are certain savings plans "to the extent that the plan, contract, annuity, or account is exempt from federal income tax, or to the extent federal income on the person's interest deferred until actual payment of benefits to the person" under the Internal Revenue Code (Property Code section 42.0021); college tuition funds (including IRS section 529 funds and accounts established under Subchapter F (Education Code ch. 54,) which are exempted under section 42.0022; and the cash value of annuities and life insurance policies exempted under section 1108.001 of the Insurance Code—at least to the extent those items are exempt from garnishment, attachment, execution, or other seizure under Chapter 42 generally. *See* Part VI, ch. 34: *Homestead Protections in Texas*.

The Cash Problem

Cash is the most vulnerable of all assets, even in Texas. What should a debtor do with it when pursued by creditors? Options are to (carefully) convert it to homestead-exempt assets such as the home or vehicles; use it for reasonable expenses (e.g., retaining an attorney, paying the IRS, paying a child's tuition, etc.); and progressively and incrementally withdraw it from the bank over time. The conversion process can be tricky, particularly if a lawsuit is already pending. If challenged, a debtor must be able to credibly assert the "ordinary course of business" defense of Property Code section 42.004. In other words, such transactions should be accomplished in the orderly course of business or personal life for purposes that can be justified independent of threatened or pending litigation.

Homestead Exemptions and Registered Entities

Only individuals (not corporations, LLCs, or partnerships) may take advantage of homestead protections. This is one reason it is suggested that investors draw a red line between investments assets and the homestead.

In Texas, stock in a corporation is nonexempt personal property (Tex. Bus. Orgs. Code § 21.801) that can be subject to levy (Tex. R. Civ. P. 641; Tex. Bus. & Com. Code § 8.112), garnishment (Tex. R. Civ. P. 669), or turnover (Tex. Civ. Prac. & Rem. Code § 31.002). However, partnership and LLC interests are subject only to a charging order, which means that *if* distributions occur, and *only* if they occur, then the creditor may attach them. *See* Tex. Bus. Orgs. Code § 101.112 (LLCs), § 152.308 (partnerships).

Going Beyond Statutory Homestead Protections: Forming an LLC

Clearly, if one owns one's home debt-free or has investment property or cash balances, statutory homestead protections are not sufficient. The next level of protection is achieved by forming an LLC which accomplishes two critical goals: it creates a liability shield for protection of member-owners and, in the case of a series LLC, it creates individual compartments or series which insulate each series from the liabilities associated with other series and the company at large. Visualize a firewall between Series A, Series B, etc. The benefits? Simplicity and economy. An investor no longer needs a multiplicity of entities to safely do business.

The Two-Company Structure

A sound asset protection structure involves two LLCs, one to hold title to assets (a holding company) and the other to manage them and engage in business generally (a management company). The holding company should be a series LLC while the management company may be either a traditional or series LLC. We prefer Texas and Nevada as states of formation.

The conceptual key to this structure is that *it separates assets from activities*. The holding company stays quietly in the background, avoiding

Two-Company Structure

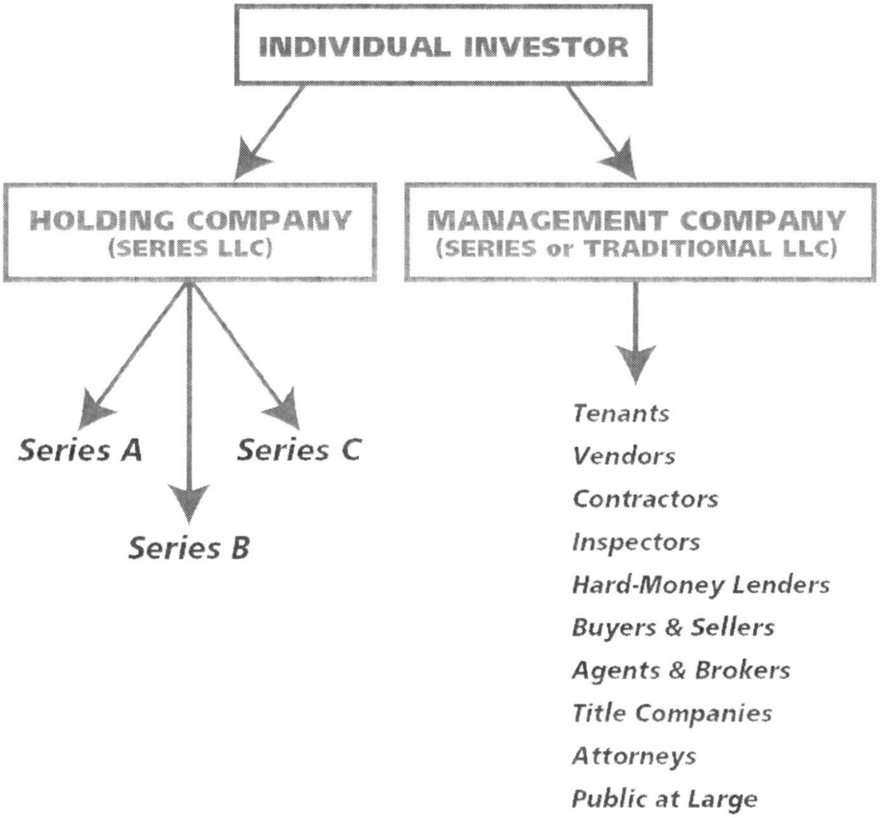

contractual or transactional privity with anyone. No one, especially tenants, should even know that it exists. The holding company's name should not even be similar to the name of the management company—and, of course, neither name should provide a clue to the identity of the investor/owner.

In contrast to the holding company, the management company is active. It collects rents, signs leases, deals with contractors and vendors, employs personnel, leases office furniture and vehicles, and otherwise engages with the public. It is a separate, stand-alone entity with no real assets, an *intentional* target for litigation. If sued, the remedy is to walk away, form a new management company, and continue business as usual.

If the result is a judgment against the old management company (a shell to begin with) the loss to the investor is minimized.

Additionally, using the two-company structure does your attorney a favor, since if the holding company is also sued he or she may successfully argue that it should not be a defendant at all. Why? Because the holding company did no business with anyone, had no privity with anyone, and therefore there is no legitimate basis for a cause of action against it.

The investor should instruct tenants, creditors, vendors, and the public generally that they are doing business with the LLC's chosen DBA. That's right, *the DBA*. Is there any reason even to tell them the name of the LLC? Not usually. If an investor is utilizing a two-company strategy, then the DBA used should be that of the management company. It is the public face of the investor's business. Invoices, payments, and the like should all be sent to the DBA and never addressed to the investor individually. When a W-9 is required, it should contain the LLC's tax identification number. The investor's personal name should not appear except perhaps in the capacity of an authorized representative who signs on behalf of the entity. Why? *Because when a personal name appears, a plaintiffs' attorney sees a potential additional defendant.*

Drafting LLC Documents

This book includes a chapter on this subject. To sum up: All LLC documents—beginning with Certificate of Formation (Texas) or Articles of Organization (Nevada) and continuing with the company agreement, the first meeting of members, and the reset—should be drafted with an eye toward asset protection. *Every company document should be prepared with the expectation that it will be intensely scrutinized by both an opposing attorney and a judge.*

Part of asset protection is deterrence. Filed documents should include provisions that discourage creditors from suing the company in the first place. For instance, the COF should contain more than the statutory minimum wording; it should go into detail concerning matters such as series separation and insulation. It should also declare two classes of membership interest—Class A for "regular" members and Class B for creditors who acquire an interest or influence (one way or another) in the company. Owners of Class B are second-class citizens. Class B is unable to vote, may not serve as manager, may not direct that assets be encumbered or sold, and may not alter or impair the company's ability to do business. What sensible plaintiffs' attorney would want to spend time and money suing a company when a victory would consist of acquiring ownership or influence over Class B? He or she certainly would not do so on a contingent fee arrangement. A substantial retainer would likely be required of the plaintiff. And that brings us back to one of the core strategies of asset protection, to wit, *exhausting an opponent's resolve and resources.*

Transferring Assets to an LLC

An essential asset protection measure is to transfer investment property out of one's personal name and into an LLC—or, if a two-company structure is used, into individual series of the holding company. For real estate, this is done by means of a general or special warranty deed. If the asset is a business or other nonrealty, then a bill of sale is generally used. Other assets may call for an assignment of interest. Executed originals should be kept in the LLC's company book.

Are due-on-sale clauses a problem in the transfer of real estate? Almost never, in spite of what lenders and Internet alarmists say. Lenders have their plates full with monetary defaults and generally do not accelerate a performing loan, especially if a property is being transferred to the borrower's personal company.

Company Maintenance

This point has been made elsewhere in this book. There are minimum actions and formalities that should be prudently observed in order to enhance preservation of the LLC's liability barrier—which, after all, is the principal reason one forms an LLC in the first place. These include well-drafted organizational minutes and a company agreement; issuance of membership certificates; minutes of annual meetings; obtaining an EIN and filing tax returns; having a company bank account; and other actions to validate the independent nature of the entity. Failure to do this sort of routine maintenance can make a company vulnerable to "piercing the veil" allegations. Such allegations are so common as to be virtually automatic in today's litigious environment. Even if they ultimately fail (as they should in most Texas cases), it is time-consuming and expensive to dispose of them. So why offer the opposition an opening on these issues in the first place? We know in advance that a creditor/plaintiff will ask to see the contents of the company book during the discovery process. It is a given. When produced, the documentation should be flawless.

Presuit Asset Protection Strategies

Asset protection strategies fall into two groups: strategies implemented in advance of collection action or suit by a creditor /plaintiff; and strategies that are feasible afterward. It is preferable to plan ahead and be prepared, since the range of pre-suit alternatives is far greater. After suit is filed, depending on the circumstances, options are reduced by laws relating to fraudulent transfers—moving assets around to defeat legitimate claims of creditors. Creditors and courts are on the lookout for these. For details, look at chapter 24 of the Business Organizations Code, entitled the "Uniform Fraudulent Transfer Act." The purpose of UFTA is to prevent debtors from placing assets beyond the reach of creditors. *See also Mladenka v. Mladenka*, 130 S.W.3d 397 (Tex. App.—Houston [14th Dist.] 2004, no pet.).

After suit is filed, the actions of a defendant may be challenged under Property Code section 42.004, which states that an exemption is lost if nonexempt assets are used to buy or pay down indebtedness on exempt assets "with the intent to defraud, delay, or hinder" a creditor. The defense? The transfer was made in the ordinary course of business as permitted by Property Code section 42.004(c). Competent planning should make effective use of this defense relatively easy.

Postsuit Strategies

Once litigation is commenced, obvious attempts to maneuver and manipulate assets will likely be detected, at least if the creditor/plaintiff is on the ball. The court may be asked to set aside or unwind an allegedly fraudulent transaction. Such transfers are generally indicated by "badges of fraud" including the following stand-out items: transfers to a family member; whether or not suit was threatened before it was filed; whether the transfer was of substantially all of the person's assets; whether assets have been removed, undisclosed, or concealed; whether there was equivalent consideration for the transfer; and whether or not, after the transfer, the transferor became insolvent as a result (i.e., made his cash or other assets disappear all at once).

Fraudulent transfer rules allow courts to reach back up to two years. Waiting until one has no recourse remaining other than to engage in an obviously fraudulent transfer is simply poor AP.

In postsuit strategy, it is important to move assets in such a way that they fall within the ordinary course of business (or, as we expand upon the concept, the "ordinary course of life and business"). One needs to be able to convincingly claim that a certain action would have been taken anyway, for good reasons that have nothing to do with avoiding a creditor's claims. After all, life does not end merely because a lawsuit has been filed. People continue to engage in commerce, buy houses and vehicles, move residences, make new investments, and otherwise go about the business of living and supporting their dependents.

The Discovery Process

How do creditor/plaintiffs find out when you move your assets around? Principally, by using the discovery process (interrogatories, requests for production of documents, and depositions—all under oath) to inquire into a debtor/defendant's transactions. The scope of this process can be wide indeed, reaching back several years. Failure to fully respond is grounds for contempt, although "fully respond" should never be interpreted as supplying more information than is absolutely necessary. Creditor/plaintiffs may do research on a defendant, particularly if the debt is substantial, but most have only the information that a debtor voluntarily gives them in pre- and postjudgment discovery. Contrary to popular fiction, where the computer whiz hits a few keys and then summarizes a person's entire life and finances, the Internet has yet to reach the point where it reveals everything about everyone.

The most pernicious discovery occurs postjudgment, since creditor/plaintiffs can then go beyond the facts of the case and compel disclosure of sources of income as well as the location and value of assets, even assets that are legally exempt and cannot be touched. This can be a headache because the creditor/plaintiff may nonetheless attempt to go after such exempt assets, forcing a debtor/defendant to seek court protection. One can see why it is important that the defending attorney make a creditor/plaintiff fight vigorously for every bit of information provided in responses to discovery.

AP Level 1: Basic Asset Protection for Investors (the Texas Series LLC)

(1) form a series LLC to own and manage investment properties and businesses in separate series, establishing insulation and multiple liability barriers;
(2) file an assumed name certificate (DBA) for this company and utilize the DBA in business dealings, contracts, leases, etc.;
(3) establish a checking account for the company under its DBA and have checks, letterhead, cards, etc. printed that way and phone numbers listed that way;
(4) transfer properties held in personal names into individual series of the holding company (Series A, Series B, etc.) using deeds that cite series protections;
(5) separate homestead and other creditor-exempt items from investments and businesses, then reduce debt on

these items in order to maximize protections afforded by the Property Code and Texas Constitution; and

(6) form a living trust for the homestead to avoid probate, transfer the home into it, and then execute a pour-over will to transfer other assets to the trust upon death.

AP Level 2: Two-Company Structure (the "Texas Two Step")

(1) establish a Texas series LLC or Nevada series LLC to own and hold—but not manage—investment properties and businesses (a holding company, which has no privity with anyone);
(2) form a separate, stand-alone Texas LLC (no cross ownership) to act as a shell management company to acquire properties and then after closing transfer them to the holding company; meanwhile the management company signs leases and contracts and deals with tenants, vendors, contractors, and the public; income passes through to the holding company as consulting fees and returns to the management company, if needed, as management fees;
(3) file assumed name certificates (DBAs) for both the holding company and for the management company and utilize these names in all dealings;
(4) establish checking accounts for each company under their respective DBAs and have checks, letterhead, cards, etc. printed that way, and phone numbers listed that way;
(5) transfer properties held in personal names into individual series of the holding company (Series A, Series B, etc.) using deeds that cite series protections;
(6) separate homestead and other creditor-exempt items from investments and businesses, then reduce debt on these items in order to maximize protections afforded by the Property Code and Texas Constitution;
(7) form a living trust for the homestead to avoid probate, transfer the home into it, and then execute a pour-over will to transfer other assets to the trust upon death.

AP Level 3: Texas-Nevada Combination (the "Two-State Solution")

(1) establish a Nevada series LLC to own and hold, but not manage, investment properties and businesses (a holding

company) achieving a measure of physical and legal distance plus anonymity from Texas plaintiffs;

(2) form a separate stand-alone Texas LLC (no cross ownership) to act as a shell management company (no significant assets) to acquire properties and then after closing transfer them to the holding company; meanwhile the management company signs leases and contracts and deals with tenants, vendors, contractors, and the public; income passes through to the holding company as consulting fees and returns to the management company, if needed, as management fees;

(3) file assumed name certificates (DBA's) for both the holding company and for the management company and utilize these names in all dealings;

(4) establish checking accounts for each company under their respective DBA's and have checks, letterhead, cards, etc. printed that way, and phone numbers listed that way;

(5) transfer properties held in personal names into individual series of the Nevada holding company (Series A, Series B, etc.) using deeds that cite series protections;

(6) separate homestead and other creditor-exempt items from investments and businesses, then reduce debt on these items in order to maximize protections afforded by the Property Code and Texas Constitution;

(7) form a living trust for the homestead to avoid probate, transfer the home into it, and then execute a pour-over will to transfer other assets to the trust upon death.

Role of Trusts in Asset Protection

Trusts come in all shapes and sizes so do not be fooled—there is no standard form of a living trust, land trust, or anonymity trust that is good for all purposes in all states. Texas has its own trust laws and practices and any trust agreement used must be compliant to be effective. So long as it is drafted properly, a trust can be useful in providing:

(1) anonymity, (although as noted previously this may generate issues with title companies and require clean-up prior to sale);

(2) ease and privacy of transferability, since beneficial interests can be assigned without recording a deed or other instrument; and

(3) probate avoidance, since beneficiaries acquire their interests automatically without probate or court intervention.

Caution: A trust does not have a liability barrier as does an LLC, so trusts standing alone are insufficient for asset protection. Trusts are merely one tool in the investor's toolbox.

Since both title companies and courts want to see a trust agreement before conceding that a trust actually exists, a written trust agreement must always be prepared.

Apart from investment land trusts, there are also living trusts (see the chapter on this subject) which are a valuable probate-avoidance device for the homestead. Anyone who has probated an estate is familiar with the procedural nightmare that can occur when dealing with attorneys and judges who will happily reduce your castle to rubble.

Anonymity and an LLC

An investor's goal should be to achieve maximum anonymity combined with the liability barrier created by one or more LLCs. Such a strategy creates legal, practical, and psychological obstacles to a potential creditor/plaintiff.

An LLC provides a measure of anonymity depending on the amount of information that is disclosed in the Certificate of Formation (or Articles of Organization in the case of Nevada). The COF requires three names and addresses: the registered agent (physical address only), the initial manager (a post office box is acceptable), and the organizer (often the attorney).

Anonymity begins at LLC formation. Avoid using the home as the registered address. Disclosing it hardly enhances anonymity, nor does it prevent a constable from banging on your door at 5:30 a.m. to serve a lawsuit. The world is both a legally and physically dangerous place. We have even had a client whose home was bombed by an angry tenant. Tenants, vendors, contractors, and the public at large should *never* have an investor's homestead address.

The COF requires a physical address, not a box, since the constable cannot serve a mailbox. Recently, the Secretary of State has become more aggressive in checking whether or not registered addresses are really mailbox stores. They occasionally even google the address. If they think it is a box, the COF will be rejected.

It is recommended that an investor should either use his or her office address or use an attorney as registered agent of the company (which also has the benefit of invoking the attorney-client privilege under certain circumstances). Otherwise, arrangements must be made for a registered agent at a real street address, which cannot contain PMB, POB, Box, a double suite number, or any other indication of a box.

Back to the COF, which requires the designation of an initial manager. This is usually where the owner's name goes. However, a creative approach is to name an anonymity trust in this capacity, but this is an advanced technique to be used only with guidance from a specialized attorney. An additional benefit: one now has an anonymity trust, backed by a trust agreement, that is able to be utilized for other purposes beyond its role as member and manager of the LLC—including buying more property anonymously. This is an example of how the component parts of an asset protection structure can work together synergistically.

The Role of Insurance

Is liability insurance alone is sufficient for asset protection? The answer is a resounding *no*. Insurance is a passive measure. True asset protection requires one to be proactive. Asset protection experts unanimously recommend a sensible mix of insurance *and* active asset protection measures. The principal reason is that insurance can never be truly relied upon, since *insurers are in the business of collecting premiums and denying claims*. That is what they do. That is their business plan, which is why they are among the wealthiest corporations in America. Expect that every effort will be made by an insurer to exclude or avoid coverage in case of loss, particularly if a creditor/plaintiff alleges fraud, which is never covered. It may then become necessary to sue the insurance company.

Even if an insurer concedes coverage, extravagant claims made in lawsuits may (and often do) exceed available limits. Moreover, the existence of a sizable policy and umbrella may actually encourage a lawsuit because it will be perceived by the plaintiff's attorney as a tempting target. Nonetheless, having adequate insurance is a necessary evil.

Bankruptcy

Bankruptcy is the nuclear option in asset protection, being broadly effective. Even so, rules against fraudulent transfers ("preferences" in the Bankruptcy Code) apply in this area as well, and more strictly. The bankruptcy court can reach back a year or more. Also, false information in a bankruptcy petition may be investigated by the FBI. And of course bankruptcy does not discharge income taxes (although the IRS may be more likely to work with you on a payment plan), child support obligations, student loans, and any items that a filing debtor fails to list on the petition.

The Bankruptcy Code allows a debtor to choose between the federal exemptions (i.e., list of exempt assets) or the state ones. In Texas it is more common to choose the state exemptions since they are so favorable.

By and large, filing bankruptcy is an admission that previous asset protection strategies have failed. The bankruptcy trustee and the court assume control of your life. It is a last resort.

Lifestyle Considerations

One's lifestyle should be consistent with maintaining an effective asset protection strategy. In addition to all the other suggestions relating to anonymity, creating a liability shield, maximizing protections under the homestead laws, and the like, one should:

(1) avoid conspicuous consumption—live a notch below your means (at least outwardly) so as to make a less appealing target for plaintiffs and their attorneys;
(2) avoid personally guaranteeing any business debt or cosigning on others' notes;
(3) carry health and term life insurance on yourself as well as key man term life insurance on your business partners;
(4) avoid all forms of debt that do not result in an income stream, including nearly all consumer debt which, after the thrill of possessing a new item dissipates merely serves to keep you up at night;
(5) reduce all business arrangements—including those with family and friends (*especially* those with family and friends)—to a written agreement that contains an exit strategy, including buy-sell and dispute resolution provisions;
(6) diversify assets and investments, preferably within one or two LLC's, at least one of which should be a series company; and put 5 to 10% of your assets into gold, cash, and other doomsday assets. The worst case scenario could actually happen. Some think it is happening already.

Other Asset Protection Devices

There are many other asset protection devices and entities that are beyond the scope of this discussion. Included among them are:

Family Limited Partnerships. Texas FLPs (like LLCs) must be filed with the state and pertinent ownership information is revealed; also an in-state registered agent must be designated to receive service of process if the partnership is sued. So why not just form an LLC (especially a series LLC if assets are in real estate) and then move title to assets into a land trust? The result is arguably superior liability protection and anonymity. Another drawback of the FLP is its concept of a friendly lien on the homestead, not very workable in Texas.

Limited Partnerships with an LLC or Corporate General Partner. These vehicles are more complex and expensive and are usually employed in larger commercial transactions, which are beyond the scope of this book.

Asset Protection in the Real World

Total asset protection is probably not achievable, even in Texas, in spite of claims made by Internet and seminar gurus (and even some lawyers) who have never spent time in a real court of law in front of a real judge who has contempt power. Do you recall Einstein's theory that a traveling spaceship may approach the speed of light but never actually reach it? Asset protection is like that. The goal is to get as close to an ideal AP situation as possible, by using the correct structure and by layering asset protection devices.

To summarize, asset protection is ultimately about preparation and advance planning that have the effect of *establishing* a sound structure, *deterring* lawsuits, and *exhausting* your opponent's determination and resources. If you can make it difficult to find your assets and make it unacceptably expensive and time-consuming for a plaintiff's attorney to reach them, then your asset protection plan has done its job.

Chapter 32

ANONYMITY IN TEXAS REAL ESTATE

A Relatively Achievable Goal

This chapter addresses legitimate privacy alternatives for the Texas investor or business person when engaging in real estate transactions. Why is privacy important? First, because information is power, and it is preferable that your opponents have as little power as possible over you; and second, because we live in a litigious world—and offering gratuitous, vital information about yourself in the public domain provides others with a roadmap to your identity, strategy, and assets.

Every day there is a John Smith who files to form an LLC under the name "John Smith Investments LLC" and then lists himself (and often his unsuspecting wife) as initial managers at his homestead address, placing his core personal information in the public domain. Of course this investor does the filing work himself, without assistance from an asset protection attorney, because he is smarter than any lawyer—even though he may have been educated as a software engineer or a medical doctor. After all, the law is easy, right? Just a matter of filling out a few forms?

Guiding rule: every member of the public, every single business partner, every single contract party, every single buyer, every single seller, every single title company, every single attorney, every single vendor, and every single agent or broker should be viewed as a potential adversary in a lawsuit. As long as you have what they want—cash or property—it is only a matter of time before they come for you. Recognition of this reality should lead sensible investors to proactively limit exposure by implementing an asset protection plan.

Litigation Nation

Why is there so much litigation? Two reasons: first, because of contingent fee arrangements by which some attorneys take dubious cases and then utilize the legal system to harass legitimate businesspersons; and second, because the American justice system for the most part imposes no significant penalty upon those who file frivolous lawsuits.

Common Questions Pertaining to Anonymity

Three anonymity-related questions frequently present themselves: (1) How can I hold title to property without revealing that I am the true party in interest (this question has to do with status of title, i.e., where true ownership resides)? (2) How can I transfer property held in my personal name to my LLC without showing that it came from me (this pertains to chain of title, the recorded links between sellers and buyers)? (3) How can I combine the anonymity of a trust with the liability shield of an LLC?

When discussing anonymity issues, two important groups must be considered: county clerks, who maintain the real property records, and whose job includes filing documents to accurately reflect the chain of title; and title companies, which insure both the status and chain of title.

Status of Title

Title to property can be held in a surprising variety of capacities—as an individual, a corporation, a limited liability company, a general or limited partnership, in a trust, and so forth—or as a combination of any of the foregoing. Property law is flexible in this respect. What if an investor wants to hold 50% of title in his or her personal name, 25% in an LLC, and the remaining 25% in a family living trust? Not a problem. Whether or not it is wise to structure ownership in such a way is another matter.

Looking past who nominally holds title (determining who is really in control) can be a challenging exercise, but in most cases it is almost always possible to trace this information through the local real property records, DBA filings at the county or state level, or through the Secretary of State and Texas Comptroller—not to mention miscellaneous data accessible on the Internet. The exception occurs when a cautious individual or entity has made a deliberate and diligent effort to remain anonymous.

So in considering issues of anonymity, one should distinguish between *absolute anonymity*, which is difficult to achieve in an informed and interconnected world, and *relative anonymity*, which is a more attainable goal. Think of it as a sliding scale. An effective asset protection strategy maximizes relative anonymity, moving the dial as far as possible in that direction. How far can that be? It depends on the circumstances and an investor's willingness to be creative.

Note that it is possible to purchase, own, and convey property without recording transfer documents. There is no law or requirement that all deeds must be recorded. It is likewise possible to purchase, own, and convey property without ever buying a policy of title insurance or entering the offices of a title company. But the reality is that unrecorded interests are difficult to sell. Also, buyers in the real world often want title insurance, and their lenders will (by law) require it.

Chain of Title

There is no effective method of defeating, ignoring, or bypassing the chain of title. So what is the response to the question posed above, "How can I transfer property held in my personal name to my LLC (or other entity or person) without showing that it came from me?" The answer is that *you cannot*, at least not if you are going to be deeding the property to the LLC outright—as opposed, for instance, to deeding the property into a trust and then privately transferring the beneficial interest to the LLC, in which case there is the drawback of a trustee who is exposed without a liability barrier. More on this below.

Each link in the chain of title is represented by a deed or other conveyance recorded in the county clerk's office—and one cannot break the chain and still preserve one's status as record owner. A broken link equals questionable title. Questionable title equals unsellable property.

What one *can* do is arrange for the property to pass through one or more intermediate transfers so that its origin is progressively more remote in the chain. Additionally, the more these intermediate transfers have the appearance of bona fide sales for consideration, the more likely the original transferor is to remain in the background, beyond immediate scrutiny. Again, it is a question of relative rather than absolute anonymity.

Preclosing Anonymity

Acquisition of real property begins with negotiation of the earnest money contract, which calls for the name and address of the buyer. Although earnest money contracts are not recorded, they can be the start of anonymity issues, since dealing with realtors, appraisers, inspectors, surveyors, title company personnel, and neighbors leaves an extensive paper trail. And people involved in the process inevitably gossip about pending transactions.

There are two advisable choices: either purchase property in the name of an LLC or trust; or, alternatively, list a personal name for the buyer but follow it with the phrase "and/or his or her assigns." The latter provides a means of switching into the preferred method for holding title at the last minute, before closing. This option may be unavailable if the property is financed, since the lender will likely require that the principal obligor on the note and the name of the grantee on the deed to be one and the same. In that event, the investor should immediately transfer the new property into an asset-holding LLC.

Does this raise due-on-sale issues? Unlikely. It is seldom that a lender accelerates a performing loan because it has been transferred into an investor's personal company, but technically it could happen. In actual practice, the potential consequences of leaving investment property in a personal name substantially outweigh any risk involved in moving it promptly into the investor's LLC.

Returning to the subject of earnest money contracts: it is important to realize that contracts can either convey a lot of information or just a small amount of it. Be attuned to this. For instance, is there any reason to list one's home address as opposed to a post office box? A home phone versus your office or cell phone? Do not provide any more personal information than is essential to make the deal. Do not say *anything* to a realtor that you do not *expect* to be conveyed to the other side, the realtor's duty of confidentiality notwithstanding. Again, people talk.

Use of LLCs, Corporations, and Limited Partnerships as Transfer Vehicles

Another method of achieving relative anonymity in the chain of title involves establishing a registered entity (an LLC, for example) that is filed with the Secretary of State. The first step, of course, is to establish the LLC; the second is to transfer the property to the entity; the third step involves transferring an interest in the entity to some third person or entity, accomplished by means of an unrecorded "Sale and Assignment of LLC Membership Interest." The LLC continues to own the asset, but the person owning the LLC will have changed. There would be nothing in the real property records (chain of title) or in appraisal district records that reflects the principals who are now behind the LLC.

Note, however, that filed entities must file an annual Public Information Report with the Texas Comptroller listing members or shareholders. Eventually, therefore, someone truly determined to discover the real nature of the transfer may do so by accessing the Comptroller's records after the next annual PIR is filed, although this vulnerability may be mitigated by certain anonymity layering techniques. It is worth noting that this level of determination goes well beyond the average and would also take time and money; so, in the right circumstances, use of an LLC as a transfer vehicle can serve as sufficient and effective camouflage.

Limited partnerships are also common anonymity structures, particularly in larger commercial transactions. LPs are often set up as a group of corporations or LLCs with a shell entity as the general partner. These may be owned by other entities. LP's are relatively expensive structures more typically used to buy office buildings and shopping malls.

Accordingly, they are beyond the scope of this book and we will not discuss them further.

Anonymity Trusts

In an anonymity trust, title is taken in the name of, for instance, the "Series A Trust" with no mention of either the LLC or of a trustee. Those familiar with trust law will immediately object, pointing out that trusts are not legal entities—which is true—although trusts often act as if they were. County clerks have no problem accepting for filing a deed that shows a trust as grantee with no mention of the trustee's name.

The problem arises later when a title company is asked to insure title as part of a subsequent sale of the property. When it comes to anonymity trusts, title companies rush to assert "You can't do that!"—even though there is a deed of record in the trust's name that has successfully preserved anonymity for the investor during his or her entire period of ownership. The real issue is what the title company requires *now* in order to move forward, which is usually one or both of the following: produce the trust agreement for their review (no problem); and/or go back and redeed the property into the trust with specific mention of the trustee's name, also no more than a minor inconvenience—particularly if you execute *two* deeds (one that does not reflect the name of the trustee and along with a second one that does) but record only the first one. If a future title company declares that the property must be redeeded, then the investor can pull the second deed from his briefcase and say "Here it is." Result? The anonymity trust device has served its intended purpose.

We neither encourage nor discourage the use of anonymity trusts of this type. Just note that they are for aggressive investors who do not mind being lectured by a title company and doing redeeding work before sale of the property.

Assumed Name Certificates (DBAs)

Can property be conveyed "into a DBA?" Does a DBA "exist" as an entity that can hold property? The answer is *no*, not even close. An assumed name filing is, after all, merely *a public notice* that a person or entity will be using a different front name in business transactions. It does not in and of itself establish a new entity, nor is there the equivalent of a trust agreement behind it. The result is that use of a DBA alone to hold title to property likely means there has been no transfer at all. Title insurance would be unavailable for conveyances out of the DBA. Result? This practice is fatally flawed and should be avoided.

Having said the foregoing, it is nonetheless true that DBAs are highly useful devices in anonymity layering. As a rule, each LLC an investor owns should do as much business as possible through its DBA. A bank account should be opened in the DBA name and checks should be printed that way. Leases and contracts should be signed using the DBA. Even though research at the county clerk's office may uncover underlying ownership behind the DBA, an assumed name is nonetheless an important part of the process.

Anonymity Using a Two-Company Structure

It is best to separate activities from assets. Assets should be held in an LLC (preferably a series company that stays out of sight and does little or no public business) while dealings with tenants, contractors, vendors, and the like should be conducted by a separate shell management company. The two-company structure can be effectively used for anonymity purposes without any add-ons other than the usual DBAs for each company. For instance, the management company can purchase properties (and, in so doing, do business with a seller, one or more brokers, rehab contractors, etc.) and then, after closing and fix-up, transfer the property to the holding company, which is largely immune from a successful lawsuit because it has no connection (privity) with anyone.

As a result of this strategy, the owner of the holding company is relatively remote and anonymous by a couple of steps—not a perfect strategy (none is) but a very good one. In certain cases, it may be useful split the two LLCs between two states, what we call the "two-state solution."

The Chinese Puzzle Box

Another alternative is to establish an entity within an entity—an LLC that is owned by another LLC, for instance. If this is your choice, we recommend that the primary operating LLC be a Texas company owned by a Nevada LLC. We favor the series LLC in most cases because of the additional firewall protection between individual series. One can go a step further and establish a three-level puzzle box—a Texas LLC that is owned by a Nevada LLC that is owned by an offshore LLC (e.g., a company based on Belize or Panama). This provides good anonymity and almost unbeatable asset protection if structured correctly.

Mixing Trusts and LLCs: LLC as Beneficiary of a Trust

Benefits can be achieved by mixing a trust and an LLC. There are a couple of possibilities. Before discussing those, it would be useful to answer two common questions: yes, an LLC (or a series of an LLC) *can* be the beneficiary of a trust; and no, an LLC *cannot* be the trustee. The trustee must be a natural person unless an entity is approved as a trustee by the state (a marathon process involving massive disclosure).

One option is to utilize an LLC as a beneficiary of a land trust. This method consists of three steps: first, creating an anonymity trust, of which the LLC is the 100% beneficiary; second, conveying property into the trust by recorded warranty deed; and third, establishing a series (Series A, for example) to own and hold a 100% beneficial interest in the trust.

But what about a liability shield? Trusts have none. The trustor and trustee are personal-ly exposed—and this is the principal drawback of this structure, since persons acting in these roles are very often named individually in suits against the trust.

The reader is cautioned against non-lawyer seminar gurus who make overblown claims concerning trusts and asset protection systems they are marketing. These are almost always of questionable legality and effectiveness. Such schemes are seldom suitable for Texas which has a unique Property Code and Business Organizations Code.

Chapter 33

ASSUMED NAMES

Don't Leave Home without One

The use of one or more assumed names or "DBAs" is an important part of an overall asset protection plan. Why? Because asset protection is, at least in part, about layering of incremental obstacles to a potential plaintiff. The more hurdles a plaintiff and his attorney have to get over in order to get to you and your assets, the better. The objective is to *deter*, *discourage*, and *deplete* a potential plaintiff's resources. Although assumed name records are publicly available for inspection, sometimes online, this is an additional level of research that—believe or not—some plaintiffs will be too lazy to undertake.

Public Interest in Disclosure

What is the intent of the statute requiring the filing of a DBA? Both simple and practical: public disclosure of the identity of the true party in interest and the location at which that party may be served with process if suit is filed. The premise behind that law is that it is in the public interest to be able to ascertain whom to sue and where service of process may be physically achieved.

From a disclosure perspective, DBA filing requirements operate in favor of potential plaintiffs. There is, however, a sense in which they favor defendants. Suits are filed everyday against assumed-name defendants, particularly at the justice court level. Consider a hypothetical auto dealership, "Northside Chevrolet." If a suit is filed against Northside Chevrolet, it is subject to immediate dismissal upon motion by Northside's attorney. Why? *Because Northside Chevrolet is not a legal entity*. It is merely the assumed name of someone else, almost certainly a corporation or LLC with a liability barrier that is doing business under the name Northside. The result is that the plaintiff must now go home, do research, and refile the case (paying additional fees and costs in the process) against the true principal behind the DBA. The legal entity may not even have its business headquarters in that county, requiring a request for out-of-county service of process, another delay and expense. A certain percentage of plaintiffs will instead give up at this point.

Law Applicable to Assumed Names

There is no statutory limit on the number of DBAs an individual or company may have, either at the state or county level. A filing is good for 10 years and fees are nominal. A DBA may also be terminated or abandoned by the filing of a certain form. Go to the county clerk's website in the county in which you are headquartered or in which you propose to operate. For state-level filings, go to www.sos.state.tx.us/corp/forms and complete Form 503. This form requires an applicant to state the counties in which an assumed name will be used. If the entity will potentially use its assumed name in all counties in Texas, check the box for "All."

Texas Business & Commerce Code chapter 71—the "Assumed Business and Professional Name Act"—requires a notarized DBA filing for individuals, companies, and others under the following circumstances:

§ 71.002. Definitions

(2) "Assumed name" means:

(A) for an individual, [if the enterprise proposes to operate under] a name that does not include the surname of the individual;

(B) for a partnership, [if the enterprise proposes to operate under] a name that does not include the surname or other legal name of each joint venturer or general partner;

(C) for an individual or a partnership, [if the enterprise proposes to operate under] a name, including a surname, that suggests the existence of additional owners by including words such as "Company," "& Company," "& Son," "& Sons," "& Associates," "Brothers," and similar words, but not words that merely describe the business being conducted or the professional service being rendered;

(D) for a limited partnership, [if the enterprise proposes to operate under] a name other than the name stated in its certificate of formation;

(E) for a company, [if the enterprise proposes to operate under] a name used by the company;

(F) for a corporation, [if the enterprise proposes to operate under] a name other than the name stated in its certificate of formation or a comparable document;

(G) for a limited liability partnership, [if the enterprise proposes to operate under] a name other than the name stated in its application filed with the office of the secretary of state or a comparable document; and

(H) for a limited liability company, [if the enterprise proposes to operate under] a name other than the name stated in its certificate of formation or a comparable document including the name of any series of the limited liability company established by its company agreement.

The filer must include the physical address of its place of business. If the proposed county of business is different from the county where the enterprise is headquartered, then a DBA must be filed in both counties.

Suppose you have a Nevada LLC and want to operate under an assumed name in Dallas or Houston, may you file an assumed name certificate in either county (or both) and do so? Absolutely. The statute expressly includes both domestic and foreign entities within its scope.

State versus County Filing of DBAs

Obtaining a DBA is a logical next step after forming an LLC. But where should the filing occur—at the county clerk's office or with the secretary of state? Under Business and Commercial Code section 71.103, the DBA must be filed as at both levels: "The corporation, limited partnership, limited liability partnership, limited liability company, or foreign filing entity shall file the certificate in the office of the secretary of state and in the office or offices of each county clerk as specified by Subsection (b) or (c)." Notice that the statute says *and* when referring to state and county filings, although filing with the Secretary of State is frequently overlooked by smaller companies who often file only in their local county.

At the county level, the county clerk will want to determine if a proposed DBA is available. The customary standard is that your proposed name must not be the same as or deceptively similar to another entity's filed assumed name within that county. At the state level, however, the DBA filing is purely a notice filing, meaning that it is not necessary to first ascertain if a certain name is available. Just create a name and file Form 503.

Texas has 254 counties. If you are obtaining a county-level assumed name for banking purposes and everyday usage, does it matter in which county you file? Surprisingly, no. Even if you are doing business in Houston, a bank will usually accept a DBA from El Paso County for purposes of opening an account and ordering checks in the assumed name. Another noteworthy point: there is currently *no central database* linking the assumed name records of Texas counties. From an asset protection/anonymity perspective, therefore, it may be useful to consider obtaining your company's DBA far from its true base of operations and in a county whose DBA database is not yet online.

Trusts and DBAs

Interestingly, the statute does not mention trusts, which are a common asset protection device. Are these covered by the law? Must a trust file a DBA if the trust is doing business under anything other than its complete formal name? Our view is in the affirmative, even though trusts are technically not stand-alone legal entities, though they often act as such in the real world. A trust likely falls under the term "company," at least for purposes of this law; and "company" is defined as "a real estate investment trust, a joint-stock company, or any other business, professional, or other association or legal entity that is not incorporated, other than a partnership, limited partnership, limited liability company, limited liability partnership, or foreign filing entity." But this is actually good news. If one has a land trust and is doing business with it then one *should* acquire an assumed name and use it.

A Series LLC Doing Business Through One of Its Series

What about individual series of a series limited liability company? Series are, in many respects, sub-companies and are largely empowered to behave that way. Business Organizations Code section 101.605 provides that an individual series has the power (1) to sue and be sued; (2) to contract; and (3) to hold title to real and personal property. In order to fulfill these functions at the series level (rather than at the level of the company at large), the series must operate or hold title under its own name (for example, as "ABC LLC—Series A") which in turn requires that the series obtain an assumed name certificate. Why is this so? *Because the series is not, as a technical matter, an independent legal entity; and since it is operating under a name other than the name stated in the company's COF, it must have a DBA on file.* Moreover, to be fully compliant, the DBA filing must take place both at the county and state levels.

The basic assumed name filing for a series LLC would be in the name of the company doing business as an individual series. For example: "ABC LLC doing business as ABC LLC—Series A." Section 71.103 would require such an assumed name filing both in the county where Series A does business and also at the office of the Secretary of State.

An Individual Series Doing Business on Its Own

What about filing an assumed name certificate for a specific series—for instance "ABC LLC—Series A DBA Ace Investments?" County clerks have no problem with this formulation and are more than willing to accept your DBA filing fee. However, the Secretary of State until now has rejected it with the following notation: "Our records do not show an entity by the name shown on the document which was submitted for filing." In other words, the Secretary of State is taking a strict stance here, i.e., that the individual series of a series LLC are not in and of themselves separate legal entities. Therefore, in the State's view, they cannot have assumed names. Since, for asset protection purposes, we would nonetheless prefer to throw a cloak of anonymity over individual series, we must for now be content with series DBA filing at the county level only—unless the Secretary of State revises its interpretation of the statute. As it turns out, this works sufficiently well for asset protection purposes.

Banks and Series DBAs

As to banking, the importance of having a DBA for Series A, Series B, Series C, and so forth is relevant if one chooses to open a bank account solely and specifically for the use of an individual series. A bank will require an assumed name certificate if "ABC LLC—Series A" wants to open an account in the name of "Ace Investments" and have checks printed that way. Having such a DBA also entitles the series to lawfully print business cards and stationery that read "Ace Investments" with no disclosure that the principal behind the scenes is in fact an individual series of a series LLC.

Title Companies and DBA Requirements

Title companies are also sensitive to DBA issues. Expect that if a company (whether traditional or series) has not filed a required assumed name certificate it will be asked to do so before closing on either the purchase or sale of real property.

As a practical matter, neither banks nor title companies appear to care whether one's assumed name certificate is issued by the Secretary of State or by the local county clerk, just so long as a filed certificate exists.

Statutory Penalties

Will one go to the penitentiary for failing to file for an assumed name? No. Penalties for failing to fully comply with the Assumed Business and Professional Name Act are generally mild:

> **§ 71.201. Civil Action; Sanction**
>
> **A person's failure to comply with this chapter does not impair the validity of any contract or act by the person or prevent the person from defending any action or proceeding in any court of this state, but the person may not maintain in a court of this state an action or proceeding arising out of a contract or act in which an assumed name was used until an original, new, or renewed certificate has been filed as required by this chapter.**
>
> **In an action or proceeding brought against a person who has not complied with this chapter, the court may award the plaintiff or other party bringing the action or proceeding expenses incurred, including attorney's fees, in locating and effecting service of process on the defendant.**

In a civil suit, then, a violator may need to immediately file an assumed name certificate in order to proceed with the prosecution or defense of a suit. It may also be ordered to pay the costs and fees associated with inconveniencing the other party. These are not heavy sanctions. There is, however, a criminal penalty for an intentional violation (whatever that may be):

> **§ 71.202. Criminal Penalty: General Violation**
>
> **(a) A person commits an offense if the person:**
>
> **(1) conducts business or renders a professional service in this state under an assumed name; and**
> **(2) intentionally violates this chapter.**
>
> **(b) An offense under this section is a Class A misdemeanor.**

We are unaware of an abundance of prosecutions in this area. Why? As with most criminal offenses, the district attorney must prove *criminal intent*. It is far more likely that a person or company failing to fully comply inadvertently overlooked the details of the statute. Forged or fraudulent filings, however, are a more serious matter—a third-degree felony. *See* Bus. & Com. Code § 71.203.

Entitlement to Exclusive Use of an Assumed Name

The filing of an assumed name certificate does *not* assure exclusive use of a DBA and is *not* the equivalent of obtaining a trademark or copyright:

> **§ 71.157. Effect of Filing**
>
> **This chapter does not give a registrant a right to use the assumed name in violation of the common or statutory law of unfair competition or unfair trade practices, common law copyright, or similar law.**
>
> **(a) The filing of a certificate under this chapter does not in itself constitute actual use of the assumed name stated in the certificate for purposes of determining priority of rights.**

Even if one obtains a DBA in the local county, there are still 253 other Texas counties (not to mention the Secretary of State's office) where someone else may lawfully file to use the same or a similar assumed name.

Having said that, the filing of an assumed name will likely, over time, build and increase one's entitlement to the assumed name as a matter of common law. The name acquires public acceptance and recognition in the area in which it is used. County clerks, of course, aid in this process by declining to issue identical assumed names to rival enterprises within their borders. A DBA is nonetheless no substitute for obtaining a proper trademark or copyright, which is a highly technical field. Consult an expert.

It should also be noted that an assumed name certificate is not a business license, which is not required in Texas except for specific industries. Nevada, on the other hand, charges $200 annually for its required LLC business license.

LLC Bank Accounts and DBAs

Forming an LLC, whether traditional or series, and then failing to get a DBA and do business under it reflects an incomplete process from an asset protection perspective. Get the required DBA and one or more optional DBAs. As many activities as possible should be conducted under a DBA name. There is simply no good reason to make it easy for a potential plaintiff to know the identity or location of the true party in interest behind either an entity or a transaction.

Use of DBAs with a Two-Company Structure

When utilizing a two-company structure, both LLCs should obtain and utilize assumed names.

As a practical matter, the choice of name for an LLC is far less important than the DBA. Most clients unnecessarily spend considerable time and energy choosing an LLC name that unwisely includes or reveals their personal names or other sensitive information. Something generic for the LLC is always better, accompanied by a catchy assumed name.

Chapter 34

HOMESTEAD PROTECTIONS IN TEXAS

Power to the People (and to Their Homes, Cars, Horses, etc.)

This chapter outlines unique protections available to an individual's residence and personal property by what are commonly referred to as "Texas homestead laws," found in Texas Constitution article XVI, section 50 and Property Code chapters 41 and 42. Our focus is on Texas law, not rules or exemptions under federal or bankruptcy law. It is worth observing, however, that bankruptcy rules are tougher on debtors than Texas law. Generally speaking, if a debtor can stay out of bankruptcy, hunker down, and maximize Texas state protections, that is the preferable course.

The homestead has always been sacred in Texas, reaching back to the Republic of Texas and even before. *See* Stephen F. Austin, *Code of Civil Regulations* (1824). The Texas Constitution (section 28) and Property Code section 42.001(b)(1) provide that the homestead of a family or single adult is protected from forced sale for purposes of paying debts and judgments except in cases of purchase money, taxes (both ad valorem and federal tax liens against both spouses), owelty of partition (divorce), home improvement loans, home equity loans, reverse mortgages, liens predating the establishment of homestead, refinance loans, or the conversion or refinance of a lien on a mobile home that is attached to the homestead. Other liens are void. Further, even a permitted lien must be in writing and signed by both spouses to be valid. The protection of the homestead combined with the prohibition against garnishment of wages has long made Texas a destination for debtors.

It is quite possible to make a good salary (no monetary limit), own a paid-for million dollar home, drive a paid-for car, have numerous judgments against you (from Texas or other states), and be reasonably secure under Texas law from creditors—although dealings in current cash accounts may be severely restricted. As to the home itself, there is no dollar limitation on its exempt value. *McCombs*, 659 F.3d at 507.

Asset protection planning in Texas relies on constitutional and statutory homestead protections plus formation of an LLC (or a two-LLC structure) for investments, with the goal of utilizing anonymity techniques whenever feasible. Add a living trust to the mix, and asset protection and basic estate planning can be effectively integrated.

Homestead laws are liberally construed by the courts. *London v. London*, 342 S.W.3d 768, 776 (Tex. App.—Houston [14th Dist.] 2011, no pet.). "Indeed, a court must uphold and enforce the Texas homestead laws even though in so doing the court might unwittingly assist a dishonest debtor in wrongfully defeating his creditor." *PaineWebber, Inc. v. Murray*, 260 B.R. 815, 822 (E.D. Tex. 2001). Unless a judgment debtor owns investment real estate, cash or cash-equivalent on deposit, or a business with attachable inventory—or engages in detectable fraud in concealment of assets—a Texas judgment against an individual may be uncollectable.

Homestead protections are available only to individuals—not corporations, partnerships, or LLCs—and they do not encompass investment or business assets (which should be held in an LLC); nor is a debtor's ownership in corporations, partnerships, or LLCs protected from the consequences of a judgment. Such business interests are non-exempt personal property.

What is a Homestead?

The answer is not as obvious as one might think. Although a person's homestead is primarily a question of intent, it must be based in a real property interest. For instance, neither a mobile home nor a boat qualify. But a vacant lot can be homestead if the owner has reasonable expectations of building a home on it; a leasehold estate (rental property) can be homestead; a life estate may also qualify; and even a beneficial interest in a trust that holds real estate can be homestead.

Property Code section 41.002 supplies the following size limitations:

(a) If used for the purposes of an urban home or as both an urban home and a place to exercise a calling or business, the homestead of a family or a single adult person not otherwise entitled to a homestead shall consist of not more than 10 acres of land which may be in one or more continuous lots, together with any improvements thereon.

(b) If used for the purposes of a rural home the homestead shall consist of:

(1) for a family, not more than 200 acres, which may be in one or more parcels, with the improvements thereon; or

(2) for a single, adult person, not otherwise entitled to a homestead, not more than 100 acres, which may be in one or more parcels, with the improvements thereon.

The statutory definition applies to realty and fixtures, not movable personal property. Movable, non-affixed items are not considered part of the homestead and are not exempt from execution unless included in the list of exempt personal property under Property Code section 42.002 (details below).

A person may claim an urban homestead or a rural homestead but not both. What constitutes "urban" versus "rural" has been the subject of litigation. It is a fact issue that differs from case to case. Once established, however, the initial characterization of the property as urban or rural continues even if the nature of the surrounding area changes. *United States v. Blakeman*, 997 F. 2d 1084 (5th Cir. 1992).

Also, one may not have both an urban residential homestead and an urban business homestead (a place to exercise a calling or business). To qualify, the homestead must be used either for residential homestead or as both residential homestead and business homestead. Tex. Const. art. XVI, § 51; Tex. Prop. Code § 41.002(a); *Majeski v. Estate of Majeski*, 163 S.W.3d 102 (Tex. App.—Austin 2005, no pet.).

The act of living upon and utilizing real property essentially settles the issue of whether or not it is homestead. The possession and use of land by one who owns it and who resides upon it makes it homestead in both fact and law. "Once property has been dedicated as homestead, it can only lose such designation by abandonment, alienation, or death. After the party has established the homestead character of the property, the burden shifts to the creditor . . . to disprove the continued existence of the homestead." *Wilcox v. Marriott*, 103 S.W.3d 469, 472 (Tex. App.—San Antonio 2003, pet. denied).

A family may have only one homestead—which raises the question, what is a family? That is a flexible definition in Texas so long as the head of household is legally or morally required to support a least one other family member. Individual family members may not claim separate homesteads.

Moving to Texas

Can persons from other states declare their intent to reside in Texas and designate a protected homestead there? Yes. If the issue is raised in court, it will be a fact issue to determine whether or not such a declaration was made in good faith (or with the obvious intention of defrauding creditors) and if there is some actual occupancy of the property as well as perhaps a Texas driver's license, voter registration card, etc. This is not a difficult test since there is no minimum number of days a person must physically reside in Texas in order to claim a homestead. If someone has multiple lawsuits and judgments, then moving to Texas to establish a homestead may be an excellent asset protection strategy, particularly if it can be done in the ordinary course of life and business. After all, people move to Texas every day for many good reasons.

Moving from One Homestead to the Next

Property Code section 41.001(5)(c) states that "[t]he homestead claimant's proceeds of a sale of a homestead are not subject to seizure for a creditor's claim for six months after the date of sale," permitting homestead protections to be rolled over from one homestead to the next—notwithstanding the perverse inclination of title companies to collect judgments upon sale of the homestead. *Taylor*, 777 S.W.2d at 570.

Designating a Homestead

It is useful, both for ad valorem tax purposes and for protection from creditors, to file an affidavit designating the homestead in the real property records of the county in which the property is located. Tex. Prop. Code § 41.005. However, for protection from creditors, this is not strictly necessary. The homestead arises automatically when required legal conditions occur. *Graham v. Kleb*, Civ. Act. Nos. H-07-2279, H-07-2878, 2008 WL 243669, at *4 (S.D. Tex. Jan. 29, 2008) (not selected for publication). Also, if a person receives a homestead tax exemption then creditor protection is automatic.

A creditor is on notice that homestead protections will apply if the debtor occupies a homestead. "When a homestead claimant is in actual occupancy of his homestead, it will be deemed that a lender or encumbrancer acted with knowledge of the occupant's right to invoke the rule of homestead." *Sanchez v. Telles*, 960 S.W.2d 769, 772 (Tex. App.—El Paso 1997, pet. denied). Moreover, the homestead is presumed to endure. "Once property has been dedicated as homestead, it can only lose such designation by abandonment, alienation, or death. After the party has established the homestead character of the property, the burden shifts to the creditor . . . to disprove the continued existence of the homestead. In other words, a homestead is presumed to exist until its termination is proved." *Wilcox v. Marriott*, 103 S.W.3d 469, 472 (Tex. App.—San Antonio 2003, pet. denied). Once obtained, homestead rights are not easily lost. A homestead claimant may even temporarily rent the property so long as another homestead is not acquired. Tex. Prop. Code § 41.003.

It is not necessary that a homestead claimant actually reside on the property at the time homestead is claimed. "A homestead exemption may be established upon unoccupied land if the owner presently intends to occupy and use the premises in a reasonable and definite time in the future, and has made such preparations toward actual occupancy and use that are of such character and have proceeded to such an extent as to manifest beyond doubt the intention to complete the improvements and reside upon the place as a home." *Farrington v. First Nat'l Bank*, 753 S.W.2d 248, 250-51 (Tex. App.—Houston [1st Dist.] 1988, writ denied). The key issues are *intent* and *preparation*. Generally, however, in order to make a conclusive and indisputable homestead claim, a person must have a present and exclusive possessory interest in the property.

A person may also execute an affidavit disclaiming particular property (and, optionally, designating other property) as homestead, and a lender is entitled to rely on such an affidavit in making a loan that will be secured by nonhomestead property. This is typically referred to as a "nonhomestead affidavit."

Although there is a conceptual overlap, the homestead protection laws should not be confused with the homestead tax exemption as reflected on the rolls of an appraisal district, which is designed to lower ad valorem taxes on homeowner-occupied property.

Judgments against the Homestead

These are a headache. Texas courts have ruled that although a judgment lien may be unenforceable against a homestead, it may nonetheless constitute a cloud on title, even if it is invalid. *Tarrant Bank v. Miller*, 833 S.W.2d 666 (Tex. App.—Eastland 1992, writ denied). This may result in a title company refusing to issue insurance unless a seller/debtor's judgments are paid, notwithstanding the six-month rollover protection. The homeowner's remedy is Property Code section 52.0012 which provides a statutory method for securing a release of a judgment lien against homestead property—but only for judgments abstracted after 2007. *See* Part VI, ch. 35: *Lien Removal*.

Protection of Personal Property

It is not just realty that is protected. Chapter 42 of the Property Code states that personal property valued at $60,000 for a family or $30,000 for a single adult (exclusive of liens) is exempt from garnishment, attachment, execution or other seizure so long as it is on the following list:

§ 42.002. Personal Property

(1) home furnishings, including family heirlooms;
(2) provisions for consumption;
(3) farming or ranching vehicles and implements;
(4) tools, equipment, books, and apparatus, including boats and motor vehicles used in a trade or profession;
(5) wearing apparel;
(6) jewelry not to exceed 25 percent of the aggregate limitations prescribed by section 42.001(a);
(7) two firearms;
(8) athletic and sporting equipment, including bicycles;
(9) a two-wheeled, three-wheeled, or four-wheeled, motor vehicle for each member of a family or single adult who holds a driver's license or who does not hold a driver's license but who relies on another person to operate the vehicle for the benefit of the nonlicensed person;
(10) the following animals and forage on hand for their consumption:
  (a) Two horses, mules, or donkeys and a saddle, blanket, and bridle for each;
  (b) 12 head of cattle;
  (c) 60 head of other types of livestock; and
  (d) 120 fowl; and
(11) household pets.

If the value of the personal property exceeds the specified dollar amounts, then the excess property is subject to levy pursuant to Property Code section 42.003, although this seldom occurs as a practical matter.

Income and Wages

Pursuant to Property Code section 42.001(b)(1), "current wages for personal services, except for the enforcement of court-ordered child support payments" are exempt "from garnishment, attachment, execution, and other seizure." This includes severance pay. Note that wages are expressly exempted from the $60,000 family limit and the $30,000 single adult limit. Additionally, "unpaid commissions for personal services not to exceed 25 percent" of these limits are also protected.

Can you create a corporation, LLC, or partnership that will pay you wages so that you can declare them exempt? Quite possibly, so long as it can be shown that the corporation, LLC, or partnership is truly a distinct entity that independently conducts business and declares income. Justifying such measures almost always comes down to the "ordinary course of business" defense (see below).

Case law imposes some caveats, however, on the protection of wages. "Once wages are received by the debtor, they cease to be current wages and are not exempt from attachment, execution or seizure for the satisfaction of liabilities"—although this is not true of Social Security payments. 42 U.S.C. § 407. In other words, cash in hand from whatever source is usually vulnerable. It can be attached, and very easily so if it resides in a bank or investment account. Also, the term "current wages" is interpreted to mean a regular salary or hourly pay, *not* compensation paid to an independent contractor. Payments to independent contractors are not protected. *See Brink v. Ayre*, 855 S.W.2d 44 (Tex. App.—Houston [14th Dist.] 1993, no writ). This is surely an unjust gap in the overall regime.

Additional Exemptions

Retirement plans (IRAs and 401(k)s) are exempted under section 42.0021 so long as contributions do not exceed the amount that is deductible under current law. Rollover proceeds are exempt for 60 days.

Also exempted under section 42.0021 are certain savings plans "to the extent that the plan, contract, annuity, or account is exempt from federal income tax, or to the extent federal income on the person's interest deferred until actual payment of benefits to the person" under the Internal Revenue Code.

College tuition funds (including IRS section 529 funds and accounts established under Subchapter F, Chapter 54 of the Texas Education Code) are exempted under section 42.0022.

Exemption for Life Insurance and Annuities under the Insurance Code

Insurance Code section 1108.001 adds the cash value of annuities and life insurance policies to those items which are exempt from garnishment, attachment, execution, or other seizure under Chapter 42 of the Property Code. This section "applies to any benefits, including the cash value and proceeds of an insurance policy, to be provided to an insured or beneficiary under . . . an insurance policy or annuity contract issued by a life, health, or accident insurance company."

No Exemption for Fraudulent Intent

Property Code section 42.004 provides that an exemption is lost if non-exempt assets are used to buy or pay down indebtedness on exempt assets "with the intent to defraud, delay, or hinder" a creditor. This reaches back two years for liquidated claims, one year for unliquidated or contingent claims. However, proving such intent (and thereby getting a transfer set aside) can be challenging for a creditor. Additionally, Property Code section 42.004(c) offers the debtor a defense if the transaction occurred in the ordinary course of business. As a practical matter, this definition may be expanded to include "the ordinary course of business and life."

It remains the burden of the creditor to both discover such transfers and prove that they were impermissible. Judgment creditors vary widely in the energy and determination they expend on postjudgment collection efforts. For instance, most judgment creditors will send postjudgment discovery demanding disclosure of assets; but many creditors do not even bother to do this, perhaps electing to wait until the debtor attempts to sell non-exempt real property and a future title company requires that the judgment be paid. Creditor aggressiveness in any particular case is unpredictable.

Here is an interesting example of fraudulent intent: a failed builder, owing millions on notes that he signed or guaranteed, conspired with his wife to file for divorce and then transfer substantially all of their community assets to the wife in the settlement. After the divorce was final, the husband filed bankruptcy showing few or no assets and sought to discharge the debts. The bankruptcy trustee notices that the husband never moved out of the couples' very expensive home, and he rightfully became suspicious. Not a surprise.

In a recent novel, a fellow who absconded with 50 million dollars was told by the man chasing him: "You took too much money. If you had just taken 5 million, we would have written it off. Now we will chase you to the ends of the earth." So the size of the debt is also a factor.

Role of a Living Trust

The Texas Constitution and the Property Code already provide the homestead with substantial asset protection. However, placing the homestead into a living trust can add some anonymity and, when joined with a pour-over will, accomplish a measure of estate planning as well, since the delay and expense of probate (although modest in Texas) are reduced or eliminated. Why? Because the living trust does not die, and title therefore remains in the trust regardless of the death of one of the beneficiaries. Also, Property Code section 41.0021, entitled "Homestead in a Qualifying Trust," specifically allows a homestead to be transferred into a living trust without losing its exempt character.

Investment Properties and Business Assets

Homestead law has been heavily litigated, and any steps taken by either a creditor or debtor are subject to case-by-case review by a court with results that may occasionally be difficult to predict. Nonetheless, maximizing statutory and constitutional homestead protections is an important part of asset protection. However, investment properties and business assets do not receive the same treatment, so investors should plan accordingly. As a rule, investment properties should be kept separate from the homestead and placed in an LLC, preferably a series LLC which has the ability to compartmentalize assets and insulate them from liabilities associated with other company assets.

Chapter 35

LIEN REMOVAL

Procedures for Removing Different Types of Liens

Sooner or later, most investors will be confronted with the need to remove a lien. This chapter addresses procedures available to secure the release of the following types of liens:

(1) invalid mechanic's and materialman's liens ("M&M liens");
(2) judgment liens against the homestead;
(3) child support liens; and
(4) fraudulent liens.

Tax liens (for ad valorem taxes as well as federal income tax liens resulting from the tax debt of both spouses) are expressly permitted by Texas Constitution article 16, section 50(a). There is no removal procedure for such liens other than entering into a payment arrangement with the taxing authority. Death and taxes, remember?

The Title Commitment

The existence of a lien, often discovered when a title company checks the county real property records and produces a title commitment in anticipation of a sale or refinance, adversely affects a property's marketability. This is so because a title company may demand that the lien be paid and released as a condition of issuing a title policy—regardless of whether the lien is valid or not. The title company is being asked to insure title and is going to look after its own interests first and foremost. Fair? Probably not. A fact of life? Yes.

The First Step in Lien Removal

The first step in lien removal is to contact the judgment creditor or its attorneys, inform them that the lien is invalid (see Part One below) or is currently showing against the homestead (see Parts Two and Three below) and then make formal demand that the creditor execute a release (or a partial release, as the case may be)—or legal action will be taken without further notice. Creditor attorneys are knowledgeable concerning potential liability for their clients, so they will often cooperate and advise the creditor to sign a release. Sometimes, however, this does not happen and it will be necessary to proceed with additional action.

The best way to commence the process is to ask your real estate lawyer to send an explanatory demand letter with an already-prepared release enclosed, ready to be signed by the creditor. This approach has credibility. Note that any old release will not do. *The release must be carefully and correctly drafted or (1) the creditor may not sign it, and/or (2) a title company may not accept it.*

PART ONE: STATUTORY PROCEDURE FOR REMOVING INVALID M&M LIENS

The Bias of Texas Law

It is no secret that Texas law is biased in favor of the worker who supplies labor and materials in new construction, whether residential or commercial. The M&M lien is enshrined in Texas Constitution article XVI, section 37, which states:

> **Mechanics, artisans and materialmen, of every class, shall have a lien upon the buildings and articles made or repaired by them for the value of their labor done thereon, or material furnished therefor; and the Legislature shall provide by law for the speedy and efficient enforcement of said liens.**

This constitutional lien is in addition to the statutory mechanic's lien available pursuant to Property Code sections 53.001 et seq. All of this legal protection assumes that contractors and subcontractors will act in good faith, timely comply with notice requirements, and file only liens that reflect money legitimately owed them. But this is not always, nor even usually, the case. It has been said that the majority of liens filed in Texas are defective in some way, and that is probably true. In addition, there are always nefarious characters who file wrongful or invalid liens in an effort to shake down an owner or stop a closing until they are paid.

General Rule Applicable to M&M Liens

Property Code section 53.157 lists six ways that a mechanic's lien may be discharged of record. The best method is to file a release. Four other methods listed in the statute require the filing of a bond. The sixth means of discharge is failure by the lienholder to foreclose within the statute of limitations, which is two years.

Removal if No Release or Other Discharge Pursuant to Section 53.157

What if the mechanic's lien is alleged to be invalid or defective? Property Code section 53.160 provides an expedited procedure for removal of an "invalid or unenforceable" lien from any real property, whether homestead or not. Grounds must be among those specified in the statute, specifically:

> **(1) notice of claim was not furnished to the owner or original contractor as required by section 53.056, 53.057, 53.058, 53.252, or 53.253;**
>
> **(2) an affidavit claiming a lien failed to comply with section 53.054 or was not filed as required by section 53.052;**
>
> **(3) notice of the filed affidavit was not furnished to the owner or original contractor as required by section 53.055;**
>
> **(4) the owner complied with the requirements of section 53.101 and paid the retainage and all other funds owed to the original contractor before:**
>
> > **(a) the claimant perfected the lien claim; and**
> > **(b) the owner received a notice of the claim as required by this chapter;**
>
> **(5) all funds subject to the notice of a claim to the owner and the perfection of a claim against the statutory retainage have been deposited in the registry of the court and the owner has no additional liability to the claimant;**
>
> **(6) when the lien affidavit was filed on homestead property:**

(a) no contract was executed or filed as required by section 53.254;
(b) the affidavit claiming a lien failed to contain the notice as required by section 53.254; or
(c) the notice of the claim failed to include the statement required by section 53.254; and

(7) the claimant executed a valid and enforceable waiver or release of the claim or lien claimed in the affidavit.

Filing Suit to Remove an M&M Lien

The least expensive means of contesting a wrongful or invalid M&M lien would be to file a countervailing affidavit in the real property records, but this would merely state one's sworn opinion that the lien is invalid, perhaps for some title company to evaluate with regard to a future transaction. It would not remove the lien.

Section 53.169 prescribes the approved procedure for removing the lien. Although the statute talks about a "motion to remove a claim or lien," it is better practice to file a suit, obtain a case number and court assignment, get service on the defendant, and then file the motion. This method allows the plaintiff to pursue all available avenues of relief against the defendant (including fraud and deceptive trade practices, for example) that go beyond the scope of the statutory motion.

Procedural Requirements

The motion procedure requires that the defendant (i.e., the person who filed the lien) be given at least 21 days' notice of the hearing. The motion should be supported by relevant documents and at least one sworn affidavit. The hearing is an evidentiary hearing, a "mini-trial," and testimony will be taken for the record. The judge then rules and the effect is immediate. There is no requirement that 30 days elapse before the ruling is final, as is the case with final judgments. A certified copy of the order should be filed in the real property records and forwarded to any title company that may be involved. Sale of the property can then proceed without further delay.

Section 53.156 provides that "the court may award costs and reasonable attorney's fees as are equitable and just." An affidavit of attorney's fees and costs should be attached to the motion.

It is at the discretion of the plaintiff as to whether or not, following a ruling on the motion, the underlying suit should continue or be dismissed. It is likely that this decision will turn on whether or not the ruling itself provides the plaintiff with sufficient compensation.

PART TWO: RELEASE OF JUDGMENT LIENS AGAINST THE HOMESTEAD

Two Sets of Rules Apply

In order to determine which rules apply, one needs to determine if the judgment in question was abstracted before or after Sept. 1, 2007.

Judgment Liens Abstracted after September. 1, 2007 (New Law Applies)

Property Code section 52.0012(c) deals with judgment liens against the homestead which are abstracted after that date. Note the use of the word "abstracted." If the judgment was rendered before this key date but it was not abstracted until afterward, then the new law would apply.

A judgment lien does not attach to a judgment debtor's exempt real property, including the debtor's homestead. It can be difficult, however, to persuade a title company that they should ignore a judgment. A title company's automatic, self-serving reaction is usually to require that all liens be cleared. The homeowner should resist this pressure and insist on his or her homestead rights.

As is true with other liens, the first step in the process under the new law is a demand letter—in this case, a 30-day letter to the judgment creditor and its attorney. If there is no response, Property Code section 52.0012 provides that a judgment debtor may file a "Homestead Affidavit as Release of Judgment Lien" which "serves as a release of record of a judgment lien established under this chapter." The affidavit must be in proper form, meeting all requirements of the statute. However, if the judgment creditor files a contradicting affidavit, and if after filing such contradicting affidavit a purchaser or mortgagee of real property acquires the purchaser's or mortgagee's interest from the judgment debtor, then the debtor's affidavit does not act as a release of the judgment lien with respect to the purchaser or mortgagee.

The following is a checklist for evaluating whether or not this procedure applies in a particular case. A title company will not insure over a homestead lien using the new law unless:

1. the abstract of judgment is recorded after September 1, 2007;

2. a 30-day demand letter has been sent by CM/RRR to the creditor and its attorney enclosing a copy of the affidavit that is intended to be filed, with evidence of homestead status included;

3. proof exists (e.g., a signed USPS green card) that the creditor and its attorney received the letter and affidavit at least 30 days prior to the date that the affidavit was recorded;

4. the title company's plant is certified to the 31st day following the mailing of the letter and affidavit;

5. no contradicting affidavit is recorded by the creditor;

6. the size of the property does not exceed 10 acres, if urban, or 200 acres, if rural (100 acres if the debtor is single); and

7. the proposed purchaser or lender is a bona fide third party, paying money for or lending money against the property.

Judgment Liens Abstracted Prior to September 1, 2007 (Old Law Applies)

In the case of judgment liens abstracted prior to September 1, 2007, the old law as set out in the1992 case of *Tarrant Bank v. Miller*, 310 Ark. 179, 833 S.W.2d 366 (1992), applies. *Tarrant Bank* decided that a judgment creditor may be liable in damages if it fails after demand to give a partial release of a judgment as to the debtor's homestead. The best approach to removing an older lien would therefore be to send the creditor's attorney a demand for a partial release accompanied by a credible threat of litigation if the release is not signed.

The Flaw in the Process

There is nothing in the statute that *requires* a title company to accept the affidavit provided for in section 52.0012 (the new law) and then go forward with closing and issuing one or more title policies. In other words, the law is not self-enforcing. Title companies, being the conservative institutions that they are, may hesitate or refuse to go along. As in other situations, it may be necessary to shop title companies until one is found that is amenable to this process.

What Does the Attorney Need from the client?

When asking that an attorney initiate the process of removing a lien from the homestead, the client should be prepared with a number of items: (1) a copy the abstract of judgment (if a copy of the judgment itself is available, supply that as well); (2) a copy of the warranty deed to the homestead; (3) a print-out from the local appraisal district indicating that the property is classified as homestead (sometimes there is a notation that it is "HS"); (4) the name and address of each judgment creditor and/or its attorneys; and (5) correspondence between the judgment creditor and the client.

Note item (4). Clients often expect a lawyer to be able to locate their creditors as part of the lien removal process. This may not be a reasonable assumption, since lawyers are not usually also investigators. Demand letters may be returned labeled "no such address" or the like. If an investigator is needed, the client should be prepared to bear that expense.

PART THREE: RELEASE OF CHILD SUPPORT LIENS

Texas Family Code section 157.3171 establishes a process by which an obligor may obtain the release of a child support lien against the obligor's homestead. The procedure involves the filing of an affidavit and is identical to that contained in Property Code section 52.0012 (discussed above). The law states that "the obligor is considered to be a judgment debtor under that section and the claimant under the child support lien is considered to be a judgment creditor under that section." The person claiming the lien may file a contradicting affidavit: "If the claimant files a contradicting affidavit as described by Subsection (d), the issue of whether the real property is subject to the lien must be resolved in an action brought for that purpose in the district court of the county in which the real property is located and the lien was filed." If the property is in the same county in which a divorce or action for child support was had, then the court that heard the case would likely have jurisdiction over the lien issue as well.

PART FOUR: REMOVAL OF FRAUDULENT LIENS

Removal of a Fraudulent Lien

There are instances where a purported lien or claim against real property is outright fraudulent. Subchapter J of the Government Code provides three forms of relief in the event a fraudulent instrument is filed. The first is based on action to be taken at the clerk level. If a court clerk or county clerk has a "reasonable basis" for believing that a filed document is fraudulent, section 51.901 provides that the clerk shall, after giving notice, "(1) request the assistance of the county or district attorney to determine whether the document is fraudulent before filing or recording the document; (2) request that the prospective filer provide to the county clerk additional documentation supporting the existence of the lien, such as a contract or other document that contains the alleged debtor or obligor's signature; and (3) forward any additional documentation received to the county or district attorney."

What would provide a reasonable basis for a clerk to take action? Someone would likely have to point out the issue or supply the clerk with an appropriate affidavit.

The second avenue of relief is provided by Government Code section 51.902 and is based on action by the person aggrieved by filing of a fraudulent judgment lien:

§ 51.902. Action on Fraudulent Judgment Lien

> **A person against whom a purported judgment was rendered who has reason to believe that a document previously filed or recorded or submitted for filing or for filing and recording is fraudulent may complete and file with the district clerk a motion, verified by affidavit . . .**
>
> **requesting a judicial determination of the status of a court, judicial entity, or judicial officer purporting to have taken an action that is the basis of a judgment lien filed in the office of said clerk[.]**

If the motion is successful, a district judge will rule that the instrument in question not be accorded "lien status."

A third type of action is contained in Gov. Code section 51.903 and again requires the action and initiative of the person who was harmed by the fraudulent instrument:

§ 51.903. Action On Fraudulent Lien On Property

> **A person who is the purported debtor or obligor or who owns real or personal property or an interest in real or personal property and who has reason to believe that the document purporting to create a lien**

> **or a claim against the real or personal property or an interest in the real or personal property previously filed or submitted for filing and recording is fraudulent may complete and file with the district clerk a [Motion for Judicial Review of Documentation or Instrument Purporting to Create a Lien or Claim] verified by affidavit . . .**
>
> **requesting a judicial determination of the status of documentation or an instrument purporting to create an interest in real or personal property or a lien or claim on real or personal property or an interest in real or personal property[.]**

Since instruments "purporting to create an interest in real or personal property" are expressly mentioned, this statute includes fraudulent deeds filed in the county clerk's real property records.

Section 51.903 supplies a statutory form of "Motion for Judicial Review of Documentation or Instrument Purporting to Create a Lien or Claim." The motion asks the district court to find that the document or instrument:

> **(1) IS NOT provided for by specific state or federal statutes or constitutional provisions;**
> **(2) IS NOT created by implied or express consent or agreement of the obligor, debtor, or the owner of the real or personal property or an interest in the real or personal property, if required under the law of this state or by implied or express consent or agreement of an agent, fiduciary, or other representative of that person;**
> **(3) IS NOT an equitable, constructive, or other lien imposed by a court of competent jurisdiction created by or established under the constitution or laws of this state or the United States; or**
> **(4) IS NOT asserted against real or personal property or an interest in real or personal property. There is no valid lien or claim created by this documentation or instrument.**

Note that if the court so finds, it nonetheless makes no finding as to the underlying claim, which can still be litigated—only as to the filing of the document or instrument in question.

Penalties for Fraudulent Liens

Chapter 12 of the Civil Practice & Remedies Code addresses "Liability related to . . . a fraudulent lien or claim filed against real or personal property." A person who knowingly and intentionally files a fraudulent lien may be held liable in civil district court for the greater of $10,000 or actual damages, exemplary damages, and recovery of attorney's fees and costs. It is also a criminal offense. *See* Tex. Penal Code § 37.01. If applicable, a cause of action under Civil Practice & Remedies Code section 12.002 should be included in any suit against the lien claimant.

Filing of a fraudulent lien may under certain circumstances also form part of a cause of action under the Deceptive Trade Practices Act. Tex. Bus. & Com. Code §§ 17.44 et seq.

Chapter 36

EQUITY STRIPPING FOR ASSET PROTECTION

The Importance of Perception in the Public Records

Equity stripping is the art and science of making a business appear to be worth less than it really is. It has been said that perception is everything, an aphorism that is definitely true in asset protection. If a review of public records indicates that a potential target company is in debt and its assets are encumbered by liens, why would a plaintiff file and pursue an expensive lawsuit in order to wind up with an uncollectable judgment? If the company appears judgment proof, will a contingency-fee attorney take the case?

Core Documents

The core documents of an equity-stripping system are

(1) a secured promissory note in a substantial amount (at least $1 million);
(2) a line-of-credit agreement supplementing the terms and conditions of the note;
(3) a deed of trust and security agreement listing real and personal property collateral subject to a lien to secure payment of the note;
(4) a company resolution authorizing the loan; and
(5) a presigned release of note and lien.

Only the deed of trust and security agreement is filed of record, but that is enough. This document states clearly that both a company's real estate and its furniture, fixtures, and equipment are subject to a lien to secure repayment of a very sizeable amount of money. The other equity-stripping documents are kept with the company record book as documentary support. The most important of these is a presigned release of note and lien which is held in reserve until it is necessary or advantageous to file it. After all, one should never allow the filing of a lien without a reliable means of getting that lien released later.

The note is payable on demand. The borrower should be an investor's limited liability company. If the borrower is a series LLC, the note should state that all series are jointly and severally liable for payment, not just the company at large. The identity of the lender may vary. This firm favors utilizing a Nevada company (or more specifically a DBA thereof). The Nevada component makes it marginally more difficult for a plaintiff to obtain information or subject the lender to compulsory document production in a Texas court.

The Role of Deterrence

Recall that a key principle of asset protection is deterrence. Deterrence in the form of equity stripping affects the process at two possible points: first, when the plaintiff and his lawyer perform due diligence (as they should) on the available assets of their target before launching an attack; and second, after suit is filed during document production, when the defendant produces copies of the note and the deed of trust and security agreement—documents which, at least on paper, vastly reduce net worth. Given the soaring expense of litigation, most plaintiffs would then pause and carefully evaluate the prospects for a tangible recovery. After all, a lawsuit is just another form of investment, and a rational plaintiff is looking for a return on that investment. Similarly, a plaintiffs' attorney who has accepted the case on a contingency basis may be wary. The attorney may even go to the client and demand a substantial retainer if the case is to proceed. Result? The lawsuit may end there.

Equity Stripping and the Two-Company Structure

As elsewhere described in this book, we recommend a two-company structure for most real estate investors: one LLC as a management company, and another a stand-alone holding company. Activities are thereby separated from assets, greatly minimizing risk. Since in this system the management company is already a shell, it is the holding company that should be considered as a candidate for equity stripping.

Is equity stripping a form of fraud against creditors?

The answer to this question is *absolutely not,* so long as it is handled correctly. After all, the note merely *authorizes* advances of up to $1,000,000. It does not indicate how much money (if any) has *actually* been advanced. Moreover, all documents relating to the transaction are entirely in order. The deed of trust and security agreement (the only recorded document) merely states the maximum loan amount and reveals nothing further about advancements or other details of the loan agreement.

It would be a different matter if one is queried during the discovery process as to how much of the loan had been advanced. One should never be untruthful in discovery; however, it is a corollary to this rule that one should provide only the minimum information necessary to be adequately responsive. If the plaintiff does not ask, then the defendant is not under an obligation to provide gratuitous information.

The Issue of Existing Lienholders

Unless one's company is fortunate enough to own its properties outright, then there will be existing lienholders to consider when it comes to equity stripping. First-lien deeds of trust recite that the priority status of their lien must be preserved or the borrower will be in default. Is this a problem? It should not be. The reason is that the deed of trust and security agreement used for equity stripping expressly states that its lien is inferior to earlier liens of record.

It is paradoxical that it may be in your best interest to appear less wealthy than you are, but it is nonetheless true in the world of asset protection.

Chapter 37

FRAUDULENT TRANSFERS

The Eyes of Texas Creditors Are Upon You

According to the Texas Uniform Fraudulent Transfer Act ("TUFTA" contained in Business Organizations Code section 24.002(12)), a transfer "means every mode, direct or indirect, absolute or conditional, voluntary or involuntary, of disposing of or parting with an asset or an interest in an asset [tangible or intangible], and includes payment of money, release, lease, and creation of a lien or other encumbrance." This is an extremely broad definition. Under what circumstances is a transfer considered fraudulent?

The largest percentage of fraudulent transfers are transactions conducted with an affiliated person or entity without payment of reasonably equivalent value in return. According to section 24.004(d), "'Reasonably equivalent value' includes without limitation, a transfer or obligation that is within the range of values for which the transferor would have sold the assets in an arm's length transaction." Combine the definitions of "transfer" and "value" and it is clear that intentionally moving assets out of reach of creditors can indeed be a challenge.

Applicable Law

TUFTA is located in chapter 24 of the Business and Commerce Code. Also relevant is Tax Code section 111.024 dealing with tax liability on the part of recipients of fraudulent transfers, as well as Penal Code section 32.33 ("Hindering Secured Creditors"). Federal bankruptcy law relating to this topic is found at 11 U.S.C. § 548 but will not be discussed, since this book addresses Texas law exclusively.

Of particular interest is TUFTA section 24.005(b)(1)-(11) which includes a *nonexclusive* list of eleven factors that may be used in determining actual fraud:

(1) the transfer or obligation was to an insider;

(2) the debtor retained possession or control of the property transferred after the transfer;

(3) the transfer or obligation was concealed;

(4) before the transfer was made or obligation was incurred, the debtor had been sued or threatened with suit;

(5) the transfer was of substantially all the debtor's assets;

(6) the debtor absconded;

(7) the debtor removed or concealed assets;

(8) the value of the consideration received by the debtor was not reasonably equivalent to the value of the asset transferred or the amount of the obligation incurred;

(9) the debtor was insolvent or became insolvent shortly after the transfer was made or the obligation was incurred;

(10) the transfer occurred shortly before or shortly after a substantial debt was incurred; and

(11) the debtor transferred the essential assets of the business to a lienor who transferred the assets to an insider of the debtor.

No one of the foregoing factors will determine a court's decision, but if several of these factors exist in a given case then it is likely that a court will make a finding of fraud on the part of the debtor. *Walker v. Anderson*, 232 S.W.3d 899, 914 (Tex. App.—Dallas 2007, no pet.) (citing *G.M. Houser, Inc. v. Rodgers*, 204 S.W.3d 836, 843 (Tex. App.—Dallas 2006, no pet.)). Under TUFTA, the creditor must carry the burden of proving the elements as to each alleged fraudulent transfer by a preponderance of the evidence. *Id.* at 913 (citing *G.M. Houser*, 204 S.W.3d at 842-43).

Under section 24.002(2) of TUFTA "asset" does *not* include property to the extent it is encumbered by a valid lien (i.e., the transfer extends only to the debtor's equity); property to the extent it is generally exempt under nonbankruptcy law (details below); or an interest in property held in tenancy by the entireties to the extent it is not subject to process by a creditor holding a claim against only one tenant, under the law of another jurisdiction.

An action by a creditor under TUFTA must be brought within one to four years, depending on which section of TUFTA is cited as a cause of action by the creditor. *See* Tex. Bus. Orgs. Code § 24.010.

Assets Exempt under State Law

The TUFTA definition of "asset" does not include exempt assets under non-bankruptcy law including the Texas homestead laws contained in article XVI, section 50 of the Texas Constitution and in Property Code chapters 41 and 42. However, Property Code section 42.004 provides that a transaction may be set aside if nonexempt assets are used to buy or pay down indebtedness on exempt assets "with the intent to defraud, delay, or hinder" a creditor. This reaches back two years. However, proving such intent (and therefore getting the transfer set aside) can be difficult, particularly if the debtor asserts that the transaction occurred in the ordinary course of business, which is a solid defense in Texas.

Postjudgment Discovery

Judgments are final after thirty days, after which postjudgment discovery (interrogatories, requests for production, and depositions directed at the defendant by a judgment creditor) are commonly used not only to determine the location and value of the defendant's assets but also whether or not there is a trail suggesting fraudulent transfers. The scope of this process can be wide indeed, reaching back several years. A debtor can be held in contempt (fine or jail) for failing to provide responses.

Fraudulent Transfers and the IRS

In re Wren Alexander Investments LLC, No. 08-52914-RBK, 2011 WL 671961 (Bankr. W.D. Tex. Feb. 17, 2011), illustrates the difficulty in moving assets beyond the reach of the IRS. In this case, the IRS successfully argued that the taxpayer's transfer was fraudulent (1) under BOC section 24.006(a) since the taxpayer did not receive reasonably equivalent value in exchange and was insolvent at the time of or became insolvent as a result of the transfer, and (2) under section 24.005(a) since the transfer was made with "actual intent to hinder, delay, or defraud" a creditor, present or future.

Implications for Asset Protection Planning

As noted elsewhere in this book, asset protection strategies fall into two groups: strategies implemented in advance of collection action and suit by a creditor/plaintiff; and strategies that can be put into effect afterward. After suit is filed, creditors are on the lookout for the movement of assets to defeat their legitimate claims. A Texas defendant may be limited to attempting to convert nonexempt assets into homestead-exempt items (one's primary residence, cars, etc.), holding cash at home, and prepaying certain key items (taxes, attorney's fees, and the like which are unlikely to be questioned as fraudulent).

EVICTIONS, FORECLOSURE, & LITIGATION

Chapter 38

EVICTIONS

Forcible Entry and Detainer

Eviction (referred to as "forcible entry and detainer" or "FED" for short) is a judicial process by which an owner recovers possession of real property and, if appropriate, a judgment for unpaid rent, attorney's fees (if any), and court costs against a tenant or occupant. Evictions are conducted in justice courts which are located in various neighborhood precincts around Texas counties. Justice courts have original jurisdiction over possession of real property and authority to decide cases involving damages up to $10,000.

The landlord's objective is usually to gain a writ of possession and a judgment. However, because collecting judgments against residential tenants can be quite difficult in Texas (there is an extensive list of assets that are exempt from execution) the residential landlord may occasionally choose to be content with a judgment for possession only.

Basic Law and Procedure

Evictions are governed by Property Code section 24.01 and Rules of Civil Procedure 738 through 755. An eviction is appropriate if there exists a landlord-tenant relationship (with or without a written lease) or if a person is occupying real property without authority to do so. The only issue to be decided in an eviction case is which party has the superior right to immediate possession. *Cuellar v. Martinez*, 625 S.W.2d 3, 5 (Tex. Civ. App.—San Antonio 1981, no writ).

In the case of month-to-month tenancy (e.g., after a lease is expired) with no tenant default, the landlord may give a month's written notice that the landlord desires possession. No more than that need be said. If the tenant does not leave, then eviction can be filed. If there is a default such as failure to pay rent, then a written "3-day notice to vacate" should be given, after which the landlord may file an FED.

The eviction should be filed with the justice of the peace in whose precinct the property is located. At the hearing, the judge will determine which party has the superior right to possession and what damages (e.g., back rent, attorney's fees, and court costs), if any, will be awarded to the landlord. These are the only issues to be considered by the court. A counterclaim by the tenant, regardless of subject matter or merit, is *not* permitted in an FED. Such tenant suits must be brought by separate action in any court (including that same justice court) where venue and jurisdiction are appropriate.

Appeals: Cash Bonds versus Pauper's Affidavit

Within five calendar days of judgment, the tenant may (with or without good reason) appeal to the local county court at law. The appeal results in the file being packed up and sent to the county courthouse where it will be heard de novo (as a new case). The justice of the peace will set a cash appeal bond which may be three times the monthly rent. However, the cash bond may be waived if the tenant files an affidavit stating that he or she cannot afford it. The content of the "pauper's bond" or "pauper's affidavit" is now prescribed by statute and is considerably more complex than it used to be.

Once a pauper's affidavit is filed, the landlord has the right to request a hearing and contest the affidavit, alleging that the tenant does in fact have sufficient resources for the bond. The tenant can be questioned on the subject of his or her assets and income. It is generally pointless to go through this exercise, however, since pauper's bonds are almost always approved by justices of the peace, and the file is then turned over to county court.

If the tenant does not appeal within five days, the judgment of the justice court becomes final and the landlord may proceed to the enforcement phase by obtaining and serving a writ of possession. This requires going to the county clerk's office and paying a nominal fee. The constable then serves the writ, but first usually posts a notice on the tenant's door allowing 48 hours to move out. After that, the constable may show up with a truck, forcibly evict the tenant, and put the tenant's possessions in storage where charges accrue at the tenant's expense.

Pauper's Bond Appellants

Important: A tenant who files a pauper's affidavit must pay a month's rent to the justice court pursuant to Property Code section 24.0054(a) and do so *before* the file is shipped to county court:

> **During an appeal of an eviction case for nonpayment of rent, if a tenant fails to pay one rental period's rent into *the justice court* [italics added] registry within *five days* [italics added] of the date the tenant filed a**

pauper's affidavit in accordance with Rule 749b(1), Texas Rules of Civil Procedure, and section 24.0053, the justice court *shall* [italics added] issue a writ of possession, without hearing, in the filing of a notice of default by the appellee. A writ of possession under this subsection may be executed immediately, and the sheriff or constable shall execute the writ as soon as practicable.

This provision gives landlords an effective remedy at the justice court level, without having to wait until the entire eviction file is transferred to the county clerk's office and set up as a new case.

Rule 749b Motion in County Court

The eviction appellate system may appear unfair, but it can be turned to the landlord's advantage: If the pauper's bond is approved, and the county court takes over, the tenant is then obliged to begin making monthly rental payments to the court and continue to do so during the pendency of the appeal. If the tenant fails to do this (and most do) the landlord may seek *immediate* possession from the county court based on motion pursuant to Texas Rule of Civil Procedure 749b, which permits a tenant to remain in possession only so long as the following requirements are met:

(1) Within five days of the date that the tenant/appellant files his pauper's affidavit, he must pay into the justice court registry one rental period's rent under the terms of the rental agreement.

(2) During the appeal process as rent becomes due under the rental agreement, then tenant/appellant shall pay the rent into the county court registry within five days of the due date under the terms of the rental agreement.

(3) If the tenant/appellant fails to pay the rent into the court registry within the time limit prescribed by these rules, the appellee may file a notice of default in county court. Upon sworn motion by the appellee and a showing of default to the judge, the court shall issue a writ of restitution.

Cash or Surety Bond Appeals

If an appeal bond (cash or surety) is posted, there is no *requirement* that the tenant pay rent while the appeal is pending. Even so, it is good practice for the landlord's attorney to file a motion requesting payment of rent into the court registry based on the theory that no one should live for free, an argument to which judges are generally receptive. A preferential setting should also be requested if the county court in question does not already automatically provide such a setting in eviction cases.

The bad news for landlords? If the tenant is a professional deadbeat who has played this game before, the property may be tied up for months.

Postforeclosure Eviction

The remedy of foreclosure is available to lenders if the borrower defaults. Specified notice and other requirements must be followed if the foreclosure is to be valid. Tex. Prop. Code §§ 51.002 et seq. Foreclosures are held in Texas on the first Tuesday of each month between 10 a.m. and 4 p.m. The successful bidder (likely the lender) gets a trustee's deed which cuts off all junior liens including purchase money liens and mechanics liens. This gives the new owner *title*; the next step is to obtain *possession*.

If the occupant of residential property is "a tenant at will or by sufferance" then the new owner under the trustee's deed must give the usual three-day notice to vacate, file an FED petition in justice court, get it served, have it heard by the justice of the peace, and then wait five days for a final judgment and a writ of possession. The new owner must then wait until the constable posts a 48-hour notice on the door and then forcibly removes a former borrower who is otherwise unwilling to leave. Elapsed time? Often three to four weeks, and even then the former borrower may appeal, possibly gaining additional free-rent time in the property.

Section 24.005(b) has been amended to provide that new owners who have purchased foreclosed property must give a residential tenant in good standing at least 90 days' notice to vacate so long as the tenant continues to pay rent to the new owner. The intent here is to bring state law more into line with federal law (see below).

Protecting Tenants at Foreclosure Act of 2009

This important federal legislation modifies the usual eviction process for tenants who remain in possession following a foreclosure sale. The statute actually speaks of a "bona fide lease or tenancy" at a monthly rate which must not be substantially less than market rent. If the tenant has such a lease or tenancy, then the tenant may stay until the lease expires or until expiration of the 90-day notice which must be given by the new owner, whichever is longer. If the tenant does not have a lease (i.e., is residing in the property month-to-month) or has a lease that is terminable at will, then the Act permits the tenant to remain in the property for up to 90 days after notice, after which time the tenant may be evicted in the customary manner. Section 8 tenants may have additional rights.

Tenants with a written lease should be prepared to show this document to the lender's foreclosure attorneys or, if an eviction has been filed, to the justice of the peace in order to confirm their right to stay in the property.

What if there is a wrongful foreclosure case pending in district court? Can the district court enjoin the eviction?

Not usually. The reasoning involves a distinction between disputes concerning *possession* and disputes concerning *title*. Generally, justice courts have original jurisdiction over possession issues, Tex. Prop. Code § 24.004, and district courts have original jurisdiction over title issues, Tex. Const. art. V, § 8; Tex. Gov't Code § 26.043. Rule 746 also provides that the "merits of the title shall not be adjudicated" in justice court.

However, the jurisdiction of the district court pre-empts the justice court on issues of possession when questions of title and possession are so integrally linked or intertwined that possession may not be determined without first determining title. In such cases, and only in such cases, may the justice court be deprived of jurisdiction. *Mitchell v. Armstrong Capital Corp.*, 911 S.W.2d 169, 171 (Tex. App.—Houston [1st Dist.] 1995, writ denied). Note that in Harris County, the county courts at law have the benefit of an exception under the Government Code and may hear title issues.

Collecting Judgments from Tenants

The key objective for the owner is to gain a writ of possession. Obtaining a judgment for monetary damages against a residential tenant in Texas is usually an empty formality since such judgments are seldom collected. Texas has long been a safe harbor for debtors, and both the Texas Constitution and the Property Code exempt a long list of real and personal property from execution upon a judgment. The average residential tenant has very little that a landlord will be allowed to take and, since garnishment of wages is unconstitutional, collection is problematic.

What does the attorney need from the client?

When asking that an attorney initiate the eviction process, the client should be prepared to supply (1) a copy of the lease agreement; (2) copies of any correspondence or demand letters; and (3) a brief summary of the specific items of monetary and technical default.

Chapter 39

FORECLOSURES

Both an Investment Opportunity and an Expedited Remedy

The remedy of foreclosure is available in the event of a borrower's monetary default (nonpayment) or technical default (e.g., failure to pay taxes or keep the property insured). In order to determine if there has been a default, the loan documents—the note, the deed of trust, the loan agreement, and so forth—should be carefully examined. Notice and opportunity to cure requirements contained in these documents must be strictly followed if a foreclosure is to be valid.

Foreclosures may be judicial (ordered by a court following a judgment in a lawsuit) or non-judicial ("on the courthouse steps"). Most foreclosures in Texas are nonjudicial. These are governed by chapter 51 of the Property Code and are held on the first Tuesday of each month between 10 a.m. and 4 p.m. at a designated spot at the county courthouse. The effect of foreclosure is to cut off and eliminate junior liens, including mechanic's liens, but not tax obligations.

Notices of foreclosure sales must be filed with the county clerk and posted (usually on a bulletin board in the lobby of the courthouse) at least 21 calendar days prior to the intended foreclosure date. Notices are entitled "Notice of Trustee's Sale" or "Notice of Substitute Trustee's Sale." They provide information about the debt, the legal description of the property, and designate a three-hour period during which the sale will be held. In larger metropolitan areas there are foreclosure listing services which publish a monthly list of properties posted for foreclosure.

Required Notices to the Borrower

Notices to the defaulting borrower must be given in accordance with Property Code sections 51.002 et seq. and the deed of trust. The content of foreclosure notices is technical and must be correct to insure a valid foreclosure that cannot later be attacked by a wrongful foreclosure suit. Clients often protest when their lawyer advises re-noticing the debtor—"But I've already sent them an email telling them they are in default." Not good enough.

Usually, two certified mail notices to the borrower are required, the first being a "Notice of Default and Intent to Accelerate" which gives formal notice of the default and affords an opportunity for the borrower to cure it (at least 20 days for a homestead, although if the deed of trust is on the FNMA form, 30 days must be given). Note that S.B. 766 and S.B. 472, which did not make it out of committee in the 81st Legislature, would have extended the 20-day period. This legislation may be revived in the future. Many lawyers consider it best to routinely give a 30-day notice.

After the cure period has passed, a "Notice of Acceleration and Posting for Foreclosure" must be sent at least 21 days prior to the foreclosure date. This second letter must also specify the location of the sale and a three-hour period during which the sale will take place. A notice of foreclosure sale should be enclosed. This notice is also filed with the county clerk and physically posted at the courthouse. If there is going to be a change in trustees it is also necessary to file a written appointment of substitute trustee.

Notices are addressed to the last known address of the borrower contained in the lender's records (this is the legal requirement), but it is wise for the lender to double-check this to avoid later claims by the borrower that notice was defective. It is prudent to send notices by both first-class and certified mail. Why? The reason has to do with Texas's mailbox rule, i.e., that a notice properly deposited in the U.S. mail is presumed to be delivered. "Common sense . . . dictates that regular mail is presumed delivered and certified mail enjoys no [such] presumption unless the receipt is returned bearing an appropriate notation." *McCray v. Hoag*, 372 S.W.3d 237, 243 (Tex. App.—Dallas 2012, no pet. h.). A careful lender will send notices to *all* likely addresses where the borrower may be found.

Other lienholders (whether junior or senior) are not entitled to notice. Depending on the first lienholder's strategy, however, it may be useful to discuss the issue with them.

If the borrower is able to cure, a reinstatement agreement should be executed unless the terms of the debt have been changed (e.g., payments have been lowered) in which case a hybrid reinstatement/modification agreement or even a new note may be appropriate.

Notice to the IRS

The best practice is to do a title search prior to foreclosure to determine if there is an IRS tax lien or other federal lien. If so, notice must be given to the IRS and/or the U.S. Attorney at least 25 days prior to the sale, not including the sale date. 26 U.S.C. § 7425(c)(1). If this is not done, any IRS tax lien on the property will not be extinguished by the sale. Note that the IRS also has 120 days following the sale to redeem the property, although this seldom happens. The successful bidder on an IRS-liened property is therefore not entitled to breathe a sigh of relief until the 121st day.

Fair Debt Collection Practices Act

The Fair Debt Collection Practices Act (15 U.S.C. §§ 1601 et seq.) requires that a borrower be given 30 days to request and obtain verification of the debt. The lender may give notice of default, accelerate the debt, and even post for foreclosure in less time, but the foreclosure sale itself should not be conducted until the 30-day debt verification period has expired.

There is also an equivalent state statute (the Texas Debt Collection Practices Act) contained in Finance Code chapter 392. Failure to provide verification of the debt when the borrower has requested it in writing has serious penalties under both laws.

Due Diligence by the Investor Prior to Foreclosure

Buying property at foreclosure sales is a popular form of investment but it contains traps for the unwary. The investor's goal is to acquire instant equity in the property by paying a relatively modest sum at the foreclosure sale. However, apparent equity can evaporate if the property is loaded down with liens. It is advisable, therefore, to check the title of the property that will be sold. Is the lien being foreclosed a second or third lien? If so, then the first lien (usually a purchase-money lien held by a mortgage company) will continue in force. First liens are king. They are not extinguished by foreclosure on an inferior lien. What about IRS liens? Improvement liens? Liens imposed by homeowners associations? Any or all of these could consume whatever equity might otherwise have existed in the property. If an investor is unsure as to which liens will be wiped out in a foreclosure sale, then copies of each lien document should be pulled and taken to the investor's real estate attorney for review.

As far as researching title is concerned, every professional investor should ultimately acquire the skills to go to the real property records in the county clerk's office and do this unaided. One should obtain copies of the warranty deed and any deeds of trust or other lien instruments. Alternatively, a down-date report from a title company may be requested.

If more information is needed about the property itself, one can contact the trustee named in the Notice of Trustee's Sale. Trustees vary in their level of cooperation but are often willing to provide additional information if they have it. They may have a copy of an inspection report on the property which they may be willing to share. One might even be able to arrange to view the property if it is unoccupied.

The investor should also check the military status of the borrower, since Property Code section 51.015 prohibits non-judicial foreclosure of a dwelling owned by active duty military personnel or within 9 months after active duty ends. Knowingly violating this law is a Class A misdemeanor.

Property Condition

It goes without saying that the investor should physically inspect the property if at all possible, although one should not trespass on occupied property to do this. It is legal, however, to stand in the street (public property) and take photos.

When one buys at a foreclosure sale, it is "as is." Property condition is therefore important. When buying residential properties in particular, an investor should be especially curious about condition of the foundation (learn to recognize signs of settlement), whether the property is flood-prone, and whether or not there may be environmental contamination (generally not a problem if the house is in a restricted subdivision). It is usually best to avoid any property that suffers from one or more of these deficiencies. Other items that involve significant expense are the roof and the HVAC system.

The past or continuing presence of hazardous substances can impose huge potential liability (particularly on commercial properties) since both Texas and federal law provide that any owner of property (including the investor) is jointly and severally liable with any prior owner for cleanup costs. The Texas Commission on Environmental Quality ("TCEQ") maintains a web site at www.tceq.state.tx.us where the environmental history of a property can be researched.

Valuation

It is, of course, important not to bid more than the equity in the property (fair market value less the total dollar amount of the liens, if any, that will survive the foreclosure sale). So how does one discover fair market value? Again, it is a question of getting the right information. One of the best ways to do this is to obtain a comparative market analysis or broker price opinion (BPO) from a realtor.

Last-Minute Bankruptcies

Foreclosures can be rendered void by last-minute bankruptcy filings. Some professional investors will check with the bankruptcy clerk's office the morning of the sale to make sure that the borrower has not filed under any chapter of the U.S. Bankruptcy Code *before* they bid on the property. Note that the bankruptcy clerk's office opens at 9 a.m. and bidding commences at 10 a.m. Checking bankruptcy filings is a wise precaution if the borrower has previously filed or threatened bankruptcy. It can be cumbersome and inconvenient to get money back from a trustee on a void sale.

Conduct of the Sale

Foreclosure sales in the larger counties can seem chaotic, with many sales going on at once. There are two general types: sales by trustees (usually attorneys) for individual and institutional lenders and sales by the county sheriff for unpaid taxes. Sales are held at the location designated by the commissioners of the county where the property is located—often the courthouse steps or close by.

The sale is conducted by the named trustee unless a substitute trustee has been duly appointed and notice of the appointment has been filed of record. As a practical matter, the foreclosing trustee is usually the attorney for the lender.

There is no standard or required script for a trustee to follow in auctioning property, although trustees usually recite the details of the note and lien, the fact that the note went into default, proper notice was given, the note was subsequently accelerated, and the property is now for sale to the highest cash bidder. The trustee has a duty to conduct the sale fairly and impartially and to not discourage bidding in any way (this can result in "chilled bidding," which is a defect). A trustee may set reasonable conditions for conducting the foreclosure sale and may set the terms of payment (e.g., by cash or cashier's check). However, these conditions and terms must be stated prior to the opening of bidding for the first sale of the day held by that trustee.

Bidding at the Sale

The investor should remain in motion, talking to the trustees, until finding the right trustee with the right property. Caution: do not let the excitement of the sale cause you to exceed your preestablished maximum bid.

The lender often bids the amount of the debt plus accrued fees and costs, so this bid can be anticipated. If the sale generates proceeds in excess of the debt, the trustee must distribute the excess funds to other lienholders in order of seniority and the remaining balance, if any, to the borrower.

If the investor is the successful bidder, he or she should be prepared to make payment "without delay" or within a mutually agreed-upon time. In order to be prepared, seasoned bidders carry with them some cash plus an assortment of cashier's checks in different amounts made payable to "Trustee." If the high bidder is for any reason unable to complete the purchase, then the trustee will reopen the bidding and auction the property again. The successful bidder will, within a reasonable time, receive a trustee's deed or substitute trustee's deed which conveys the interest that was held by the borrower in the property—no more, no less.

Property Code section 51.009 states that a buyer at a foreclosure sale "acquires the foreclosed property 'as is' without any expressed or implied warranties, except as to warranties of title, and at the purchaser's own risk; and is not a consumer." The "consumer" part of that statement is meant to prevent any DTPA claims.

Elapsed Time

Compared to other states, Texas has a streamlined non-judicial fore-closeure process that is nearly as quick as an eviction. The minimum amount of time from the first notice to the day of foreclosure is 41 days, unless the deed of trust is a FNMA form, in which case the time is 51 days, although it is never wise to cut these deadlines that close. Why risk a void sale or give the borrower a possible wrongful foreclosure claim?

The advantage of a foreclosure over an eviction is that there are no effective defenses to the foreclosure process except for the borrower to block it with a temporary restraining order or file bankruptcy. For either option, the buyer needs money and probably an attorney.

Deficiency Suits

In the event that proceeds of the foreclosure sale exceed the amount due on the note (including attorney's fees and expenses), then surplus funds must be distributed to the borrower. More often, however, the price at which the property is sold is less than the unpaid balance on the loan, resulting in a deficiency. A suit may be brought by the lender to recover this deficiency any time within two years of the date of foreclosure. Tex. Prop. Code § 51.003. Federally insured lenders have four years. As part of a defense to a deficiency suit, the borrower may challenge the foreclosure sales price if it is below fair market value, and receive appropriate credit if it is not. Any money received by a lender from private mortgage insurance is credited to the account of the borrower. One case states that the purpose of this "is to prevent mortgagees from recovering more than their due."

For borrowers, deficiencies can be as significant a loss as the foreclosure itself since the IRS deems the deficiency amount to be taxable ordinary income.

Servicemembers Civil Relief Act

The Servicemembers Civil Relief Act ("SCRA"), 50 U.S.C. app. § 501, which was passed in 2003 completely rewrites the existing 1940 law by expanding protections for those serving in the armed forces. Except by court order, a landlord may not evict a servicemember or dependents from the homestead during military service. The SCRA provides criminal sanctions for persons who knowingly violate its provisions.

Right of Redemption

There is no general right of redemption by a borrower after a Texas foreclosure. The right of redemption is limited to:

> (1) *Sale for unpaid taxes.* After foreclosure for unpaid taxes, the former owner of homestead or agricultural property has a two-year right of redemption (Tax Code section 34.21a). The investor is entitled to a redemption premium of 25% in the first year and 50% in the second year of the redemption period, plus recovery of certain costs that include property insurance and repairs or improvements required by code, ordinance, or a lease in effect on the date of sale. For other types of property (i.e., nonhomestead), the redemption period is 180 days and the redemption premium is limited to 25%.
>
> (2) *HOA foreclosure of an assessment lien.* Prop. Code section 209.011 provides that a homeowner may redeem the property until no "later than the 180th day after the date the association mails written notice of the sale to the owner and the lienholder under section 209.101." A lienholder also has a right of redemption in these circumstances "before 90 days after the date the association mails written notice . . . and only if the lot owner has not previously redeemed." These provisions are part of the Texas Residential Property Owners Protection Act designed to reign in the once arbitrary power of HOAs (Chapter 209 of the Code). Note that an HOA is not permitted to foreclose on a homeowner if its lien is solely for fines assessed by the association or attorney fees.

An investor should be prepared to hold the property and avoid either making substantial improvements to it or reselling it until after any applicable rights of redemption have expired.

Postforeclosure Eviction

Foreclosure gives the new owner *title*; the next step is to obtain *possession*, and the procedure for doing this is outlined in the previous chapter. It is generally necessary to give the usual 3-day notice to vacate and file a forcible detainer petition in justice court. After judgment, the new owner must wait until the constable posts a 48 hour notice on the door and then forcibly removes a former borrower if that person is otherwise unwilling to leave.

An investor should build eviction costs into the budget from the beginning. It is advisable to hire an attorney for the first couple of evictions, after which an investor will likely be prepared to handle them solo. Never, however, attempt to conduct an eviction appeal to county court without an attorney.

As discussed in the chapter on evictions, there are both state and federal protections for tenants. Both Property Code section 24.005(b) and the federal Protecting Tenants at Foreclosure Act of 2009 require at least 90 days' notice to vacate so long as a tenant continues to pay rent.

Stopping a Foreclosure Sale

It is a myth that lawyers can wave a wand and, with a phone call or nasty letter, stop foreclosure. Attorneys have no such power. It is a fact that foreclosure *can* be stopped, but the only sure way to do so is to file a lawsuit *and* successfully persuade a judge to issue a temporary restraining order *prior* to the foreclosure sale. After the sale occurs, the remedy that remains—a suit for wrongful foreclosure—is slightly different. Relief may be limited to a money judgment if the property was sold at foreclosure to a third party for cash (a bona fide purchaser or "BFP"). If a BFP is in the mix, the possibility that the property itself can be recovered by the borrower is near zero.

Clients will often report that they have been engaged in reinstatement negotiations with the lender, usually consisting of numerous phone calls and messages, and ask if that is sufficient to avoid a scheduled foreclosure. The answer is a resounding *no*. Unless there is payment of the arrearage *and* a signed reinstatement agreement, the foreclosure will almost certainly go forward, even if the client was talking settlement with the lender just the day before. Note that reinstatement agreements must be in writing and signed by both parties. *Phone calls mean nothing in this business.*

Clients will sometimes state that they don't want to sue the lender; they just want to get a restraining order to stop the foreclosure. The lawyer must reply "Sorry, it doesn't work that way, you can't split the two." A restraining order is an ancillary form of relief, meaning that it arises from an underlying suit. In other words, there must be an actual lawsuit in place to provide a basis for requesting a TRO. Fortunately, the suit and application for the TRO can be filed simultaneously and a hearing obtained usually within a day.

There is an additional issue: a borrower must have grounds for legal action or possibly face penalties for filing a frivolous suit. Some clients have difficulty understanding this. "Why," they ask, "can't you just go and get a TRO for me?" The answer is that the lawyer must give the judge at least some credible basis for granting equitable relief.

So why don't more people sue to stop a foreclosure? Money. A person in financial distress will have difficulty coming up with cash. Here is the blunt truth: if a borrower or investor cannot readily write a substantial retainer check to an attorney for purposes of suing a lender, then that person has no business in the expensive world of litigation.

Wrongful Foreclosure Suits

After the sale, a suit for wrongful foreclosure can be filed if there are grounds for alleging that the loan documents (e.g., the note and deed of trust) were defective in some way; if the notices leading up to the foreclosure were done incorrectly; or if there was some alleged impropriety in the sale itself. Note that there is no requirement that the sales price be fair. A sale cannot be set aside because the consideration paid is allegedly inadequate because it is less than market value. *Sauceda v. GMAC Mortg. Corp.*, 268 S.W.3d 135, 139 (Tex. App.—Corpus Christi 2008, no pet.). To prevail in a wrongful foreclosure suit based on inadequate sale price, three elements must be proven: (1) grossly inadequate consideration; (2) defective foreclosure notices or sale; *and* (3) a causal connection between the defect and the inadequate consideration. If the notices and sale were correctly done, then the sale will be valid even though the sales price was lower than market value.

As a general rule, it is far better for a borrower to obtain a restraining order to stop a foreclosure than it is to bring suit after the fact. Texas law favors the finality of foreclosures, making wrongful foreclosure suits an uphill battle. If the property was sold to a third party who has no knowledge of any claims or alleged defects there is little chance that the borrower will get the property back. The third party is a protected BFP, and any remedy for the borrower will therefore likely be limited to monetary damages. Bottom line? If in doubt about whether or not a foreclosure is going to occur, file suit and attempt to get a temporary restraining order to stop it. "Wait and see" is the worst possible strategy in this case, since it is always more difficult to correct the situation after the foreclosure sale has occurred. The judge will likely ask without much sympathy, "Why, since you knew about these various alleged defects, did you not take action to stop the foreclosure?"

If a wrongful foreclosure suit is being considered, it should be filed quickly so that notice of the suit (a notice of lis pendens) can be filed in the real property records. If the lender was the successful bidder, this notice may effectively prevent the lender from transferring the property to a BFP.

Note that the action available under Property Code section 51.004 (discussed above) is different from a wrongful foreclosure remedy per se. Relief is granted if the court finds that the fair market value is greater than the sale price, but only in the context of a deficiency claimed by the lender.

The cruel fact for borrowers is that wrongful foreclosure suits face challenges from the beginning. Is that fair? You decide. It is, however, undoubtedly the bias of Texas judges, whether one approves or not.

A plaintiff can realistically expect the following in a wrongful foreclosure lawsuit: (1) The lender will *not* rush to settle, since lenders pay high fees to large litigation firms to fight tooth and nail to avoid doing the right thing; (2) written discovery (interrogatories, requests for production, and requests for admission) from the plaintiff will be nearly entirely objected to by lender's counsel, so extensively as to make the responses essentially useless (a deposition will therefore be required); (3) lender's counsel will remove the case from state court to federal court where judges are more conservative and lenders can use Federal Rule 12(b)(6) to dismiss the case. This rule permits dismissal if the borrower's complaint fails "to state a claim upon which relief can be granted," which happens more often than one might think. A change of courts can also create complications for the attorney representing the borrower, who may be accustomed to practicing in state rather than federal court. The attorney may be an experienced state court lawyer, but may not even be licensed in federal court. This is common as federal practice becomes more of a specialty among lawyers.

Prolonged Negotiations for a Modification

Clients often report that they were engaged in prolonged negotiations to modify their existing loan prior to the foreclosure sale. Of course, these communications were conducted by phone and there is no signed written agreement binding the lender to stop the sale, so there is likely no basis for a wrongful foreclosure suit. Do lenders pursue this strategy intentionally, so as to make it appear that they are willing to be reasonable, when in fact it is in their interest to foreclose instead? Opinions vary.

Chapter 40

TEXAS LITIGATION

A Nuts and Bolts Tour for Investors

This chapter is designed to acquaint investors with basic rules and procedures involved in Texas litigation. For our purposes, "litigation" refers to the filing and prosecuting of a real estate-related lawsuit, or defense against one, in the county civil courts at law or the civil district courts. We will not discuss divorce cases, criminal defense, or litigation in federal court.

The cost and complexity of litigation has doubled in the last 10 years, in no small measure due to the impact of computers and technology. What is capable of being done with all our electronic gadgets is now expected to be done. Ironically, the result is more, not less, paper. A prime culprit is the "docket control order" or DCO, also called a "scheduling order," generated by the clerk's computer. In times past these orders contained only a few dates, including the discovery completion date, the date by which experts were to be designated, and a trial date. DCOs have now expanded to include many more dates and deadlines. Meeting dates and deadlines is the attorney's professional obligation, not only to the client but also to the court, and therefore attorneys must be prudent when signing on as attorney of record. The attorney must not only be confident that the case has merit but that the client has the commitment and financial means to pursue litigation at today's level of expense.

Contingency fee arrangements are usually unavailable in real estate and business cases (since there is generally no insurance pot of gold at the end of the rainbow) so the client will be required to post a substantial initial retainer. Many attorneys require an initial retainer of $5,000 to $10,000 (plus costs such as filing fees) with supplementary retainer installments to follow. Larger firms may require up to $25,000 up front. There is a reason for these retainers. For attorneys, there are few situations more frustrating than being in a lawsuit governed by a complicated DCO while stuck with a client who cannot or will not pay the bills for the work that order requires. Although most suits settle before trial, the client must be able to see the process through to its bitter end if necessary.

In contemplating filing or defending against a lawsuit, one should keep in mind three cardinal rules, which shock clients when they learn them: (1) *There is no such thing as a perfect case and yes, that includes yours*; (2) *no one ever gets exactly what they want in court and yes, that includes you;* and (3) *litigation always costs more than you think it will.*

References to rules in this chapter are to the Texas Rules of Civil Procedure.

Evaluating the Case

A good case consists of (1) facts that clearly show liability, and (2) monetary damages in an amount that makes the process worthwhile. *Both factors must be present.* Good liability facts are not helpful if there is no real monetary loss; and large damages will not help a plaintiff who cannot show a clear path to holding the defendant legally liable. One or more established causes of action (fraud or breach of contract, for example) must apply. Note that *legal* liability is not the same as *moral* liability. The justice system, like every human institution, is imperfect. It is unable (and unwilling) to right every wrong.

As a rule of thumb, there should be at least $15,000 in actual damages to make it worthwhile to file a suit in county or district court. Plaintiffs with $5,000 and $10,000 cases should consider filing a small claims action in justice court where an attorney is not required. Otherwise, such cases are not cost-effective. The days when it was reasonable to hire an attorney for a low-damage claim are gone. A breach-of-contract claim in a real estate transaction of, say, $2,500 is *not* the basis for a lawsuit. It is a business write-off.

If an investor is contemplating litigation, the first step is to consult with a real estate litigator to go over the facts, review and analyze documents, and evaluate the potential for success. At the initial meeting, the client should be prepared with copies of all relevant documents and correspondence as well as a written summary and a timeline of events. The prospective litigant should also be ready to demonstrate that he or she can afford the litigation. If the client arrives prepared, most attorneys can evaluate a case in an hour. As is the case with major medical decisions, a second opinion may be a good idea.

Representing Oneself as a Pro Se Litigant

Because of mushrooming complexity, representing oneself as a pro se litigant is no longer practical for nonattorneys except in small claims cases in justice courts, which hear controversies involving up to $10,000. Justice courts are also handy because they are located in various neighborhood precincts. For many, jp court may be the best option, but even there one sees more and more attorneys at the bench, and few things are more foolish than a pro se litigant attempting to match wits or knowledge of the rules with a trial lawyer. It goes without saying that representing oneself at higher court levels—county court or district court—is inviting trouble. The Rules of Civil Procedure, the Civil Practice & Remedies Code, and the Rules of Evidence govern trial work. These are complicated even for lawyers who appear in court frequently. They can appear illogical, incomprehensible, and Byzantine to others.

Note that corporations and limited liability companies are required to have an attorney in Texas. They are not permitted to represent themselves, either in filing or answering a lawsuit.

Obligations of the Client

A client cannot expect to meet with an attorney, pay a retainer, and then walk away and forget about a lawsuit. The client must be an active and essential participant, since a case in litigation will involve considerable time, effort, and expense. Patience and persistence are also required since it can take nine months or so to move a case to trial, and there are invariably bumps in the road.

The attorney-client relationship is based on trust, candor, participation, and communication. A client should tell the attorney everything pertinent to the case and provide all relevant documents.

A plaintiff who does not know the location of the person or entity to be sued should be prepared to incur the expense of a private investigator.

Clients should resist the temptation to micro-manage a lawsuit. Reach an agreement with the attorney on general goals and strategy and then let him or her do the job. Even so, no attorney can ever make a guarantee concerning the outcome of a case. Attorneys are merely the agents of their clients within the system.

Jurisdiction

The term "jurisdiction" has three aspects: first, whether a particular court is enabled by law to handle certain subjects ("subject-matter jurisdiction"); second, whether damages fall within certain monetary limits ("monetary jurisdiction"); and third, whether the court has jurisdiction over the parties and property involved ("personal jurisdiction" and "*in rem* jurisdiction," respectively). All of these requirements must be satisfied.

County courts and district courts have subject-matter jurisdiction over the full range of real estate and business matters. However, in certain counties other than Harris County, matters pertaining to title to real estate must be brought in district court. Justice courts have original jurisdiction over possession of real property, so evictions must brought there.

County courts have monetary jurisdiction up to $100,000. District courts can hear cases that exceed $500 in value, and there is no upper limit. Often, but not always, litigation in county court is cheaper and faster than in district courts.

Venue

Venue refers to the county in which a lawsuit is brought. One cannot file suit just anywhere. Venue is proper in a particular county if (1) all or a substantial part of the events or omissions giving rise to the claim occurred in that county; or (2) the defendant resides in that county or, if a corporation, does business there; or (3) the real property the subject of the suit lies in that county. If suit is filed in the wrong county, the opposing party will likely make a special appearance in order to ask for a change of venue. Failing to pay attention to proper venue results in wasted time and money.

Causes of Action

In order to be an effective lawsuit, a case must meet all the required elements of one or more causes of action. Causes of action derive from common law (legal history and tradition) and from specific statutes. Examples:

breach of contract
breach of express or implied warranty
common law fraud
statutory fraud
conversion
negligence
deceptive trade practices
conspiracy
wrongful foreclosure
slander of title
suit to quiet title
trespass to try title
suit for specific performance
suit for declaratory judgment
violation of real estate license act

These causes of action are common in real estate litigation. There are, of course, many more.

Injunctions

Injunctive relief (a temporary restraining order or temporary injunction) may also be requested after suit is filed. Injunctions are useful in preventing another party from taking certain action, such as foreclosure, that will cause irreparable harm to the applicant (Rule 680). A temporary restraining order ("TRO") is a form of emergency, equitable relief that is good up to 14 days. A TRO is granted, if at all, after notice to both sides and a hearing. A temporary injunction ("TI") requires a more thorough hearing, usually a mini-trial, at which the applicant must show a likelihood of prevailing upon the merits at trial. A TI usually remains in effect for the duration of the litigation. Finally, a permanent injunction is granted as part of a judgment and is usually for an indefinite period.

Note that a bond is always required if a TRO or TI is granted. The amount can be nominal or significant. Bonds in the amount of $5,000, $10,000, or $20,000 are common, although the amount can be set much higher. This is discretionary with the judge and is designed to protect the interests of the party against whom injunctive relief is awarded. An applicant for a TRO or TI needs to be prepared to post the cash (which is refundable if the applicant prevails in the case) within 24 hours of the hearing or use a bondsman to do so. Bondsmen will require 10-20% of the bond amount as a nonrefundable premium as well as collateral (e.g., a lien on real estate). *Do not ask your attorney to seek a TRO or TI unless you have sufficient resources with which to post a bond.*

Whether an injunction can be obtained depends on many factors including the attitude of the judge. The outcome of an application for an injunction is never guaranteed. An application for an injunction adds a significant layer of complexity and expense to a lawsuit.

Discovery

"Discovery" refers to mechanisms for obtaining information, documents, and tangible things about an opponent's case. *See* Tex. R. Civ. P. 190 et seq. Discovery can be divided generally into written discovery (requests for disclosure, interrogatories, requests for admission, and requests for production) and depositions of parties, witnesses, and experts. Discovery is necessary and it is expensive. No modern case can be effectively litigated without doing thorough discovery, which is at least partially responsible for soaring costs.

Generally, lawyers prefer to do written discovery first and then, as needed, take depositions. It should be noted that this system is broken.

Many lawyers who bill by the hour will be intentionally obstructionist and object to many interrogatories and production requests. This is at best contrary to the spirit of the rules, at worst unethical. The net effect of objecting to everything is to make depositions inevitable, since the inquiring party needs the information, one way or another, in order to prepare for trial. Depositions are time-consuming and expensive for the client, but for lawyers who bill by the hour that is just fine. Chances are you will be doing at least one deposition in your case. Average cost? Between the court reporter and legal fees, $1,200 to $1,500.

Clients occasionally question the need to do discovery, hoping to avoid the expense, but attorneys know that it is always better to go to trial with foreknowledge of the opponent's case. Their own clients will be the first to blame them if they do not.

Motions for Summary Judgment

A motion for summary judgment is an attempt to dispose of all or part of the case without proceeding to a full trial on the merits. Tex. R. Civ. P. 166a. Such a motion may be partial, i.e., limited in scope to certain issues or certain parties, or it may affect the entire case. Disposition by summary judgment is proper only when the movant establishes there are no genuine issues of material fact such that the movant is entitled to judgment as a matter of law. In evaluating a motion for summary judgment, however, the reviewing court must "indulge every reasonable inference in favor of the nonmovant and resolve any in its favor." *Nixon v. Mr. Prop. Mgmt.*, 690 S.W.2d 546, 548 (Tex. 1985). Therefore, all evidence favorable to the nonmovant will be taken as true and all doubts must be resolved in the nonmovant's favor. The practical result is that summary judgments are difficult to obtain. Judges are reluctant to deprive a party of his or her day in court.

MSJs are useful, however, when one wants to address just part of the dispute—possession of real property, for instance, leaving issues of title for trial. Or an MSJ may be a way to remove a party from a suit if that party was sued improperly in an individual capacity. In any case, MSJ hearings are limited to lawyer argument supported by documentary evidence and affidavits. Live witness testimony is not allowed.

One of the most basic criteria by which an attorney evaluates a case is whether or not it will survive an MSJ by the other side.

Mediation

Parties should expect to mediate. Most judges order it automatically (it is usually one of the deadlines in the DCO). All judges will order it if either side requests it. It may be for a half day or a full day. It is voluntary in the sense that neither side is obligated to accept any particular outcome. All aspects of mediation are confidential and (like settlement discussions) cannot later be brought up in court.

The cost of the mediator's services is usually $400 to $600 per side for a half day. Clients must come to mediation prepared with a cashier's check or money order payable to the mediator. This is collected before mediation begins. Attorney fees are in addition to this amount. While expensive, mediation is nonetheless far cheaper than trial of the case.

Clients should also come to mediation prepared to be reasonable, since it is seldom that anyone in the legal system gets exactly what he or she wants. No attorney wants a client who will not mediate or will not mediate in good faith. Incentives for settlement at mediation include (1) the cost and aggravation of continued litigation, and (2) having certainty and control over the outcome, rather than leaving it to a judge or jury who can return unpredictable and even whimsical results. Any experienced lawyer has stories about times when he or she was shocked and dumbfounded by an unexpected verdict.

Jury Trial versus Trial to the Judge

Jury trials are more suitable in cases where one desires to inflame the passions of jurors in order to get a bigger verdict. This is more likely in personal injury cases than in real estate or business cases. In the latter, technical questions of contract law and the like are usually best left for a judge to decide. The judge has the training and expertise and hears similar cases often.

Phases of the Case

The litigation process can be broken down into predictable phases:

Initial Pleadings and Discovery

- Original Petition or Original Answer
- Application for Temporary Restraining Order (TRO)
- hearing to convert TRO to Temporary Injunction (TI)
- ongoing attorney-client conferences
- settlement negotiations with the opposition
- written discovery
    - requests for disclosure
    - interrogatories
    - requests for admission
    - requests for production

Continuing Discovery/Motions/Mediation Phase

responding to written discovery
amending pleadings, including filing a counter-claim or cross action
hearings on various motions
half-day mediation
continuing settlement negotiations
depositions
motion for summary judgment
locate experts and obtain expert reports
ongoing attorney-client conferences

Pretrial Phase

ascertain compliance with Docket Control Order
final amendment of pleadings
additional motions, if appropriate
supplementation of discovery responses
designation of experts by the deadline
business records affidavit
pretrial order preparation
conferences with client to prepare testimony
conferences with witnesses to prepare testimony
pretrial research and preparation
correspondence and conversations with the opposition

Trial Phase

trial of the case by judge or jury
entry of judgment

Posttrial Phase

motion for new trial/defense of motion for new trial
request for findings of fact and conclusions of law
postjudgment discovery
abstraction, execution, and attempt to collect the judgment

The total time to trial is approximately nine to twelve months, varying from court to court and county to county. Cases are usually heard in the order of oldest first. They are set for a certain term of court (often one week in county courts and two weeks in district court). During this time, the attorney, the client, and the witnesses are all on call, which can be inconvenient and expensive (if, for instance, one must pay hourly experts to sit around and wait). A judgment is final after thirty days.

Dismissal for Baseless Causes of Action

The 82nd Legislature introduced a much needed reform by creating Rule 91a, which provides that causes of action with no basis in law or fact may be dismissed within 45 days of the filing of an appropriate motion. It provides a dismissal remedy early in the process rather than having to wait for discovery to be completed to file a motion for summary judgment.

Expedited Trial

Another needed rule change pertains to "expedited actions" for monetary relief not exceeding $100,000. Rules 47 and 169 apply. Unfortunately, this innovation does not apply to actions brought under the Property Code.

Collection on a Judgment

Collecting on a judgment against an individual is difficult in Texas because of homestead laws and the constitutional prohibition against garnishing wages. If the loser has no insurance coverage, collection can be a real problem. Similarly, satisfying a judgment against a corporation or LLC may be challenging if assets have been moved out of the company name or if they are located in other jurisdictions. Attorneys are fond of saying that they could "paper the walls" of their offices with judgments obtained but never collected. That is the reality in Texas, especially when it comes to judgment debtors who are individuals.

Execution on a judgment is most likely to be successful when the defendant has cash in the bank, investment real estate, or a business with substantial inventory or receivables. If none of these is present, the plaintiff's best option may be to file an abstract of judgment in the real property records and hope that the defendant will sell property through a title company during the 10 years that the AJ remains on file.

Postjudgment Discovery

Postjudgment discovery enables a creditor to determine whether or not he is dealing with a judgment-proof debtor or perhaps a debtor who negligently failed to make an asset protection plan and whose assets are widely exposed. Written discovery require responses within 30 days. An oral deposition is also possible. The format and procedure is the same as for any trial deposition, except the focus is now on assets, their location, and their value.

Postjudgment discovery can be lengthy and brutal. Attempting to represent oneself in this process is the equivalent of swimming through piranha-infested waters.

A lawsuit is a business enterprise, and a tough and demanding one at that. It should never be taken personally. One function of the attorney is to help the client keep a cool head and evaluate the case rationally.

Legal fees and costs expended to pursue a suit represent one form of business investment. Alternatively, for instance, one could put that same money into stocks, real estate, or a gambling trip to Las Vegas. The client needs to estimate the rate of return on the investment in exchange for time, effort, and money expended. Putting dollars to work in a lawsuit represents an opportunity cost in economic terms, meaning those funds are not available for other uses. Clients who say these sorts of businesslike calculations are beside the point, that their suit is all about principle, are the first to tire of the process and quit, leaving their attorneys with egg on their faces. Attorneys do not like to quit and they do not like to lose. Clients need to have both the fortitude and the finances to support their attorney's efforts to thoroughly litigate and win the case.

Chapter 41

MEDIATION

An Effective Alternative to the Courtroom

Mediation is a form of settlement conference guided and supervised by a mediator who has either been chosen by the parties or appointed by a judge. The Rules for Mediation put it as follows:

> *Mediation Rule 1: Mediation is a process under which an impartial person, the Mediator, facilitates communication between the parties to promote reconciliation, settlement, or understanding among them. The Mediator may suggest ways of resolving the dispute, but may not impose his own judgment on the issues for that of the parties.*

> *Mediation Rule 3. The parties consent to the appointment of the individual named as the Mediator in their case. The Mediator shall act as an advocate for resolution and shall use his best efforts to assist the parties in reaching a mutually acceptable settlement.*

Mediation Required by Contract

Contracts may require that parties mediate before litigating. An example is paragraph 16 of the TREC One to Four Family Residential Contract, so long as the "will mediate" box is checked. The intent is to provide a structured opportunity for the parties to air and resolve grievances before resorting to the courthouse. Generally, the seller should always check the "will mediate" box. The buyer, the reverse. Why? Because even though paragraph 16 goes on to state that it "does not preclude a party from seeking equitable relief from a court," a buyer wants to be under no limitation if a suit needs to be filed in order to discourage or prevent the seller from conveying the property to someone else.

Mediation during Litigation

The docket control order, generated by the court's computer for scheduling purposes, contains relevant dates and deadlines applicable to a case, and it usually includes a date by which mediation must be completed. It is generally down the road a bit, since most attorneys prefer to do at least preliminary discovery (requests for disclosure, interrogatories, and requests for production), and perhaps consult an expert, *before* mediating, so that all cards will be on the table when the parties meet to talk settlement.

Some judges will name a mediator, others leave it up to the parties to agree upon one. Even though mediation is usually ordered, the outcome (whether or not a settlement is reached) is voluntary. The parties can choose to walk away without settling and go to trial instead, leaving their fate in the hands of a judge or jury. The mediator will report an impasse and all aspects of the mediation, including offers of settlement, remain private and confidential.

Mediation versus Arbitration

The difference here involves the authority of a mediator vs. an arbitrator:

> *Mediation Rule 5. The Mediator does not have the authority to decide any issue for the parties, but will attempt to facilitate the voluntary resolution of the dispute by the parties. The Mediator is authorized to conduct joint and separate meetings with the parties and to offer suggestions to assist the parties achieve settlement.*

By contrast, in an arbitration, the arbitrator makes a final ruling just as if he or she were a judge. Arbitration is never ordered by a court (unless of course the parties have an arbitration clause in their contract) but may be agreed upon by the parties.

Effectiveness of Mediation

Why is mediation popular? Because statistics show that *it works*. Depending on which numbers you believe, 70-80% of cases settle in mediation. Attorneys know this and encourage their clients to mediate with an open mind. In fact, when a client is recalcitrant and unreasonable about settlement, attorneys can become quite annoyed—and the reason is that lawyers know better than anyone how a trial can consist of rolling the dice. Trial practice is (or should be) a branch of chaos theory. No outcome is *ever* assured in the legal system, no matter how determined the client or how capable the attorney.

Mediation promotes predictability and certainty, but this requires compromise. *You do not win your case at mediation. In fact, a good mediation is by definition one in which both sides leave unhappy.* Clients find this difficult to accept. Remember, the "legal world" is not the same as the "real world." Clients who rebel against the mediation process and insist on total victory based on principle often lose in the end.

It is a rare case when a party is justified in refusing mediation. However, if good grounds exist for doing so, the judge (after motion and hearing) can waive a mediation requirement. Judges do not like to do this for two reasons: first, they are seasoned realists who know that most cases *do* and *should* settle; and second, it assures that another case will be added to an overburdened trial docket. Do you want to alienate the judge? Object to mediation in your case. Many lawyers consider a party's refusal to mediate in good faith to be grounds for attorney withdrawal.

Rules for Mediation

Several of these Rules have already been cited in this chapter. Others include:

> *Mediation Rule 2. Whenever the parties have agreed to mediation, they shall be deemed to have made these rules, as amended and in effect as of the date of the submission of the dispute, as part of their agreement to mediate.*

> *Mediation Rule 7. Party representatives must have authority to settle and all persons necessary to the decision to settle shall be present.*

> *Mediation Rule 9. Prior to the first scheduled mediation session, each party shall provide the Mediator and all attorneys of record with an Information Sheet and Request for Mediation on the form provided by the Mediator, setting forth its position with regard to the issues that need to be resolved.*

The mediator always asks if all parties are ready and willing to mediate in good faith and work toward a settlement with an open mind. This readiness is the foundation of both mediation and dispute resolution generally, and the mediator will request that the parties make an unconditional commitment to do this. Additionally, it is important to determine that persons present have authority to settle the case. Otherwise, the process can be futile.

Impartiality of the Mediator

> Mediation Rule 4. *The Mediator will only serve in cases in which the parties are represented by attorneys. The Mediator shall not serve as a Mediator in any dispute in which he has any financial or personal interest in the result of the mediation. Prior to accepting an appointment, the Mediator shall disclose any circumstance likely to create a presumption of bias or prevent a prompt meeting with the parties. In the event that the parties disagree as to whether the Mediator shall serve on the basis of any of the foregoing conditions, the Mediator shall not serve.*

Mediators may or may not be certified. They are usually experienced attorneys or retired judges who act as shuttle diplomats in attempting to resolve the parties' differences. After a joint session in which both sides have the opportunity to make vent their grievances, the parties retire to separate rooms, and the mediator goes back and forth in an effort to promote a settlement. In doing so, the mediator points out the strengths and weaknesses of each position without taking sides.

Fees and Expenses of Mediation

> Mediation Rule 17. *The Mediator's daily fee shall be agreed upon prior to mediation and shall be paid in advance of each mediation day. The expenses of witnesses for either side shall be paid by the party producing such witnesses. All other expenses of the mediation, including fees and expenses of the Mediator, shall be borne equally by the parties unless they agree otherwise.*

Mediators do not have a financial stake in the outcome of the mediation (i.e., mediation fees are not contingent upon a settlement being reached). Mediator fees vary and are paid at the beginning of the session. Half-day mediations are common since all but complex cases can be settled in that amount of time. Half-day mediations typically cost $400 to $600 per side. Mediators often require payment by cashier's check or money order since unhappy parties have been known to go home and stop payment on their checks.

Time and Place of Mediation

> Mediation Rule 8. *The Mediator shall fix the time of each mediation session. The mediation shall be held at the office of the Mediator or at any other convenient location agreeable to the Mediator and the parties, as the Mediator shall determine.*

Mediations are scheduled for half a day or for a full day, but may continue longer with consent of the parties. "Midnight mediations" are not uncommon, since the accumulated pressure of time will often force a compromise. One mediation this writer attended reached settlement only after the mediator broke out a bottle of whisky at 10 p.m.

Using the location of the mediation as an opportunity to serve other parties with citations, pleadings, writs, and the like (however tempting that may be) is not allowed.

Rule 14 addresses when mediation may end:

> Mediation Rule 14. *The mediation shall be terminated: (a) by the execution of a settlement agreement by the parties; (b) by declaration of the Mediator to the effect that further efforts at mediation are no longer worthwhile; or (c) after the completion of one fully mediation session, by a written declaration of a party or parties to the effect that the mediation sessions are terminated.*

After the mediation is terminated, the mediator has no further obligations other than to report the result to the court. If mediation was successful, a written summary of the settlement will be prepared and signed by the parties and attorneys before they leave.

Privacy and Confidentiality

Privacy and confidentiality are key elements in mediation. Clients often ask if family members or others may attend, participate, or observe. This is not usually permitted.

> Mediation Rule 10. *Mediation sessions are private. The parties and their representatives may attend mediation sessions. Other persons may attend only with the permission of the parties and with the consent of the mediator.*

> *Mediation Rule 11. Confidential information disclosed to a Mediator by the parties or by witnesses in the course of mediation shall not be divulged by the Mediator. . . . The parties shall maintain the confidentiality of the mediation.*

Mediators do not testify in court. Nothing said in mediation is admissible into evidence at trial. Tape recording the proceedings (either openly or surreptitiously) is forbidden. If mediation fails, it is the evidentiary equivalent of its never having occurred at all.

The Psychology of Mediation

The mediator's job is to promote settlement and be impartial in so doing. In the broadest sense, mediation is about communication—communication that may previously have happened only haphazardly or may never have happened at all. It is also a business-like endeavor, meaning that it should be stripped of emotion. Each side is encouraged to examine the costs and benefits of the available options and perceive settlement as a cold business decision. Attorneys play an important part in this analysis. They may continue to advocate but in a more muted way.

It is part of a mediator's job to challenge each party's cherished assumptions about the value of their cause of action or defense. Clients often misinterpret this and believe that the mediator is advocating for the other side. Not so. Mediation is designed to push the parties out of their comfort zones and into the zone of compromise. Mediators have the tough but essential job of overcoming the parties' resistance if the case is to settle.

Other Rules of Mediation

> *Mediation Rule 5. The Mediator does not have the authority to decide any issue for the parties, but will attempt to facilitate the voluntary resolution of the dispute by the parties. The Mediator is authorized to conduct joint and separate meetings with the parties and to offer suggestions to assist the parties achieve settlement. If necessary, the Mediator may also obtain expert advice concerning technical aspects of the dispute, provided that the parties agree and assume the expenses of obtaining such advice. Arrangements for obtaining such advice shall be made by the Mediator or by the parties, as the Mediator shall determine.*

Mediation Rule 6. The parties understand that the Mediator will not and cannot impose a settlement in their case and they agree that a settlement, if any, must be voluntarily agreed to by the parties. The Mediator, as an advocate for settlement, will use every effort to facilitate the negotiations. The Mediator does not warrant or represent that settlement will result from the mediation process.

Mediation Rule 12. There shall be no stenographic record of the mediation process, and no person shall tape record any portion of the mediation session.

Mediation Rule 13. No subpoenas, summons, complaints, citations, writs, or other process may be served upon any person at or near the site of any mediation session upon any person entering, attending, or leaving the session.

Mediation Rule 15. The Mediator is not a necessary or proper party in judicial proceedings relating to the mediation. Neither Mediator no any law firm employing Mediator shall be liable to any party for any act or omission in connection with any mediation conducted under these rules.

Mediation Rule 16. The Mediator shall interpret and apply these rules.

Mediation is an opportunity for both sides to exert control over the outcome of their dispute rather than leaving it to an unpredictable and expensive trial process. Clients who ardently believe in the rightness of their position may resist this process, but it must happen if settlement is to occur.

Chapter 42

JUDGMENTS IN TEXAS

Collection Is Not as Easy as You Think

Any discussion of judgments in Texas needs to be broadly divided into two parts: first, the process of obtaining a judgment (which, after all, is only a piece of paper signed by a judge) and second, actually collecting on the judgment. The second part may be more challenging, since Texas is a state notoriously favorable to debtors. It is unconstitutional to garnish wages in Texas, and an individual's home and vehicles are usually beyond reach. Unless a judgment debtor has a going business with valuable inventory or cash flow, rental property, or cash in the bank, collecting on a judgment may be problematic. Often, the creditor's attorney receives word from the constable that he is unable to collect and is returning the writ of execution *nulla bona*.

Finality of Judgments

One can only obtain a judgment after filing a lawsuit and complying with the rules of civil procedure in order to either prevail at trial or obtain a judgment by default. After the judgment is signed, the court clerk will not issue a writ of execution until it is at least 30 days old (21 days in justice court) at which time the judgment is considered final. This postjudgment waiting period exists so that the debtor has ample time to file a motion for new trial as a prerequisite to appeal. If the motion is granted, or if the debtor files an appeal, then execution efforts must cease.

Homestead Exemptions

Many Texas debtors have numerous judgments against them but live in expensive homes. They can do this because the entire homestead equity is exempt from execution. What constitutes a debtor's homestead? *See* Tex. Prop. Code § 41.002 (definition). Within broad parameters, a homestead is what a person intends it to be. A rental property or even a vacant lot can be homestead if the owner has reasonable expectations of building a home on it. Moreover, Property Code section 41.001(5)(c) states that "proceeds of a sale of a homestead are not subject to seizure for a creditor's claim for six months after the date of sale." This expressly permits homestead protections to be rolled over from one home to the next.

Certain personal property is also exempt under chapter 42 of the Property Code. Personal property valued at $60,000 for a family or $30,000 for a single adult (exclusive of liens) is exempt from garnishment, attachment, execution or other seizure so long as it is on the statutory list. This includes home furnishings, clothes, jewelry, firearms, and vehicles—even 12 head of cattle. Retirement plans (including rollover proceeds) are exempted under section 42.0021 so long as contributions do not exceed the amount that is deductible under current law. College tuition funds are exempted under section 42.0022. It is important to note that homestead protections are available only to individuals, not LLCs or corporations.

Writ of Execution

Once issued, the writ of execution is sent to the constable (or sheriff, in some counties) who charges a fee for attempting to collect. The reality is that these officers may not try very hard—no flashing lights, no guns drawn. Often, the constable will knock at the debtor's door early in the morning, present the judgment, and ask if there are any assets available to satisfy it. If the debtor says "no," then the officer may withdraw and send the unsatisfied writ back to the court. Unless the creditor's attorney can direct the officer to a specific, known, nonexempt asset for attachment or garnishment, then the collection process may come to halt.

Postjudgment Discovery

Judgment creditors, often at a disadvantage in Texas, have an important collection tool: postjudgment discovery which includes interrogatories, requests for admission, and requests for production. Tex. R. Civ. P. 621a. This discovery can be incredibly complex since rules pertaining to limits on trial discovery do not apply post-judgment.

The purpose of postjudgment discovery is (1) to ascertain whether or not the debtor possesses non-exempt property sufficient to satisfy the judgment; and (2) to determine if the debtor has fraudulently hidden assets. In addition to written discovery, it is possible to delve into these matters by taking the debtor's deposition, although written discovery generally comes first. Note that if a debtor who has been properly served fails to answer post-judgment discovery, he or she may be held in contempt by the judge, resulting in a fine or even jail. Tex. R. Civ. P. 215.

If actionable information is obtained, the judgment creditor can approach the court and request a writ of attachment, Tex. R. Civ. P. 641;

Tex. Bus. & Com. Code § 8.112, garnishment, Tex. R. Civ. P. 669, or a "turn-over order," Tex. Civ. Prac. & Rem. Code § 31.002.

Abstracting the Judgment

It is normal procedure for the creditor to request an abstract of judgment from the clerk and then file that abstract in the real property records (Note that judgment records and real property records are often located in different computers). The AJ stays on file for 10 years but may be refiled for successive 10-year periods. Filing the abstract puts the public on notice that the judgment exists and attaches to non-exempt real property of the debtor. Title companies will search for these AJs to determine if they should collect from sales proceeds to satisfy them. This represents a problem for any judgment debtor who is trying to sell property out of his own name, including homestead property. Even though a judgment lien does not attach to, and does not constitute a lien on, a judgment debtor's homestead, it can be difficult to persuade a title company to ignore a judgment and go forward with closing. A title company's self-serving reaction is to minimize risk and require that all liens be cleared.

Filing an AJ is often the only realistic way that a judgment creditor has to collect, in some cases years after the judgment was obtained.

The Debtor's Homestead

A homestead is exempt from forced sale so long as the property remains the homestead of the debtor. *Exocet Inc. v. Cordes*, 815 S.W.2d 350, 352 (Tex. App.—Austin 1991, no writ). Property Code section 52.0012 provides an expedited statutory method for securing a release of any judgment lien against homestead property, available only for AJ's filed after September 1, 2007.

Section 52.0012 provides for the filing of an Affidavit that must substantially comply with the appearing in this section of the Property Code. Filing of the affidavit must be preceded by a 30-day notice sent certified mail and addressed to the judgment creditor and its attorney of record. The letter must contain a copy of the affidavit that the homestead owner intends to file in the real property records. The requirements of the letter and the affidavit are highly technical and should be done by an attorney knowledgeable in this procedure. The judgment creditor may contest the homeowner's action by filing a contradicting affidavit if there is reason to believe that the homeowner's affidavit is false. The ultimate result, if this procedure is followed to the letter, is that the homeowner's affidavit serves as a release of the judgment lien as to the homestead property. *See* Part VI, ch. 35: *Lien Removal.*

Enforcement of Judgments from other States

Unfortunately for Texas debtors, this is not as difficult as it used to be. Enforcement of "foreign judgments" is governed by Civil Practice & Remedies Code chapter 35, also referred to as the "Uniform Enforcement of Foreign Judgments Act" or "UEFJA." The UEFJA provides that a foreign judgment may be authenticated as follows: (a) at the time the foreign judgment is filed, the judgment creditor or the judgment creditor's attorney must file with the clerk of court an affidavit showing the name and last known address of the judgment debtor and the judgment creditor; (b) the clerk then mails notice of the filing of the foreign judgment to the judgment debtor at the address given; and (c) the notice must include the name and address of the judgment creditor and, if the judgment creditor has an attorney in Texas, the attorney's name and address. So long as this procedure is followed, and so long as the judgment is not being appealed in its original jurisdiction, the creditor will have access to post-judgment discovery and other remedies allowed under Texas rules.

The result is that a foreign judgment may be enforced and collected in Texas just as any other judgment, with one limitation: Civil Practice & Remedies Code section 16.066(b) provides that the foreign judgment may not be enforced in Texas if 10 years have passed since the judgment was rendered in its home state or after the judgment debtor has resided in Texas for 10 years.

Chapter 43

CHARGING ORDERS

Can a Judgment Creditor Seize Your LLC Membership?

Much is made in asset protection circles about charging orders and the circumstances in which they may occur. What is a charging order? It is a judge's order enabling a creditor to intercept and receive any distributions, payments, or proceeds from a specific entity to the judgment debtor. The judgment creditor becomes, in effect, a court-ordered lienholder and assignee of any such funds. It is important to distinguish the applicability and effect of a charging order from the outright attachment or seizure of a judgment debtor's interest in the entity. It is similarly important to identify which entities may be subject to a charging order. In Texas, these are limited liability companies and partnerships (general and limited).

Unlike an LLC membership interest or partnership interest which is subject to a charging order, corporate stock may be seized and sold at public auction. Stock in a corporation is nonexempt personal property, Tex. Bus. Orgs. Code § 21.801, that can be subject to levy, Tex. R. Civ. P. 641; Tex. Bus. & Com. Code § 8.112, garnishment, Tex. R. Civ. P. 669, or turnover, Tex. Civ. Prac. & Rem. Code § 31.002.

Law Applicable to Limited Liability Companies

The law relating to charging orders on LLC membership interests is found at Business Organizations Code section 101.112:

> **(a) On application by a judgment creditor a member of a limited liability company or of any other owner of a membership interest in a limited liability company, a court having jurisdiction may charge thc membership interest of the judgment debtor to satisfy the judgment.**
>
> **(b) If a court charges a membership interest with payment of a judgment as provided by Subsection (a), the judgment creditor has only the right to**

receive any distribution to which the judgment debtor would otherwise be entitled in respect of the membership interest.

(c) A charging order constitutes a lien on the judgment debtor's membership interest. The charging order may not be foreclosed on under this code or any other law.

(d) The entry of a charging order is the exclusive remedy by which a judgment creditor of a member or of any other owner of a membership interest may satisfy a judgment out of the judgment debtor's membership interest.

(e) This section may not be construed to deprive a member of a limited liability company or any other owner of a membership interest in a limited liability company of the benefit of any exemption laws applicable to the membership interest of the member or owner.

(f) A creditor of a member or of any other owner of a membership interest does not have the right to obtain possession of, or otherwise exercise legal or equitable remedies with respect to, the property of the limited liability company.

The charging order is an exclusive remedy. In other words, the judgment creditor gets paid *if and when* distributions from the LLC occur. The charging order is therefore not tantamount to taking over the membership interest of a debtor or seizing control of the company. Moreover, the creditor may not attach the debtor's membership interest; force its sale or transfer; or (absent a judgment piercing the veil) reach any assets of the LLC itself.

What if the LLC pays a member a salary for services? Is this a "distribution" subject to a charging order? No. Such a salary would not be subject to garnishment since it is exempt under Property Code section 42.001(b)(1) which provides that "current wages for personal services, except for the enforcement of court-ordered child support payments" is exempt "from garnishment, attachment, execution, and other seizure." This includes severance pay.

The exclusive nature of a charging order does not limit a creditor's remedies once a distribution has been carried out. Distributed funds or assets become non-exempt personal property *once they are received the debtor* and may therefore be reached by attachment, garnishment, or turnover. *Stanley v. Reef Secs., Inc.*, 314 S.W.3d 659 (Tex. App.—Dallas 2010, no pet.).

Law Applicable to Partnerships

The law relating to charging orders on partnership interests mirrors the law applicable to LLCs and is found in Business Organizations Code section 152.308:

> **(a) On application by a judgment creditor of a partner or of any other owner of a partnership interest, a court having jurisdiction may charge the partnership interest of the judgment debtor to satisfy the judgment.**
>
> **(b) To the extent that the partnership interest is charged in the manner provided by Subsection (a), the judgment creditor has only the right to receive any distribution to which the judgment debtor would otherwise be entitled in respect of the partnership interest.**
>
> **(c) A charging order constitutes a lien on the judgment debtor's partnership interest. The charging order lien may not be foreclosed on under this code or any other law.**
>
> **(d) The entry of a charging order is the exclusive remedy by which a judgment creditor of a partner or of any other owner of a partnership interest may satisfy a judgment out of the judgment debtor's partnership interest.**
>
> **(e) This section does not deprive a partner or other owner of a partnership interest of a right under exemption laws with respect to the judgment debtor's partnership interest.**

(f) A creditor of a partner or of any other owner of a partnership interest does not have the right to obtain possession of, or otherwise exercise legal or equitable remedies with respect to, the property of the partnership.

Asset Protection in Anticipation of a Charging Order

Sound asset protection practice requires that planning and strategy take place well in advance. Once a lawsuit is threatened or filed, it is more challenging to find legitimate ways of reorganizing or redistributing one's assets so as to reduce vulnerability to postjudgment collection efforts. One method is to form an LLC with two classes of membership: Class A and Class B. The company agreement should define Class B as any membership interest that has been substantially influenced or made subject to a collection device or court order, including a charging order. The conversion of Class A to Class B occurs automatically if that occurs. The effect? Class B members have no power to vote, serve as officers or managers, inspect the books, or compel the sale of company property. Class B membership is effectively worthless unless the LLC is dissolved.

Asset Protection after a Charging Order: Fraudulent Transfers

Property Code section 42.004 seeks to restrain fraudulent transfers, including the pay-down of exempt assets, if undertaken "with the intent to defraud, delay, or hinder" a creditor. This reaches back two years for liquidated claims, one year for unliquidated or contingent claims. However, proving intent may be a difficult task if the judgment debtor goes about his or her business in an orderly, incremental fashion that can plausibly be described as normal, or at least justifiable on grounds independent of litigation concerns. Tex. Prop. Code § 42.004(c).

CPSIA information can be obtained at www.ICGtesting.com
Printed in the USA
LVOW13s0527190913
352986LV00004B/12/P

9 781622 873951